Strangeways

A Prison Officer's Story

Neil Samworth

W F HOWES LTD

This large print edition published in 2018 by
W F Howes Ltd
Unit 5, St George's House, Rearsby Business Park,
Gaddesby Lane, Rearsby, Leicester LE7 4YH

1 3 5 7 9 10 8 6 4 2

First published in the United Kingdom in 2018
by Sidgwick & Jackson

A CIP catalogue record for this book is available
from the British Library

ISBN 978 1 52884 569 4

Typeset by Palimpsest Book Production Limited,
Falkirk, Stirlingshire

Printed and bound by
T J International in the UK

For Yvonne Francis Samworth,
my mum

'The degree of civilization in a society can be judged by entering its prisons.'

FYODOR DOSTOEVSKY,
The House of the Dead, 1862

CONTENTS

AUTHOR'S NOTE

Where necessary, names have been changed to protect the innocent – and on occasion the guilty.

PROLOGUE

He was twisted, I'll give him that: quite definitely a firestarter too. And like me, he was the type who'd made a career out of prison – only in his case on the wrong side of the bars.

Riley was his name, self-harming his game, which brought him more grief than anyone else. He'd had a hard life and it showed. A serial arsonist who would never be free, he was destined for a high-security hospital, this creature and a half. Think Gollum in *The Lord of the Rings*, only not as good looking.

He was the kind of prisoner it is easy to hate, the sort who mean constant mither. Thomas Riley had a history with cell fires and back in the day he had done himself serious harm. He'd tied his trackie bottoms at the ankles, filled the legs with sugar and set them alight. Now sugar melts, of course, and so did his calf muscles, pretty much. He couldn't walk for ages and it all added to his horrific appearance. He didn't so much talk as squawk. At one time he must have been somebody's son, someone's child, been taken to the park and that. Yet here he was now, a stunted fucking thing.

Cell fires are a hazard in every prison, Strangeways included. The likeliest places are segregation units, where the most disruptive inmates are housed, although the forensic or hospital wings have their share. I'd worked on healthcare a while by now and developed an intuition around the mentally ill prisoners that mainly – with us officers and nursing staff – made up the place. The majority of cell-burners didn't intend to go up in smoke; it was about manipulation. They wanted to cause us as much trouble as they possibly could.

I was on nights and sensed something was up with Riley. He seemed weirder than usual, strangely possessed, so I laid a hosepipe along the floor to his cell, just in case. As usual on healthcare at night, the lights were out and he had his music on. He'd often stay up all hours. After a while, I got to thinking it were a bit loud and didn't care for his song choice either. 'Firestarter' by The Prodigy was blaring out and I'm more of a Def Leppard man, me. I looked through the little glass hatch in his door. Sure enough there he was, facing the window, off on one, dancing away like Keith Flint.

'Boom! I'm the trouble starter, punkin' instigator . . .'

Now he's really into it, this lad. He's got a lighter in one hand and, while I'm watching, bends down and gives it a flick – the signal I need. I drop the hatch – which is maybe a foot and a half wide – and insert the end of the hosepipe.

'Tommy,' I say, but he's ignoring me. 'Tommy!'

The hems on his trackie bottoms are aglow and spark into flame just as he starts on his T-shirt. 'Tommy!' At last he reckons to twig and turns around just as a jet of water hits him in the face.

Keith is still giving it some – for the minute anyway – but this lad is speechless. He's not dancing any more either. He's stood facing me, lighter in hand, saturated top to bottom.

Up and down goes the spray while he glares back, fuming. I move on to the bedding and bunk until everything else is just as wet as he is. I even turn the hose on that fucking ghetto blaster and give that a soaking. Which finally shuts The Prodigy up as well.

Good job well done, I closed the hatch and went into the office, where a nurse sat doing paperwork. 'Cell fire,' I said and she leapt to her feet. 'Don't worry. Dealt with.' Old Gollum still had his lighter, but there was nothing left to set fire to. After that, he went on intermittent watch – five times an hour we'd have to look in on him.

In winter, them cells got cold and at around three or four o'clock in the morning Riley rang his bell. So off I strolled.

'All right, Tommy?'

'Fucking 'ell, Mr Samworth. I'm freezing in here.'

'Well, kid, if you're going to set yourself on

fire . . . Would you like fresh bedding?' Yeah, he would. 'What about that lighter then?' He handed it over. 'Cup of tea, Tommy?' I offered, ever the professional.

'Yeah,' he said, adding a nice sarcastic, 'please.'

No one can fully prepare you for cell fires. There are big scary people in jail, but when a blaze gets going it's something else again.

Another lad came to us from HMP Wakefield, or 'Monster Mansion' as it's known, due to all the perverts. Wakey holds prisoners long-term and is more laid-back than Strangeways, which is high security and remand. It must be like coming from a monastery to the Haçienda – a massive change. He wasn't happy, this kid. He'd only been there half a day when he torched his TV and, after covering himself in wet towels, hid under the bed. The wing was full of smoke. I'd just gone off shift so heard about it the next day.

Once they'd dragged him out, his punishment was interesting. He was placed on report and the adjudication was sent to the police, as happens in serious cases. Very unusually, in my experience, the Crown Prosecution Service (CPS) took it on – cell fires are a grey area, and every other case I saw was handled in-house – and he became the first prisoner ever to get lifed-off via video link. Before lighting that blaze, he'd been on a life sentence that isn't life at all. The shortest I've seen is eighteen months; more often they are anything up to thirty-five years. He now got whole of life.

Currently, there are about 400 prisoners in the estate that will never go free. The urban myth that there are only five is fake news. Some want locking up forever. The murderers of Lee Rigby will always be a threat, our arsonists too. Reckless endangerment doesn't cover it. There were over 200 people on that wing – staff and prisoners – whose lives he could have ended.

Reports of serious assaults in prison, knife attacks, cell fires, the throwing of urine, spitting even, regularly go to the CPS. Yet they still don't take enough cases up. What happens in prison stays in prison. My jaw was cracked once, but nothing ever came of it. You get the impression you're expected to be there to be punched – well, bullshit. I may be six foot tall and weigh seventeen stone, but not everyone has such physical presence. When it comes down to it, a prison officer is just a civil servant.

Every day in prison is a story of endurance and aggression in a culture where few dare ask for help. Our jails are creaking catastrophically due to shortages of cash and a genuine will for change, unless by that you mean interference by pen-pushers, box-tickers and politicians, who have never faced the reality of working on a prison landing in their life and would shit blue lights if they were ever asked to do so.

Rage: I know all about rage. I saw plenty of it when I joined the prison service, and it's what was in me when Strangeways chewed me up and spat me out. The job will do that to you. In Britain, it's not just cells that are going up in smoke. It's the prison service itself. And until we get serious about extinguishing the flames, there is a danger they will burn out of control.

CHAPTER 1

GOOD MORNING, JUDGE

Growing up where I did there was always a chance you'd be a criminal, just by virtue of who you knew. Environment is a big part of it. I've had friends go to prison – not all of them bad people. Okay, they did bad things, but it's often where circumstance led them.

As a teenager in Sheffield, on the other side of the Pennines, I'd had one or two run-ins with the law myself. It was only for fighting on nights out, nothing serious – fists not knives or booting people on the deck. For a while in my youth I liked nothing better than an all-in brawl and wound up in court four times in twelve months. You'd go before a judge, apologize and get slapped with a caution and £80 fine.

A few years back I went out with a gang of old mates. They knew I was a screw and ripped me all night. Towards closing time, they gave me warning that they were going to get stuck into these other lads who'd been following us, suggesting I got out of there. That scrap made the front page of the *Sheffield Star*.

One pal used to deal drugs. If I was skint he'd

say, 'Deliver for me.' I wasn't interested. It wasn't really morality. I put another mate on the bones of his arse in touch.

One night just after I'd been kicked out of the sixth form, a mate and I were off out when a Rover 2000 pulled up. We knew the lad in it from school.

'Do you want a lift?'

As we pulled away, this cop car came the other way, and suddenly we were off; he was hammering it. Only then did it dawn on me that the car wasn't his. Fortunately, he got some distance and dropped us off before the police caught him up. He got jail time for that. Mates go on to be crooks, thugs and drug dealers – that's just how life is.

The last time I got in trouble, I was picked up for fighting and then also got accused of vagrancy: I'd given my last £20 to my mates so they could go for a curry. I'd been in front of this judge before and he called me a problem child, although I'd just had my twenty-first birthday. He sent me to see a doctor, who told me I was 'absolutely barking' – there is a fag paper's width between insanity and genius, he said, and he wasn't sure which side I was on.

Anyway, I never went to court again, mainly because I never got caught, and by twenty-five I had calmed down. By then I was channelling my aggression into rugby union.

I'd been all right at school, though detested the place. It was only due to rugby that I hung around until sixth form, before they 'asked me to leave'.

That was fair enough: my head wasn't in it. I lived for rugby: prop or blind-side flanker. At seventeen I started playing for Sheffield Tigers Colts and, after getting the shit knocked out of me to begin with, developed a reputation. In my early twenties, though, I'd started really piling the weight on and got up to twenty-two stone. Too heavy. A mate said, 'Enough of this,' and we did a *Rocky IV*, running uphill with bricks on my back, shit like that. I'd no time for getting into bother.

When I applied for the prison service, I did worry that those teenage indiscretions might be on my file, but nothing was said about them. I reckon it all stood me in good stead anyway, because I can see where some cons are coming from, how they got where they did. But by the time I joined the prison service I'd grown up quite a lot. The horrors I'd seen long before I got to Strangeways would mature anyone fast.

My road into HMP Manchester was winding. It began, as I've said, in South Yorkshire, in 1962. My first forty years were spent in Sheffield, around half of it living with my mam and sister. Our dad left us to it when I was two. I'm not keen on calling him my dad, as that conjures an image of someone always there, looking after you. He never was. When I was about fourteen, there was a knock on the door. I'd just come in from school. A bloke stood on the step.

'It's Neil, isn't it? Do you know who I am?'

'Yeah, my dad,' I said, and shut the door right in his face. We did carry on seeing his parents a couple of times a year: they were always good to us.

To begin with we lived in Walkley, quite a poor area south of Hillsborough. Mainly, however, I remember us living with our nan in Vernon Terrace, Crosspool, which was more affluent. It was a crowded three-bedroomed house. There were us three, Mam's sister Auntie Pat, her four kids – she was getting divorced – my nan and granddad, who had Parkinson's, and Uncle Don, Mam's twin brother, who kipped in the attic. At one point we had his fiancée squeezed in as well. Next door were Auntie Freda, Nan's sister, who baked more than Mary Berry – we had a strong sense of family.

Mam worked three menial jobs, cleaning or whatever, trying to provide for us. Her maiden name was Pilling; Samworth was my dad's name. He chose Neil too, but no one other than my nan ever used it. My mam always called me Sam, and even my nan towards the end of her life switched to Sam too. One or two dicks in the prison service tried it on by shouting 'Neil' at first, but not for long.

Aside from having no dad, we were your typical working-class Yorkshire brood, loads of us about, plenty of funerals and weddings. My sister and me had politeness instilled in us. Treat your elders with respect; say please and thank you. If someone offers you a sandwich, take it – which was never a problem for me because I like my grub; always have done. We had nothing: a new pair of school shoes meant hard times.

Until I was fifteen, I can only remember Mam going on one date. That changed when she met my stepdad, the first guy to show her respect, although I didn't get on with him at first – teenage angst, most likely. I came to see how he was good for her and good to us. Before he came along we had jack shit. Holidays had been camping in Wales with Uncle Don and Auntie Pat, same place every year: nothing materialistic, just loads of love, so we were lucky. A lot of kids don't get that.

The night before we were to play Old Brodleians, near Halifax, my mam told me she and Terry were getting married the next day. I was as surprised as you'd expect.

'Well,' she said, 'we've been together a while, and I know you love your rugby.'

It was her way of saying that I didn't need to come. That's how we were: no fuss! I was happy for them – Terry looked after her, and she started enjoying life. I was happy for me and all, because the players always got hot pie and peas at Old Brods.

My mother was thirty-eight years old when she left us, and to say her death was a shock doesn't come close. She fell down and banged her knee, that's all, a part of her she'd had bother with in her youth, requiring a couple of operations. To

11

begin with she was confined to bed, but gradually felt worse – couldn't get downstairs on her own – and eventually had to go to hospital. At first I didn't think it was serious: you wouldn't, would you? I was still living at home at the time, but Terry had to ask me to go visit.

Four or five days later I went to see her again and, although there was no indication of anything fatal, something in my gut said otherwise. On my way home from that second visit I had to pull my motorbike over by the side of the road. I took my helmet off and found myself sobbing my heart out. She was dying. I knew it.

Within days they'd got her on life support: her immune system had just shut down, and twenty-four hours later that was that. She'd only been in there a fortnight. It was devastating, not only for me but also for my sister, Auntie Pat and the rest of the family. One day right as rain, the next gone. I still can't get my head around it.

Some people light candles to mark the day a parent dies. I don't know the exact date, other than it was in 1983 and around my twenty-first birthday. I know my mam's birthday, 17 May, when I shed a tear thinking about her. But not the day she died. Blanked it out, I suppose.

Terry and Mam had met when I was fifteen, so they were together around six years in total. He didn't want me to go to the chapel of rest, but I did: the first time I'd been on my own with Mam since she passed away. It was horrible. She looked nice and peaceful, but they hadn't done a very good job of disguising the post-mortem scars on her head. I had a cry and gave her a kiss, knowing nothing I would ever do in life could be worse than seeing my mother like this.

After the funeral, Terry and I took her ashes to Lodge Moor, a lovely part of the world with its crags looking out towards Derbyshire, where we'd decided Mam would like to be. I'd spent a lot of my childhood there. It was a beautiful day and we went for a walk on the golf course towards a large rock we used to run around as kids. When Terry launched the ashes, though, there was a sudden gust of wind. Blowback. We were covered: eyes, ears, up the nose, the lot, as though we'd fallen down a chimney. We had a good laugh and could then get on with life.

In the garden of rest on City Road in Sheffield there's actually a plaque Terry placed there in her memory, though I've never seen it. That's me: it's how I deal with things – I'm not one for stuff like that, posting soppy messages on social media and the like. She's in my heart, and that will do.

I suppose it's losing my mam so young that has helped shape me as an adult. You've got to crack on, haven't you? Get things done, because everything can change in a second.

Mam's death was one of three events that knocked me sideways in quick succession. I also got married, stupidly – it lasted six months, if that

– and fractured my skull playing rugby, although it wasn't operated on.

Thing is, I hadn't realized what I'd done at first and went out as usual after the game on the Saturday night. Same thing Sunday night, few beers and what have you, still feeling a bit woozy. Monday morning, I looked in the bathroom mirror and my eye wasn't moving – not up and down, not side to side, nothing. I went straight to A & E and ended up at the Royal Hallamshire, where a scan revealed a clot the size of my fist on my brain. If I'd gone in on Saturday, the consultant said, they'd have kept me in and I'd have been on a drip. The fact that I'd been out all weekend drinking and was still alive meant they would just give it time. I was told to take it easy for a couple of weeks; get any more headaches come straight back. I spent the next eighteen months going back and forth to that clinic. It took twelve months for my eye to start moving again. I'd double vision for a while and went deaf in my left ear, which I still am. Most of the patients were little kids with jam-jar-bottom glasses, so I was sat on little stools while nurses waggled Mr Men pens in front of my face. I survived.

Workwise, after leaving school at seventeen I'd done a youth training scheme in engineering. Despite failing the exam – I was more interested in rugby and going on the piss – it led to my first job at a knife manufacturer in Sheffield, where there's a lot of that about. Ninety-nine hours for ninety-nine quid. It was an eye opener – only thirty lads to four hundred women. If you bent over a machine you got back-scuttled. Your arse would be purple. One lass took her teeth out and kissed me – I was there four years at a time when sexual harassment wasn't seen as the serious issue it is today. Even that place had its tragic side though. I got my first proper taste of how I'd react in a crisis.

It came about when a kitchen knife got stuck between a pair of rollers that dropped horizontally to polish the blades. The machine stopped moving and the kid who tried to unjam it forgot to switch it off. He tried to pull the knife free, and the thing sprang back to life, dragging his arm in up to the top. It took the lot, muscle, sinew, fat, you name it; there was a big bulge at his shoulder. Rollers get hot, so it burned him too. Not surprisingly he passed out, so we had to take it in turns to hold him up. It took a fitter twenty minutes with spanners to unwind the machine and get him clear. People complain about health and safety – I've done it myself – but sometimes, you know, it does make sense.

It was at the knife factory that I met the lass I married. Even as we were going to the registry office, I was saying to Mark, my best man, 'Let's sack this and go on the ale.' By the time he'd argued me around we were in the car park with people stood around waiting.

The next place I worked at had a bloke on an

invalid scooter who'd been there years. One day, a bit of metal broke off a spinning-machine, size of a house brick, and hit him full on in the face, killing him instantly. He was splattered as if by a shotgun, poor sod.

By Christmas 1984, what with everything going on, I'd ballooned up to twenty-one stone, was divorced, and in a very short space of time ended up in a squat. Fortunately I'd another engineering job by then, but otherwise, bare floorboards, no heating, no water or bath, fuck all. I'd do my twelve-hour shift at the factory, get showered there either side of it, then pub, chippy and home at eleven, head down in sleeping bag. Repeat. Repeat. Repeat. That was my life for eighteen months, so I know what it's like to be homeless, although I did have food in my belly and I was working.

Then I was made redundant, so I was out of work too. Come Christmas 1985, I was starving and by that time had another mouth to feed, a dog I kept for company. We'd follow the old Express Dairies milkman around and swipe potatoes and other produce off people's doorstep. Well, I would. The dog had no hands. Once a week I'd walk around to my nan's for a hot meal, but I was too proud to go every day, cap in hand. This was when the Tories put a clamp on benefits and wanted people to move around the country – Tebbit's famous 'on your bike' speech. I'd had no money for two months when one of the neighbours began bringing me a bag of groceries once a week, which was very good of them, and I made it last. On Christmas Day, the dog and me had potatoes four ways: chips, jacket, mash and roasties, with gravy. I've been homeless and I've been starving, but not at the same time. How people who are both of those manage, I really don't know.

Things did look up. My dog went to live with my uncle and I could afford to rent again after I got a job manufacturing drill chucks. I was there seven years; secure employment saved my skin. I was shit at it to begin with, but when they got a new line in from France I moved over to that and never looked back. Well, not until the company was sold off to China. When we arrived for work one day, the gates were chained.

My second marriage was a happier affair. She was a nurse and we were together fifteen years until we began to drift apart. By 1998 we'd split up. I then lodged with Julie, a friend of a friend, for three-and-a-half years. That helped me out, settled me down and got me back into a routine that now involved a college massage course run by Alison, the wife of our rugby club president. I got into aromatherapy, Indian head massage, reiki healing – your alternative Japanese stuff, all a bit spiritual and out there. I even began to teach it. I got £40 a night, two nights a week, for that.

I was also a bouncer. Friday nights at Gatecrasher in Sheffield – earplugs recommended – or at Hanrahans, a trendy wine bar that attracted thugs and celebrities. Jarvis Cocker, Phil Oakey . . . we had them all in there. One famous, er, face was Dane Bowers, who made that sex tape with Jordan. He had a meal with his mate and gave the waitresses and chefs a hundred quid tip. He did the same with the bar staff, who never got tipped usually. On the way out he shook my hand, forty quid in it. Never judge a book by its cover – a useful life lesson.

Hanrahans was also where I first had a gun put in my face. Two local gangsters rocked up, hard as fuck, and people were fearful. They had a beef with the manager and pointed the shooter at me.

'Can we come in for a drink?'

'I'm on £9 an hour, of course you can.'

That emptied the bar. There were no last orders that night.

Then a mate of mine's cousin gave me the number of a company set up by former prison officers. He was an officer himself and told me I should call them. They dealt in female-only secure mental health units – for some reason called 'forensic units' – that come in varying degrees, like prisons. High-security units include places like Rampton and Broadmoor. In medium-security units people can't get out unless supervised.

The two places this company had were medium security. They were after hired muscle essentially, although the job was far subtler than that. I told them I'd been a doorman for a while, got the job and worked there two years. I'd done nothing like it before. It was a great experience, though quite stressful and certainly challenging.

The units I worked at looked like renovated hotels over two floors. One was just outside Chesterfield, the other in Mansfield. They housed anyone from schizophrenics to girls who'd been hospitalized back in the day because they got pregnant out of wedlock. When I started I was asked to have a read of a few case files, not too many as that would get in my head. It pulled me up short.

The vast majority of patients – aged twenty to around sixty – had been harmed or raped as children by supposed friends and family. One, abused by her parents, was put in the custody of her grandparents, who continued the abuse. At seventeen, she'd cut her grandad's throat and stuck a stiletto heel in Grandma's head. When I met her she was a pensioner, her entire life since spent in mental institutions. A standard life sentence would have seen her released after fifteen years. Put someone healthy in a place like that and they can become unwell just through learned behaviour: stay around mentally ill people and you can take on their traits.

The company wanted us to be as natural as possible, because the unit was these women's living space. But I was a male in a female environment, so had to be careful how I behaved. No walking around arms folded like a bouncer on a door. If somebody went off on one, you'd sit with her while she had dinner, take her into the garden, perhaps, or go shopping. One patient I'd been watching was lying quietly on her bed when a pool of blood began billowing around her. She asked me to get a nurse, who found a piece of metal she'd used to cut herself.

That woman had some heft about her – a lot of psychiatric patients do. One side effect of anti-psychotic drugs is weight gain, especially for women. Imagine being mentally unwell, size ten and going in hospital. Two years later you're a size twenty-two and have put on eight stone. Not good. She'd gone through the top layer of skin and a layer of fat: her intestines were protruding. The nurses made no fuss. There was no rushing about.

'All right, love, we'll get you off to hospital,' one said calmly.

Her stomach was stapled, and the next day she was back with us.

But it was endless. The Chesterfield unit had about thirteen lasses upstairs and seven or eight down, who were more of a handful. Mansfield had twenty in total, again over two floors. Some days there might be forty staff, because if one kicked off, they all did. In the morning, someone self-harming would get upset. Then another would, and another, until by the end of the day the place was bouncing. They could be violent as well. You'd get punched, spat at, bitten and we had to use as little force as possible to restrain them.

One self-harmer was pinned to the floor for

thirty-six hours, on and off. She had cut herself and began pulling the stitches out. At one point, when we'd got her calmed down, she was allowed back to her room. She slammed the door and immediately smashed her head against a mirror. It went on like that. She'd relax, you'd think it was over, and then *bam!* We rotated staff, put pillows under her head, turned her over, got her up for a cup of tea, and she'd harm herself again . . . I spent a thirteen-hour shift with her. We were talking to her all the time . . . 'would you like a drink' . . . 'are you going for a cigarette' . . . and when we'd let her up she'd run straight into a wall, smash a cup on her head or something. She was sedated for a while, but then off she went again.

All in all, it was a very intense job yet also fulfilling. I enjoyed chatting to the women; their stories were fascinating. It felt worthwhile, like I was really helping people. I connected really well with some patients, many very wary of men, given their backgrounds. I was quite proud of that. The few blokes employed, former prison officers among them, could be a bit unapproachable, but I really tried. I put my heart and soul into it.

While there, I got offered a chance to work in the private prison sector.

Forest Bank, Salford, was as good as new. A Category B men's nick – originally designed as a maximum-security Cat A, but immediately down-graded one level below for reasons I don't know.

It had opened in January 2000, the year before I arrived. There are four categories of prison security: Cat A, whose prisoners are judged highly dangerous to the public or national security; Cat B, whose prisoners are marginally less dangerous – allegedly – but for whom escape still needs to be extremely difficult; and Cat C for lads and lasses who still need to be in a closed prison but are unlikely to try to get out. Open prisons are Cat D, where the cons can be reasonably trusted.

Private jails get a bad press compared to public ones. That's partly because when they open it tends to be with fresh-faced staff. Cons sniff weakness a mile away, so anyone raw soon gets terrorized or becomes a target. The other thing is that when you open a new prison, the rest don't send their quietest and most peaceful inmates. Obvious when you think about it: if you're at Durham prison, say, and hear you can send twenty lads to this new joint, you don't go to the wing where you keep your white-collar crooks, do you? You get rid of all the dregs – the disruptive bastards who won't toe the line. That was how it was at Forest Bank. I met several dodgy customers there that I'd later run into again and put behind their doors in Strangeways.

As I say, I enjoyed working at the female mental health units, although the full-on nature of the place along with all the other stuff I was doing (working as a bouncer and masseur) was taking its toll. I was knackered. So much so that I sold my possessions and went to India with my landlady Julie and her boyfriend on a much-needed break. I'd been mulling over the prison service for a while, some of the lads in the units talked about it, so I applied direct to Forest Bank and got offered the job. The very day I had to let them know was the day we flew home from India. It would have been dead easy to keep going as I was, floating about aimlessly, not in a relationship or anything, but my nan's voice kept coming back: 'You never regret what you do, only what you don't,' so I gave it a whirl. What did I have to lose?

Actually, part of me wanted to stay in India, and I sometimes wish I had. But then I wouldn't have met our firestarter, Thomas Riley, would I, and hundreds of twats like him.

CHAPTER 2

LIPPY KIDS

Forest Bank in Salford was a modern building, fronted by what is known as a sterile area – essentially a place that inmates never enter. In this case, it was an office block where you hung up your coat, collected your keys, handed in your phone or whatever on arrival. Then, beyond a gated vehicle space and fenced walkway, also sterile, came the prison proper.

The entry point was 'Main Street', around 150 metres long and maybe 12 metres wide. Running horizontally off that were various buildings – gym, prisoner reception, kitchens, chapel, medical centre, workshops, etc. – along either side. At the end of the street was the four-storey housing block that held the prison wings – six in total, A, B, C, D, E and F Wing, but two floors each, so A1, A2, B1, B2 and so on. All the cells on the 'ones', first floor, were doubles, around eighteen of them, accommodating two people. The 'twos' on the second floor were single occupation.

The wings were flooded with natural light because the wall at the end of each was almost totally toughened glass. The cells contained fixed furniture of the type you might find at Ikea – open wardrobes, a little table to eat at, that sort of thing, very compact and well designed. Everything was made easy. Each wing had its own exercise yard next to its gate, so there was less need to escort inmates around.

At Forest Bank, if someone had to go to work, you'd just let them off the wing and they'd walk there, perhaps thirty metres, on their own: no prison officer required. Movement was far easier than at Strangeways. Nowadays it holds more prisoners than Strangeways too, up to 1,600, yet covers only about a quarter the amount of land. Comparisons, though, would come later. However superior Salford's layout was, starting work there was still a real shock to the system.

I drove over from Sheffield to begin with and that first morning I remember sitting in my car, an hour early, just staring at the walls and crapping myself. Am I gonna be tough enough? Am I gonna have to fight people every day? What exactly am I gonna have to face? I'd done my nine weeks' training at a centre away from the prison, but this shit just got real.

Clocking on would again stand comparison with Strangeways, only not in such a positive light. Because the place was so compact and well designed, they needed fewer staff, so there weren't as many fellow officers to blend in with. And the first thing the prison did was put you on Main Street, where there might be 300 prisoners walking past you to work. They'd all be eyeballing you and making comments as they went by – 'Shitting yourself, boss?', that sort of thing. One con, passing another new officer, said, 'Boo!' The kid jumped and they all laughed. You were on your own.

Within that first week, I worked an all-dayer with young offenders on a YP (Young Persons') Wing which housed eighteen to twenty-one year olds – a nightmare population. They're not kids at that age, are they? When I was twenty-one I was tackling hairy-arsed prop forwards. That shift, which kicked off at half six in the morning, felt endless; stressful doesn't come close. They were taking the piss. At night, the prisoners were supposed to be locked up by eight o'clock. It got to half past and I had to phone for help. A manager came on with one other officer and – *bam!* – straight behind their doors. Driving back to Sheffield I wondered what the fuck I had done. There was no way I was giving up though; my nan's voice in my head again.

There were two YP wings at Forest Bank at that time, built like every other wing to hold eighty-six prisoners, though we were never quite full. A1 was for sentenced YPs, A2 for enhanced sentenced YPs. 'Enhanced' meant the lads who'd behaved well enough to earn privileges like extra visits, etc., so they were less hassle. B1 was for remand YPs, who were the worst, and B2 for enhanced remand YPs. Watching them on each floor were three members of staff, including me on B Wing. There were a lot of big lads and a lot of violent lads, it really mashed your head in. They were fighting every day, not with us necessarily but with each other. All on the juvenile estate know that these so-called children are among the most violent characters in prison. Some may not have maturity or size, but they need managing with a firm hand. Anyone who chooses to work with young offenders I applaud.

Incidents piled up and not always in Forest Bank itself. I got asked to accompany a teenager called Mark on a four-officer escort to a hospital in Liverpool. His notes described him as a violent offender and very unpredictable. There was quite definitely something odd about him, standoffish. Usually in hospitals they put prisoners in a side room, out of the way of general public. Not this time. We went in a massive waiting room, size of a church hall, never seen anything like it. It was packed, full of people and, guess what, they're not all looking at him. They are staring at us.

It was uncomfortable. Comments were being made out loud, 'Fucking screws.' I was all for drawing a line under it and taking Mark back to prison.

Then one member of the audience made a comment about battering us and the officer in charge, big bloke, bit of bottle, suddenly said, 'It's all right looking at us like this, you don't know what this twat's in for.'

'What do you mean by that?' this Scouser replied.

'Well, think.'

'Is he a fucking nonce?'

27

Now I didn't know what he was in for, even though he was on my wing, but the atmosphere changed. It got even more hostile, only now Mark was the target. Fortunately, one of the nurses saw what was happening and moved us to a side ward pronto.

Back at the prison I decided to have a nosey at his background on the computer and what I discovered didn't make for pleasant reading. He'd broken into the home of an elderly pensioner, robbed and killed him, and then gone back for a fortnight buggering his corpse. Not your average teenage misbehaviour that, is it?

Prison populations can change and, at one stage, the prison decided B1 and B2 weren't needed for YPs anymore, they were required for adults. B2 was emptied first, they wanted to change the bedding, give the place a lick of paint, but the lads already there weren't happy. In the days leading up to the change they threatened to riot and got put back behind their doors, but by the time it came to shift the B1 inmates we'd got rid of a fair few on both floors and were down to about forty or fifty prisoners to be shipped out. They were still all refusing though, every single one. So the management said we were going to take the basics first, as they are the most troublesome and mouthy.

Among them was this gang member, Yardie, a kid I got on well with, polite and no bother at all. The manager told us to get kitted up in PPE – personal protective equipment – and Yardie was first on the list. Where possible this stuff was worn in 'restraint' situations; it was practical in a fight and the look of it sent a message. Fifty restraints would make for a very long day, so being 'timid', Yardie was the ideal kid with which to lay down a marker.

'He needs to scream,' said the manager.

He screamed all right. He screamed the fucking wing down. Four of us went in, big lads the lot of us, but would he move? He would not. He fought and he fought hard. Anyone watching might see it as brutality but, as ever during restraints, it was actually controlled on our part, well organized. Yardie fought back, though, and he fought back hard, refusing to leave the wing. The noise! Anyway, eventually we managed to get him out of there.

Another lad on the wing was a proper gobshite. He was a bad boy, a bully who I didn't like at all. Five or ten minutes later it was his turn. Moments before he'd been shouting, 'Fight 'em, Yardie, fight 'em Yardie . . .' so we expected more trouble. But when we opened him up, out he came, head down, quiet, like the kid he really was, and walked off the wing. After that, the rest of them surrendered, no more trouble.

Eighteen months in that environment was more than enough for me. It felt like a thousand years. Burnout. I moved to the segregation unit, where the real bad boys go for extra punishment, or sometimes just their own protection.

At Forest Bank, seg' was basically a corridor you went through a set of double gates to enter. On the left as you went in was the office, on the right the 'special cell', a temporary holding bay for the most troublesome new arrivals, lads who were kicking off and risking their own health and that of the staff – a plinth to sit or lie down on, observation panels, no toilet and no sink. Nowadays, with human rights and that, they are a last resort. In total, we had twenty-two cells on there, single occupancy. There was also a servery, where food was dished out, an association room and outside exercise yard.

Every day, by application, prisoners in for punishment could have a phone call, an hour's exercise and a shower. That's your lot. They weren't even allowed on the servery to collect their grub. We'd fill up a trolley and take food to their cells, three at a time, pretty much locked up all day long. Those not on punishment – Forest Bank had no vulnerable prisoners wing at that point, we had eleven sex offenders with us once – did get out for a few hours a day, together in the association room. All in all, though, it was pretty miserable.

The entrance to cell seventeen, bottom of the landing on the right, was the only camera blind spot and every prisoner down there knew that. There was another small area of the exercise yard outside, but that was it. You couldn't be filmed going into that cell. If you'd a badass on, you could threaten to put them in cell seventeen and they'd fall straight into line. I'm not saying we gave them a kicking or anything, but disruptive prisoners drain resources for everyone, including their fellow inmates, so the unspoken threat was enough. It was a dangerous seg' at Forest Bank. You had to use every weapon at your disposal.

The old man was just out for a drive with his wife when he made the mistake of beeping his horn at the driver who'd just pulled out on him. A mild rebuke, you'd think, but the reaction to it was not mild at all. In fact, it was insane.

Unbeknown to his victim, Michael Kennedy was a violent maniac. Although not the biggest of lads, maybe five foot six and lightweight with it, he had the strength of a wild boar. The elderly couple were run off the road, the stunned driver dragged from his seat. Having pulled the man's arm across the bonnet, Kennedy hacked it off at the shoulder with a machete. Nor was he done yet. He got the bloke's missus out of the car and started chopping at her. Bravely or foolishly, passers-by got stuck in. It was incredible that nobody died, though any rational individual would imagine their parents or grandparents in that situation and know that they must be traumatized forever. Kennedy got a public-spirited kicking and was arrested. By any definition, he was a horrendous little creep. One day, though, I would save his life.

Behind bars, his reputation demanded that we watch him like hawks. He went on a three-staff

31

plus SO (senior officer) and Oscar One unlock, the latter being the duty manager of the jail who works off the wing but is called to it if there's an incident. Basically, that's who had to be there whenever Kennedy was released from his cell. Even lunatics can do with a proper wash and this particular Sunday I reckoned he needed a shower.

As well as being a danger to elderly drivers on the out, however, Kennedy had been flagged up as a serious threat to women: he should be allowed minimum female contact. Handy then that our Oscar One was a woman, and that aside from myself the rest of the team were too. He'd be butt naked, so I asked for more male officers, only for the SO to say, 'There's three of you, deal with it.' As usual on a weekend, we were short-staffed and when the Oscar One came down, she agreed we had enough firepower to manage the situation.

I had no worries about physically restraining this scrote – I've seen smaller who were tougher – but he was very unpredictable and sly. I'd never turn my back on anyone down there, certainly not him.

'Listen, Mickey,' I said. 'We're gonna let you out now, so no funny stuff, eh?'

We shot the bolt and he strutted out, walking straight up to one of the officers and putting an arm around her.

'Y'awright, love?' he said. 'Fancy a drink when I get out?'

Now, he wasn't attacking or assaulting anyone, but that's still inappropriate and the lass was trying to push him away. The others were undecided about what to do.

'Come on, Mickey,' I said, 'get in the shower.'

There was a bit of what he'd consider banter – sweetheart this, darlin' that – but eventually we got him down there.

As inmates in the seg' are so dangerous, the shower curtain only covers half of their body. You need to see their top to know what they are up to and talk to them. The Oscar One made a classic error.

'What are you in for?' she asked.

It's never a good idea to ask a prisoner that unless you've built some sort of rapport.

'I cut an old guy's arm off,' he said.

'You did what?'

'I cut some old guy's arm off, love.'

'Oh, how obnoxious are you?'

Kennedy looked at me. 'Mr S.,' he said, 'what's obnoxious mean?'

'That you're a horrible bastard, Mickey,' I said, and up he blew. He tore out of the shower, bollock naked, and went straight for her. I ended up restraining him, while the two officers got hurt.

This guy was tricky to get to earth, especially when slippery and wet with his todger whirling around. The thought of it is funny now, but wasn't then, especially as the person who'd insulted him fucked off quickly without pressing the alarm – at the outbreak of any incident you do that to let other staff know something's afoot, and the cavalry

33

rides to the rescue. One of the officers who got injured did so instead. More staff arrived and he went back behind his door.

Thing is, he'd been playing up for a fortnight. What he wanted to do was go back to Liverpool, but that wasn't happening. No prison takes bad boys from a segregation unit if they can help it. 'We've Michael Kennedy here, dirty protest, staff assault . . .' – he's going nowhere, is he? You tell them this, but it never gets through.

This dick's behaviour got worse. One day I went to answer a cell bell – they all have them, for emergencies (they don't get room service). The alarm wasn't Kennedy's, but as I walked past his cell I could smell smoke. When I looked in, a blaze was raging.

The flames weren't high, but the floor was orange. As dread rose in my gut I yelled a warning and got a hosepipe. The door was red hot, steaming. After cracking the bolt, I got on the ground and blasted the cell with water for a good minute. Kennedy was on the floor too, his torso smouldering. The smoke was acrid and overpowering. People were coughing and choking. Whoever else was there helped me drag him to the landing where, despite him being badly burned, we flipped him over and I began CPR, cardiopulmonary resuscitation.

When I started the compressions smoke came out of his mouth – that's what I remember most. It billowed out of his gob, you couldn't help but breathe it in. But I carried on until the nurses came and stuck a tube down his throat. Once the ambulance took him away, someone made us a brew. I was still coughing my lungs up, felt sick. One officer threw a whitey, feeling nauseous, and a governor moved him away. Fair enough.

How did it start? Who knows? They could smoke in their cells then, but we'd light the cigarettes for them because they weren't allowed lighters.

Some colleagues were critical – what had I saved that piece of shit for? Well, him croaking wouldn't have given me any sleepless nights, for sure. Kennedy was a sorry excuse for a human being. But at the same time, you are what you are. My instincts were to drag him out and start CPR, so that's what I did. I felt sorry for the lad who was traumatized. As I would discover in the years ahead, it is a job that has a habit of getting to even the toughest prison officers.

One month we had a spate of cell fires on the seg', including one started by Patrick Durr, a nonce from Rochdale. It was a run-of-the-mill job where prisoners deliberately put their gear under the bed because it's less likely to get damaged. Property is important to them – it might have taken a while to accumulate. We bagged and tagged his stuff, standard practice after a cell fire, and then disposed of it since the gear was ruined. He then put in a claim, accusing us of throwing decent clobber out. The case went to the ombudsman, a solicitor was involved, and we had to pay him out. Ridiculous, really, since he started it.

Another star turn was Harry Hammond, a well-known crook around Manchester. Alcoholic, drug abuser, he was the sort of inmate I found fascinating, being full of stories. At the time I was his personal officer; we'd each get a handful of cells and their inhabitants could bring you their problems. Boy, did Harry have problems. He'd been abused in an infamous kids' home. A solicitor came in to see him once, trying to get compensation for adults who'd been there, but Harry was having none of it. Didn't want money, and it was thousands of pounds this solicitor was on about.

'I'm an addict, an alkie . . . it's ruined my life and I don't want it coming back.'

About forty years old, covered in scars, battered stupid, prison all his life, the lad didn't have a lot to live for. I got told he'd tried to cut his own face off once by slicing around it with a knife. He admitted to it. That's not self-harm, it's desperation. If you were straight with him, though, he wouldn't necessarily be happy with your decision but would put up with it.

This particular morning, we had an SO on seg' who liked to bang heads, usually for the sake of it. My first job was to go around the cells counting heads and gathering requests. When I got to Harry he said, 'Awright, Mr S.? Can I get my exercise today?' I told him he could, yeah. He was entitled to an hour in the yard – no big deal. I was on duty all day so would make sure of it – promised him, like.

We'd have a clipboard, and would tick off answers to routine questions: did they want a shower, phone call, exercise . . . that's basically all they were allowed. On punishment, they were banged up for twenty-three hours a stretch, pretty much. You'd then hang the board up in the office for all to see, same routine every day. Prison officers are creatures of habit, just like cons, and it was important to establish a system. You could never have two prisoners out at once, for example. There was no socializing. Most of them were fucking dangerous so they needed keeping apart.

When I got back from a few other duties I noticed that this SO had crossed Harry's name off the list and we got into a bit of a barney about it. Golden rule: never break a promise to a prisoner. Rights and privileges are important to keep the peace, if nothing else, especially in a seg' unit where people can go cuckoo. The SO was the boss though, so I had no choice but to get on with it. It didn't look like being Harry's lucky day.

In my experience, people join the prison service for all sorts of reasons. Some, like me, are just hoping for reliable employment. Others, I'm sure, honestly believe they can make a difference, to begin with anyway. Jails tend not to encourage idealists. I dare say some come in on a power trip and that would certainly describe this bloke, or perhaps the service ground him down, I don't know. Quite definitely, though, most prison officers at least try to be decent people, which makes the bad apples all the more rotten.

We had a young officer on seg', an ex-squaddie, decent lad, but like a lot of officers he was a chameleon: he'd adopt the personality and attitude of those he worked with. This kid had taken to fronting-up cons, a risky thing to do when people have serious personality disorders. Seg' is not a normal wing. Harry was on his buzzer, wanting to be out, so this hero marched off and came back, chest like Foghorn Leghorn.

'The cock's still wanting exercise. Told him he's not having it.'

I looked at the SO and said this was out of order. He just shrugged.

Harry pressed his buzzer again, and when the lad returned this time he announced, 'Prick says he'll set his cell on fire.'

I looked up from my paperwork. 'And what did you tell him?'

'To fucking crack on with it, like, know what I mean?'

Great. He also said Harry had covered himself in bog roll.

'Do you not think that's a clue?'

He just gaped at me, blank.

I got up, pressed our bell. Didn't matter what the SO said now, did it? I got out the hose, walked down and, sure enough, Harry was setting himself alight. I cracked the door, soaked him through, no damage done. The fire had just been getting going, and he wasn't burning anything other than himself, although he had put a dent in the door with his boot. The SO said to put him on report, but I was having none of that. If it went to adjudication – mini-courts in which a Home Office representative tries prisoners alleged to have been disobeying orders, fighting or having drugs on their person, that sort of thing (in public jails, it's the governors who judge) – it'd be, 'I wanted exercise and they refused me it after saying I could have it . . .'

It didn't end there. Harry had also smashed his sink, so a C&R (control and restraint) team arrived. In times past, you'd get six burly lads barging into a cell, two ending up with broken jaws. It's more organized these days. As they were getting kitted up and formulating their game plan, I spoke to Harry through his door and persuaded him to pack his stuff and move to another cell peacefully. But I warned him, 'If I open this door and you kick off I'll be in bother.'

I was able to let Harry out because he wasn't on an unlock, the prison protocol dictating the rank and number of officers needed to be there for someone like Michael Kennedy, for example. In a segregation unit, everyone's on a two-officer as a matter of course: never open a cell door on your own. It all depends how volatile the prisoner is: someone like Charles Bronson can be on a twelve-officer and SO unlock.

Off Harry went and laid down on a bed in the cell opposite, good as gold. I told a governor hanging about to stand the C&R team down.

'I've moved him. That's what you wanted, isn't it?'

He laughed wryly and called me a cock.

Yet another case of a cell fire in seg' was the burglar and armed robber William Cassidy, well known throughout the system, dead now, I believe. HIV positive. Hep C. Hep B. Baghead . . . the word once reserved for glue-sniffers, but it's come to mean any drug addict. For reasons best known to himself, he chose to appeal his five-year sentence. He'd already done six months on remand, so that was four and half left, then you maybe halve that, and in reality he was looking at two years more to serve, perhaps three, for twelve or thirteen burglaries – he was a repeat offender, this guy. The appeal process is long and he ended up at the High Court in London. I don't know how, it should have been kicked out. Anyway, he had his day of fame and came back with an increase – twelve years.

When he gets back to segregation, he goes straight in his cell, drops one out and smears it over the walls – dirty protest (or dirty conditions as they are now told to call it). For two or three days he threatened staff, spat and threw his blood products from the transfusion centre which, bearing in mind he was HIV positive, ain't great. Sometimes in prison cons will pay someone to do a vile and disgusting act called 'potting' on their behalf. They'll chuck urine and faeces, the works. Cassidy was happy to muck in himself, so we put a screen around his door and a blanket on the floor so he couldn't piss under it.

Two ladies from the Board of Visitors (now called the Independent Monitoring Board) came on to see him. To be honest, I thought the BOV were jobsworths at first, and I wasn't on my own, though my opinion has since changed. They come in voluntarily, visit seg', healthcare and so on, have a part in the complaint system. Prisoners ask to see them. They are usually well-to-do and are supposed to be there for inmates and staff alike, although few officers used their services. The feeling was that they looked down on us as scumbags, while talking about rapists and paedophiles as if they were Lord John.

William Cassidy had put in a complaint. We briefed these old dears, safety pins in their skirts, about the state he was in, and recommended they speak to him from behind the screen, at a safe distance from the door. It was for their own well-being. Even in a new prison, cell doors are rarely a perfect seal. The lock side? Yeah, tight. Precision fit. The hinges at the other side, though, created a gap you could get a slice of bread through. Prisoners used to throw playing cards covered in shite out. Hence the screen. That wasn't good enough for one of them, though, who toddled off like Miss Marple to have a word. She couldn't hear him, she said, and moved to the side of the screen. 'Don't do that, please,' I warned, but up went the hand – I could talk to that. And sure enough, before long out came the golden spray. I watched the jet of piss cascading off her plaid woollen skirt.

'Ethel!' her mate shouted, and off they went, not so prim, proper and matronly any more.

The SO said to place Cassidy on report, which I did. All fell quiet for a while. I kept having a look in at him, though, and sure enough at one point saw him setting his cell on fire. People like that get to a point in their life where they've nowhere to go.

He's not usually getting out of his cell covered in shit, piss and blood, as he was. There are rules to deal with prisoners in that state. To open the door we'd have to get kitted up: PPE, white suits over that, white boots on top of your boots, easily disposed of afterwards. The big SO, good and sensible, agreed we hadn't time. I got the hose, ran to the cell and kicked the screen aside, jetting water down the sides of the door as best I could before cracking the bolt. The flames were getting higher.

The walls were red hot, smoke swirling low as a dawn mist. He'd stuck wet tissue around the cracks in the door to hide what he was doing. It had only been going a few minutes, but Cassidy was face down on the deck, unconscious and covered in bubbling shite. We dragged him out and began compressions. He wasn't alight so when the nurses arrived they got stuck in, knelt in all sorts. Most are young and female; there are very few male nurses in prison – maybe half a dozen in my time.

They made sure he was breathing and got him an ambulance. Off to hospital he went with smoke inhalation damage, master of his own downfall. That new twelve-year sentence still makes me chuckle.

CHAPTER 3

BITTER SWEET SYMPHONY

You may think there is no alcohol in prison, in which case you'd be wrong. All you need is sugar, water and fruit. Once it ferments, fill your boots. Cons are smart. They'll use Ovaltine powder because it's got yeast in. A prisoner has twenty-four hours a day and seven days a week to play games with you. If there is hooch on a wing and they know cell searches are coming, they might hide it in a bin on the landing. There is never enough staff to detect everything.

I was locking up once at Forest Bank on F Wing and got a whiff of that distinctive sweet stink. It was the usual tale at banging-up time, lads fannying about getting tobacco – known inside as 'burn' – milk or coffee, and one kid tipped me off, 'Best go up there, Mr S. Some lads in a tangle.'

The closer I got the worse the sickly whiff grew – rancid oranges, mainly. Not only that, there was a smell of vomit. I looked in: there were four of them – a dad, his son, an uncle and their mate, every last one unconscious, and the stench was nasty. The prisoners were going behind their doors then anyway, and a call went out for medical staff and an ambulance. The son, dad and uncle went off in that while the friend was shipped to healthcare. Although sparko, they had to be cuffed to officers. One of the older pair died of alcoholic poisoning.

At the inquest it was revealed that between them they'd drunk about twenty-three litres of hooch. And when tested, it was between 21 and 23 per cent proof. I got questioned: 'How did you not see it?' The new lad I'd been on shift with sat in the office all day terrified. He was about nineteen, and prison officer is not a job for a nineteen-year-old. The private sector is all about bums on seats.

One lad in seg', John Dand, an ex-young offender, was on remand for murder. He'd gone on a revenge mission with a gun and shot someone dead at a party, case of mistaken identity as it turned out. At this point in his prison career he was about twenty-two years old and had already carved quite a reputation. Now he'd been found in the prison yard, out of his head on hooch.

We'd carted him to the seg', he'd fought back, and hadn't been in long when he blacked out and began spewing. Segregation and healthcare had adjoining doors, so we took him to an observation cell in there. Around teatime, a nurse manager phoned to ask if we could take him back as he was coming around.

So off we went and there he was, hung over and booting fuck out of the door. There were four of us plus the duty Oscar One, who said, 'Right lads, you can either get kitted up or we can treat this as spontaneous.' Getting kitted up can be a ball-ache: overalls, gloves, helmets, boots, pads . . . so we decided to go in and, being a big daft Yorkshire twat, I went first, rugby tackling him to the floor. Normally prisoners comply once restrained. Not this fucker. He'd have none of it, spitting, swearing . . . taking huge swings that thankfully missed. We got him to his feet, cuffed him, but still had to take him to the floor a few times as we hauled him out of healthcare.

'Fucking hell, Dandy,' I said. 'Give it a rest. Behave.'

He kicked his legs out, trying to trip us up, butting his head. This one time he went down the Oscar tapped his head with the side of his boot, barely a touch. He was still squirming, though, so we had to manhandle him. With a non-compliant prisoner, that's a dangerous thing to do, as you are either lugging a dead weight or can be ragged all over. They teach you to be careful. And you carry them on their back. I took one arm, another guy cradled his head, my SO had the other arm and two lads wrapped his legs. Still creating, he spat right in my face, so I wiped it off with one hand and put the other over his mouth so he wouldn't be trying that again. It was a revolting thing to do.

This relocation, through a couple of gates and over fifty metres, took a good twenty-five minutes. You get out of breath. As he was non-compliant, once we got him back to seg' we put him in the special cell – bare, nothing in it. There's a couple of observation points in the ceiling, where you can go up some steps and keep an eye on them every five minutes or so, to make sure they're all right.

So we've carried this joker into the cell on his back, me on his left arm. At this point no other staff should enter. We were going to strip search him, as decently as we could, to be sure he'd no weapons to harm himself or anyone else with. The plan was to leave him with a blanket, boxers, socks, maybe a T-shirt. One lad went out, leaving four of us in there, not counting the prisoner who was now on his front, arms cuffed behind him.

At which point, the SO turned this lad's head to the side and banged him one, right on the nose. Why he did that, I don't know. Dand had calmed down a bit, but his hooter was split now, claret all over the shop. The rest of us looked at each other in disbelief – *What the fuck has he done that for?* – while our hooch-supping friend rallied in strength, calling us dirty bastards.

Somehow we managed to follow the strip search routine and eventually left the cell. As usual, there was a nurse on hand to check the prisoner was uninjured or record any cuts and bruises, and on this occasion also a healthcare manager. Neither could fail to notice fresh blood that wasn't on his face when we wrestled him in. This manager gave us a knowing look and returned from where she came.

Within half an hour, the Oscar One was walked off the premises pending investigation, accused of kicking a prisoner in the head. And what's more, the prisoner wanted to phone his solicitor citing assault. The duty manager came and got the lad out on the landing, where the three of us, including the SO who'd twatted him, stood waiting.

'You fucking bastard, Samworth,' said Dand, pointing right at me. 'You punched me in the face.'

I looked him in the eye. 'Are you sure it were me?'

He looked at the other officer there and said, 'Well, you fucking did it then,' as the duty manager glared, fit to explode.

It didn't look good, although for a while all went quiet. The SO who had cracked him likely thought it would be all right. For five days, not a word was spoken. Only the Oscar One was suspended.

Here was a quandary every officer faces, but shouldn't. I knew I'd have to put a statement in saying what happened and that it had to be honest. But if I tell them my SO punched a con, I'm a grass. Colleagues won't speak to me; I'll lose my job. Ethics and integrity can go by the wayside. My mind was in a whirl. Common sense said, *Shut the fuck up, Sam. It's a team game this and you're in the front row. Head down, arse up. Pack tight.* But my gut instinct just wasn't having it. I kept coming back to the fact that there was no need for what happened – being a prison officer is not a licence to punch the fuck out of people. It's wrong and behaviour like that disrespects and endangers your colleagues, so where's the team spirit there? Maybe if this SO had just apologized for losing his rag it would have blown over. Prisoners being what they are, if he'd said, 'Look, lad, you've fucked us about,' Dand might well have taken that. But he'd kept schtum and it was now a dodgy situation.

Eventually, a more experienced member of staff told me that he knew what had happened. 'All I'll say,' he said, 'is tell the truth.' Then he added that if I mentioned our conversation to anyone he'd deny it. I like to think I'd have done the right thing anyway but the fact is I didn't want stitching up, so felt I had nowhere left to go.

The minute I put my version in, I was suspended as per protocol. In fact, all five of us in the restraint were ordered to stay off work.

In private prisons, whenever there is what management called an adverse event – a mobile phone is found, say – the pot of government funding shrinks. Every time there's an assault, they lose brass. So the best-case scenario for Forest Bank's substantial profit margins was that incidents were rare or non-existent. Given that system, cases were rigorously assessed by the Home Office to ensure impartiality. The guy investigating us was asked to complete ours quickly as five staff members missing was a problem. Investigations can take months; this was sorted in four weeks. I did about five hours of taped interviews and got a letter clearing me. I phoned personnel and asked for a return to work date. 'We'll get back to you.'

For two or three weeks, radio silence. Then I received a letter saying the company was doing an investigation of its own based on the Home Office's. I was interviewed again, and now was accused of assault and falsifying paperwork, among other things. How? They were using the same info.

My disciplinary was ten months later and I was suspended throughout. Stressful doesn't describe it. I went to a wedding where mates turned their back. It's a bad place to be, soul-destroying. I've seen folk ruined by it. Yet it wasn't me who'd done anything wrong.

I had said that my SO threw a punch at the prisoner. When I finally saw the paperwork the same officer had put that I 'might have caught him with his elbow'. The three others denied seeing anything at all, which is what a prison officer would normally do. Imagine that, in a space two metres or so square. If I'd have said, like I was going to, that I too hadn't seen anything, I'd have been charged with assault, probably faced police charges and quite definitely been booted out.

That's how it is. If you go down that route and the real culprit then makes something up, you can be seen as the guilty one. Tell the truth and you are the bad guy. Thankfully, I was cleared again in the end and represented the company against my SO at his hearing. The governor and I were on one side of the table, he was on the other with his union rep.

Six years later, by which time I was at Strangeways, another letter arrived from London. That SO was still appealing the decision, trying to get his job back.

When I returned from suspension after twiddling my thumbs for nearly a year the segregation unit was a different place. The earlier camaraderie was extinguished. Even though the manager there was looking out for me, I still had to put up with wise-cracks, the cold shoulder – it got tiresome. I was there two or three weeks, getting into arguments with other officers all the time.

Someone asked if I'd like a move to F Wing, and I couldn't get out of seg' fast enough, but nothing changed there. I stuck it out for a while, then handed in my month's notice. I couldn't face that either, so handed over my keys and fucked off early. By the time I left what few illusions I had when starting at Forest Bank were long gone.

Fortunately, I landed on my feet. By then, thoroughly pissed off and looking for an escape, I'd applied to the HM Prison and Probation Service and actually had an offer from Strangeways. A job as a carer at a children's home came up at the same time though, so I took that instead. At that point I'd quite definitely had enough of prisons, ta very much.

There were six kids in all, not exactly locked in but well supervised. Two staff per shift, so three kids each, which wasn't really adequate when they were troublesome. It was a private house, nice gaff, with six bedrooms, so the kids could have one each. Like anywhere in this line of work, though, it had its frustrating side. They'd all come from broken homes, troubled pasts, and this was where the system failed them.

One eleven-year-old lad, who looked seven, had been abused by his dad and uncle, and as a result began showing highly sexualized behaviour. He was smoking, drinking and generally heading the wrong way. A fifteen-year-old was a flasher, with a mental age of ten. He was another who had been abused and needed therapy, but all we were really doing was supervising. Kids like that need hope and stability.

Once, I'd got them out in the park when the fifteen-year-old started ragging the other, who threw a stone the size of a cricket ball at him. It caught me on the head instead and almost knocked me out; it was my bad side as well, above my left ear. Back to the house we trudged, where the manager told me to call the police.

'He's assaulted you,' she said. 'I want him charging.'

I didn't do it, of course. An assault charge on his record as an eleven-year-old? He'd just lost his rag, is all. Kids need to be mentored and cared for. The six I helped look after will have ended up in jail anyway: they didn't know how to fit into society. You can be a role model, fine, but I might only see them for two shifts a week. Not much of one, am I?

And so the conveyor belt keeps turning.

CHAPTER 4

STRANGEWAYS, HERE WE COME

The children's home gave me a sense of responsibility that I enjoyed, despite the usual frustrations that exist everywhere today in the care industry. It felt good to be helping kids with their whole lives ahead of them – or trying to. To begin with, there was hope.

It was also good to be out of Forest Bank after all the hassle there. When the reality of the kids' futures dawned on me though, that breath of fresh air turned stale as an old lag's tab. And on a personal practical level, by then I also began to regret what I'd lost and reckoned I needed another job with more hours and longer-term security.

Let's be clear: although I was choosing to work with offenders, that wasn't because I was on some sort of social crusade. I'd just sort of fallen into it. I'd been divorced twice, forced to sell as many houses, been homeless and experienced redundancy. I had an urge to put down roots and wanted a job I could settle down in and get my teeth into, preferably with a pension attached. Having been at Forest Bank, I was confident in my abilities as a prison officer and so thought I'd try and give it a go again somewhere else. Maybe a change of scene was all I needed.

In the private sector you apply direct to the prison, as I did at Forest Bank. In the public sector you apply to HM Prisons and put down your preferences. Strangeways was only my third choice. My first was Hindley, in Bickershaw, then Risley, near Warrington, two Cat C prisons whose inmates would be a bit less troublesome than Forest Bank. As luck had it though, HMP Manchester had greater need, so under that scary tower and within those walls I went.

It might surprise you to learn that when you apply to become a prison officer in the public sector there is no formal interview. First, they give you a basic medical. Then there's a physical that most folk piss, a bit of role play and English and maths tests, all scored. That's the lot. Pass and you are in.

The training centre was away from the main prison and the first couple of days went quickly, all seemed well. Then, halfway through the first week, the men in charge went AWOL one morning: not an instructor to be seen in the classroom. Managers walked past but didn't look in. We were like, *What the fuck?* At about eleven o'clock, one boss stuck his head around the door and read out one bloke's name: he was wanted upstairs. Then he came back and, after a while, the boss said someone else's name, and off they went too.

'What's going on?' I asked.

'Can't say 'owt.'

Eventually everyone had been up but me, which was quite definitely a concern. Had I done something wrong? How could I have? I hadn't been there a week. Nobody was speaking, and by now there was a really shitty atmosphere. Then the manager came back. 'You,' he grunted, pointing a finger, 'upstairs.' Fucking hell.

There were four of them waiting: two SOs, one principal officer, or PO, and the officer who took the training. 'Sit down,' he said, and then it began. 'You're a cunt. You're a bully – you're going to fail this course.'

Every time I opened my mouth they shut me down with this barrage. 'If you pass this course, you're still going to fail. You're a cunt.' *Bam. Bam. Bam.*

After about ten minutes of this I was feeling pretty small, until finally I just about managed to ask what I'd done. 'You're a cunt and a bully and we don't like fucking bullies in this job' – and off they went again, until even they'd had enough. 'Right, fuck off.' Wow. Back downstairs I went.

We were told not to talk to each other about what had been said, but I learned later that the two lads who went up before me got similar treatment. Admittedly, I can be quite loud and bombastic, but they were both quiet and unassuming. It was a mystery. One of them was proper down, in tears. I wasn't far off myself. Coming downstairs seemed to take forever, all sorts of things going through my head. I needed this job so, cap in hand, I went in to the classroom and apologized if I'd offended anyone with my manner, 'I'm not sure what I've done, but sorry.'

I'm a bully and a cunt and am going to fail – I had a lousy night. Were they just testing us, like they do in the SAS, pushing us to see how far we would go without breaking? Maybe, though I doubt it. I reckoned it more likely that one particular trainee had dropped me – and presumably the other two – in it. Her rude and abrupt manner was a giveaway. I cracked on, determined not to rise to the bait and be given the flick while our instructor filed a daily report.

The only useful thing was a week's C&R training – where you are taught to subdue prisoners in a three-officer team using basic martial arts moves. Fantastic. You don't have to be big; it's safe for you and, while painful, safe for them as well. We did that at Forest Bank too. Every prison officer, private or public, undergoes C&R training.

Nothing else in training prepares you for life as a prison officer, certainly not homework. There was a lot of that, though, preparing for life in both prisons. A complete waste of time. At Forest Bank it was mainly about preparing for tests and if I told you that the tutor would leave the answers on his desk and say, 'Right, I'm just going for a coffee now,' I'm sure you'll get the idea. They wanted you all to pass. At Strangeways, it was more about writing essays. I'm not a studious person, but I spent ages on mine, taking them in the next day so the others could have a look, trying to be a model citizen. I'd make half a dozen copies. One task on diversity took five hours to do, and I even shared it with the trainee I assumed had dobbed us in. Normally I'd have told her where to shove it, but I bit my lip. Yes, I'm a big gobby Yorkshire twat, but I'm all right really, and don't mind shovelling shit. The last piece of homework ran to about ten pages.

The next morning the trainer put it in front of me.

'Is this yours?' Yeah. Then he put down another, identical, with this other trainee's name on it. I knew I had to be careful.

'If I told you this took all night to do, and that I make copies for people who are struggling, to help them out, like, would you believe me?' I said.

Yes, he would, he said, and it was left at that.

The training process was similar to the one I'd already undergone, just one week less of it. Nine weeks at Forest Bank, eight for Strangeways. (We spent that extra week practising interpersonal skills, which to be fair was quite enjoyable.) During the day, the C&R week aside, it was all hypotheticals . . . searching mock cells, putting on handcuffs, stuff like that. They showed you how to fill in paperwork, write reports and gave us those tests on prison rules, legal rights and such. Mainly, though, it was the sort of thing that means jack shit until you are hands on. Do your C&R training and spend some time in the jail, that's what I think. A bit of training on how to react to people with mental disorders would have been handy too. I stuck at it, though, determined to prove how much I wanted the job.

I know someone who still works in the training centre and he confirms that things haven't much changed between 2005 and now. If anything, it's become even more about just getting people passed and onto the shop floor. The population of this country is around 66 million and they're only after recruiting a couple of thousand extra staff by 2018, so this is pretty embarrassing, I'd say.

Anyway, by about week four our trainer was coming around. The good reports began to swing things my way. Even the training manager, who was also a governor, began to be won over, sending letters to compliment me on my progress.

Bizarrely, given what had gone on, when we reached the end of the course everyone had passed, including 'big bully' me. We had a celebration buffet in the training centre and the PO asked for a word.

'I don't know how you managed it,' he said. 'I was sure you were going out on your arse, but I will be happy to have you on K Wing.'

Staff allocations were on the basis of alphabetical order, so I was headed to K Wing regardless, but it was nice that the PO would be pleased to see me.

* * *

Anyone who has ever swung off the M60 and down Bury New Road will recognize Strangeways – from the outside at least – as it looms ominous and tall on its desolate northern hillside. It casts a hell of a shadow too, with walls supposedly sixteen-feet thick: part red-brick Dracula's castle, part Colditz, keeping a beady eye on the Manchester scallies, smackheads and shoppers heading off towards Deansgate below.

Despite being only a stroll from Manchester Arena, the neighbourhood ain't pretty. Along the main road is a row of shops you might take for derelict, shuttered mostly, that flog swag. Police and customs officers raid their back alleys and basements. People loiter on corners. It's your standard den of iniquity, very rundown. Then you drive up Southall Street towards a glass-fronted entrance.

Before the riots, you entered Strangeways via old gates and a turreted gatehouse that still stand. In the 1990s a new reception was added for extra security, although visitors still smuggle all sorts in. The prison's central 'watchtower' isn't the lookout point people think; it's there for ventilation. But it quite definitely adds to the gloomy Gothic menace, especially when it rains.

If those bricks could speak, they'd tell a blood-curdling story or two, without doubt. During my decade, I saw stuff that gave me nightmares by the end. And the atmosphere . . . Every hour of every day, misery, violence and fear envelop the place, but then so do boredom, frustration and dark humour. Which is just as well if you value your sanity.

I'm no history student, but since I'm writing about the joint I thought it best to dig up some background info to go with what I know from my own time inside. Hours of in-depth research – cheers, Wikipedia – reveal that the name itself comes from the site the prison was built on, Strangeways Park and Gardens, and the ancient village it's in. The jail opened in 1868, replacing the New Bailey, long since demolished, in Salford. The online Surname Database reckons the name is pre-tenth century: 'the elements of the word being from "Strang", which probably means "Strong", and "Gewaesc" – an overflow of water, so a fast-flowing waterfall is the likely explanation.' These days it's officially known as HMP Manchester, and the bosses would rather you called it that. But for most of us it's Strangeways and always will be.

Now a Grade II listed building, Strangeways was one of the first British prisons to erect permanent gallows. Hangings were common before the abolition of capital punishment in 1964, which is roughly when the jail went all male. I was interested to read that it holds the record for the world's fastest hanging. James Inglis took the drop in 1951, twenty-nine, for strangling Alice Morgan, a fifty-year-old prostitute, in Hull. Seven seconds.

Strangeways has long had a reputation for housing some of this country's worst criminals. All sorts of notorious characters were locked up there down the years, evil bastards like Harold Shipman awaiting trial, Ian Brady, in for theft before the Moors murders, the one-eyed killer Dale Cregan and the horrendous Mark Bridger, who I had a run-in with myself. Other well-known inmates include suffragettes Christabel Pankhurst and Emily Davison (who sued the jail for turning a water cannon on her – don't tell Riley), antique TV presenter David Dickinson (fraud), footballer Joey Barton (assault), Stone Roses frontman Ian Brown ('air rage') and the Irish playwright Brendan Behan, who was imprisoned there in 1947 for trying to spring an IRA terrorist.

More recently, Strangeways has had its critics, not least for a higher than average suicide rate in a city that's a national black spot for that generally. It also became infamous for the riots that kicked off on April Fool's Day 1990, when 147 staff and 47 prisoners were injured, one con lost his life and an officer died from heart failure. It was then that Strangeways had its rebrand as HMP Manchester, part of a repair and modernization programme that cost over £80 million. For all that, it's still a place you'd look at and say, 'Fuck me, I wouldn't want to be in there.'

A lot of prisoners wear those riots like a badge of honour. They were Britain's longest ever: twenty-five days. One officer I worked with admitted that the first couple of days were terrifying; then they just began counting the overtime. Two days was how long it took to get on top of the situation, but then an order came from London to retire to the gate, basically surrendering the jail to the cons. Poll tax riots had erupted down south at the same time, and the conspiracy theory goes that the government wanted media attention diverted north. The screws were in disbelief at it all, certain they'd have got the jail back within the first week otherwise.

Along with prisoners remanded into custody from courts in the local area, Strangeways holds the sort of high-security Category A cons you would not want over your garden fence. Mobile communication devices of any kind are forbidden. Prison officers and operational support grade staff (OSG) run reception, the latter working hard on low pay despite often being called on for support in dodgy situations. A key area is ECR, the electronic control room, which sends radio messages and controls the electronic gates. It's supervised by an SO and the rest of the staff in there are OSGs. When an incident explodes, they organize the troops. Nobody watches all the CCTV cameras constantly – they are everywhere but inside the cells, as we've seen, on the landings, outside the prison walls, in the yards – but everything is recorded. When an incident needs to be wound back to and viewed, it is Security who do that. At the last count, Strangeways held over 1,200 prisoners and a prison officer count of around 400 and falling. Not many of those enjoy being there either. Going in, your heart sinks.

I remember my first day there in April 2005 well, partly because it was like walking into a maze. Structurally, Strangeways is sliced in two. There's a top jail, so called because it's up the hill, where I began on the infamous K Wing, and a bottom jail with passages, stairs and gates that it took me years to work out.

In each of the two jails, the wings run away from the round centre like petals on a flower, four storeys high. Each has a ground floor, the 'ones', and usually three landings above known as the 'twos', 'threes' and 'fours'. The bottom jail houses A, B, C, D and E Wings, all of which are residential, and F Wing, with the library and education rooms. Bottom jail is quite a building, architecturally dramatic and forbidding. Think *Porridge*, Norman Stanley Fletcher and all that. The top jail has five wings, each four storeys high: G, H1, H2, I and K. There's no J Wing for some reason – I don't know why.

After the riots some lord decided that the kitchens should be set apart, otherwise the convicts could dig in for as long as their tins of beans held out.

K Wing, where I was headed, was the biggest in the North West – 200 prisoners over three landings. And policing it we had two members of staff on each. Not good odds, are they?

As soon as I entered the building, the stink hit me. Prison smells like nowhere else. Not bad exactly, not obnoxious, but just as hospitals have their own distinctive aroma, jails do too. Six hundred teenagers' bedrooms comes close to it, perhaps, another ingredient in the general mood of doom. Being an old Victorian building, Strangeways also has a musty smell and little natural light to brighten a dreary colour scheme of grey, dark blue and magnolia. Another trip online tells me the architect was Alfred Waterhouse, who also designed Manchester Town Hall. He must have done this joint on an off day. Forest Bank wasn't exactly cheerful, but at least it was new. The only modern thing here was the plastic light stripping that gave it the feel of one of those drab and gloomy inner-city underpasses you warn kids not to go down. Strangeways wasn't *in* the doldrums, it *was* the doldrums.

None of this exactly helped with my first-day nerves, of course, and the first person I bumped into looked me up and down, unimpressed.

'I've heard about you, Samworth. You're a bully . . .'

As greetings go, it isn't the warmest, especially when your accuser is your SO.

Bertie Bassett was six foot two, had a good three stone on me, and lungs to match. He might only have been a year or two older than I was, in which case he must have had a harder life. He was a heavy-set fella with a moustache and gentle face, jowly as a bulldog, topped off by a Friar Tuck hairdo, grey, what there was of it. He was a big man and big personality. To say he was loud is an understatement. He didn't talk so much as boom, like a parade ground sergeant major. If he thought you were a twat, he'd stick his barrel chest out and call you a twat. He boomed at inmates. He boomed at staff. He boomed at everyone. I've no doubt he boomed at his grandma. And didn't we love him for it.

Bertie was as straight as it comes and could also be quite jolly – everything you want in a manager, especially in prison. In public he'd support you, then get you in the office and call you a fucking idiot. We had proper slanging matches that were instantly forgotten. If you helped him, he'd help you. No holding grudges.

As for this bully business, I'd like to think that once the rest of the staff got to know me, very few held on to that initial impression. Bertie would soon know better. Big Sam is what I became – even officers taller than me called me that. They certainly couldn't knock my work ethic. I always did my bit and a little more if needed. I made a point of arriving early, half six every morning without fail. I'd go through the metal detector, collect my keys, head out into a courtyard and up the sloping main drag to top jail. This bit is a sterile area: as at Forest Bank, prisoners never access it, unless they are cuffed in a secure vehicle. Thanks to high fences and a wall, you can't see much of anything outside before you pass another creepy structure, healthcare.

As time went by, the nerves at starting a new job settled, but those early days were pretty daunting. For one thing, with Forest Bank fresh in my mind I was determined to impress, and that training allegation hadn't helped. And for another, there was just the suffocating aura of the place. No bright natural light here. It felt like you had gone back to the days of Jack the Ripper, which of course you had in a sense, only unlike all these gargoyles and gangsters and legions of other dodgy bastards you could go home for your tea. I felt the weight of authority very strongly, and was keen not to put a foot wrong. Certain other people, not so much.

One day the officer who I'd suspected began this 'bully' business came into our office, on overtime. There was only Bertie and myself in there, and of course she gave me her finest scowl.

'And can you tell me who you are?' Bertie asked her, since he hadn't seen her on any of our landings before.

'First, you tell me who you are,' she replied.

Well, that was a mistake.

'I'll give you a clue,' he boomed. 'I'm the SO here, and I'm asking you for your fucking name.' So she told him. 'Right. You're on threes with officer so-and-so. You'll need to get India Nine.'

'What's India Nine?'

'It's a radio. At ten o'clock you're doing exercise.'

Her hand shot up, all sassy, 'I don't do radios.'
'You fucking what?'
'You heard. I don't do fucking radios.'
'If you don't do fucking radios,' he boomed, 'I'll take you down the disciplinary route.'

Off she stomped to file a grievance, not that Bertie was fussed. Before long that officer left completely, having been in the job twelve months, nine of those off sick. During that time she must have filed twenty-five grievances. Even then the prison service tried its best to hang on to her. In any other walk of life, if you can't do the job, you won't stay in it. That's not the case in jail – far from it. Attracting new staff is hard enough, so those they have they do their best to hold. The prison service is not in the habit of getting rid of folk.

The flip side, though, is that when officers do have genuine issues they get little or no sympathy. It's that macho thing, you see, even among women. You mustn't show any weakness or feeling. Prison can be a very judgmental environment. HMP Manchester had a reputation for being rammed with hard nuts. Not just among the prison population, but screws as well. Pretty soon, though, I realized most of my colleagues weren't physically tough at all. Sometimes I wondered what had made them want the job. Did they think it would be like being a schoolteacher?

Whenever I lost my temper, it was because officers weren't supporting their mates or were taking shortcuts. It wasn't so much the dead bodies, self-harmers and other terrors that got through my defences – though some did – it was how people were badly treated. Given time that would be the thing that got to me most of all: the inhumanity of it.

CHAPTER 5

PRISON SONG

When I arrived at Strangeways in 2005, I'd already met a few of the prisoners because some of them had been at Forest Bank. Where you're arrested in Greater Manchester dictates the prison you go to. Manchester or Salford – you're off to Strangeways, public sector. If it's Bolton or Oldham or Wigan, you get Forest Bank, private sector. So the cons could and did swap about.

Five of us were brand new from the training centre. We looked very official in our uniform – black trousers, white shirt and numbered epaulettes, so that when a prisoner is identifying you he doesn't have to say, 'That six foot seventeen stone bald twat.' MR837 is friendlier. At one point, the entire service got to vote on a new epaulette, like anyone gave a fuck, and I became MR444. We no longer wore caps, but did have a black clip-on tie you could ditch in summer under a 'short sleeve order'.

We also had a £60 boot allowance for Doc Martens or similar, something sturdy and comfortable that would last. You were on your feet a long time. Much later, they decided that was too costly, so gave us plastic ankle boots once a year instead. They had a non-slip sole, their saving grace, but otherwise were shite and cost about £6 a pair. One of my mates was diabetic and developed a foot ulcer, which can be naughty. He went to a podiatrist who asked to see his footwear. Both boots said size eleven, but one was eleven and half, the other ten and half. He was off work for a good few months. You had to wear them though: if you didn't you weren't insured.

As for the cons, back in the day they used to wear denims and blue-and-white striped shirts that had to be tucked in, made in-house. On the yard they wore donkey jackets. Go on eBay today and that old gear – with a prison label on – can fetch £100–£200. These days the sewing shop makes grey prison tracksuits or sentenced prisoners can wear their own clothes. Skint lads are issued with standard prison boxers – one size fits all – socks, a tracksuit with no pockets, a grey sweat top and T-shirt. Prisoners who get out of line are made to wear a maroon combo known as 'corned beef', due to its colour, which they detest. Imagine you're a Salford gangster, bit of an image, and made to walk around like that. If you are one of the guys, you're going to feel like a dick.

HMP Manchester was laid out like this. A Wing was for sex offenders, nice and quiet as those wings are. Not a lot of bother. B Wing was – don't laugh

– drug free. No wing in this country – or world – is drug free. It seemed to me they picked their own prisoners: hardworking types who wanted to do their time in peace. Once, I walked up to the fours landing, where three lads were strewn across the stairs.

'What you doing up here, boss?' one asked. 'Staff don't come up here.'

B Wing staff traded on being laid-back, yet what they really were was lazy bastards who spent all day by the kettle while the prisoners ruled the roost. B Wing inmates were regularly piss tested, but there are loads of ways around that.

C Wing was for lifers, a bit brighter and cleaner than anywhere else, though not everyone was whole of life. That eighteenmonth 'life sentence' I mentioned before went to a first-time offender who killed another teenager in a knife-fight: genuinely tragic given their age and immaturity. He was on C Wing. Not much happens, although being full of murderers, when it does it's serious.

D Wing was essentially K Wing's overflow, everything you can imagine – remand, lifers, troublesome, disruptive, mentally unwell . . . you name it. Walk on C Wing, nice and light, all painted up. D Wing – shithole. However, some staff loved it. It had a bit of a buzz, a lot of testosterone flying around. 'Smiffy, you twat, get that cleaned up . . .' – down to earth, a no-nonsense place to work. Officers migrated to where they fit best. Put D Wing staff on C Wing and they'd be bored.

E Wing was like three wings in one. It housed the segregation unit, where the prisoners were locked up all day; the small Category A unit with its own special set of rules, full of highly dangerous and frequently violent criminals as defined by the Home Office; and opposite that was VP (vulnerable prisoners), sex offenders, rapists, paedophiles and other such unpopular types, who are kept separate from the rest of the prison population for their own safety, do their own exercise and have their own visits area.

I remember one VP who came to us on K Wing, quite old, hard bastard and skinny as fuck. He had white hair, no teeth, and he used to wear make-up, black tights and a sequined dress. You'd think in an environment like that he wouldn't have lasted two minutes, wouldn't you? Not a bit of it. This guy would offer folk out, staff and prisoners – he'd go to their cells and threaten to do them in. The VPs were usually no bother. They might have considered themselves powerful on the out, but inside among the real hard cases it was a different story. Mostly, they were sly enough to know it.

Manchester had an anomaly, an OP section, the term for someone designated 'own protection'. A druggie in debt to another prisoner, for example, can apply to go OP, although why anyone would do so is mystifying as often they'd go to a VP wing. Then again, a lot of OPs are also lower than a snake's belly, so keeping such horrendous company doesn't matter to them.

Having three categories all on E Wing might sound daft, but it was a good plan. Cat A lads aren't going to want to associate with perverts, are they? They have a hard and macho image to maintain. A gate separated the two areas as well, so there would be no communication or risk of anything dodgy being passed.

That was the bottom jail; in top jail you found G Wing, where all the inductions happened and prisoners coming in were processed. They were brought in in vans, put in holding cells, stripped of their property in reception and moved there, except for sex offenders who went straight to E Wing.

On G Wing, they'd get a five-day induction course in a classroom. Prisoners very often shitting themselves were told how to make phone calls, get their family in, make money, how to survive basically. Decent arrivals were kept there for a good length of time. Any shite was fast-tracked to K Wing within hours. If they had only been on G Wing a day, you knew they'd be troublesome.

I Wing stank. It was for detoxing drug addicts and alcoholics. The stench of body odour was constant. The majority had no hygiene skills; they thought baths were for keeping spiders in. A lot were repeat offenders, living on the streets. They don't look after themselves. They'd come in with nothing and go out with nothing. Other than that, with only seventy prisoners when full, it wasn't a big population to manage. They were like medicated robots too: meds in the morning, meds at dinner, meds at night. On arrival at Strangeways, prisoners got a reception pack – sweets or tobacco. That made them targets generally but on I Wing, where everyone was craving something, they were like worms in a field, circled by crows. Once they were detoxed, they'd move on to H Wing to complete their alleged recovery. There was always a steady movement of cattle.

In prison everyone reckons their original wing had the most adverse conditions. That was true for K Wing at Strangeways, where I landed when I started. We had all sorts, the entire spectrum – from brutal killers to prisoners other wings couldn't handle to sales reps in for a month for crashing a car. It meant K Wing staff developed a tough reputation, despite being no harder or better equipped than anyone else. Lads in the private sector had told me it was like Beirut, and they weren't wrong, although while I was there it was mostly kept under control thanks to Bertie and the commanding officers. But I have very fond memories of it. We knew what was expected of us. The staff and prisoners we had on those landings made prison life as volatile and exciting as it gets. K Wing was big but it ran like clockwork.

Cock of the walk was PO Pennington, one of your old-style regimental sergeant majors. He had a 'tache, dressed smart and looked the part, Fulton

Mackay with an English accent. The entrance to the top jail was named after him: Pennington's Back Passage. He was very proud of that. His withering one-liners were legendary.

Once there was a fight on the yard, 200 prisoners on exercise and only two staff supervising them. Some drugs had flown over the wall. 'Draw batons!' yelled PO Pennington, like some general on a horse on a hill. So everyone did, but couldn't do anything with them for laughing. Another time his voice came over the radio, 'Send in the second wave! We need more troops.'

Above him was the governor. We had a few in our time. At the very top of the jail is the number-one governor – the one who gets interviewed on the TV when something goes wrong – but at every prison there are a number of managers lower down who also have that title. Indeed, every prison wing has one. Among ours was the training centre PO who didn't like me at first – let's call him Captain Hurricane. Most hands-on were our three SOs, front-line managers like Bertie, rotating on shifts. Two good ones and you're laughing. Bertie's oppos were Spongebob, a vertically challenged mini-me, maybe five foot five with a flattop. People said he modelled himself on Bertie, but so what? They worked the same way. You'd argue and it would be over. Happy days. Wainers, our third SO, was a lover not a fighter, a gentle man who'd been in the job ages. He'd sweep up the administrative stuff. Unlike Bertie Bassett and Spongebob, he

wasn't one for dishing out discipline or confrontation, but was a cracking manager too.

Then there was K Wing's married couple, known
to all as Tractor and Trailer, a rare set-up.
Relationships inside were frowned upon – they led
to serious conflicts of interest: how they'd managed
to get around that I don't know. What I do know
is that it worked a treat. They'd met at HMP
Liverpool and fallen in love. Personally, I wouldn't
want anyone I loved working in prison, especially
on the same wing.

Trailer Pete was pleasant with a goatee beard
and looked like a milkman or librarian, not a
clichéd screw like me. He was as gentle as Tractor
Helen, his wife, was loveably stern, fixing you to
the spot with a knowing look over her glasses.
During the time we worked together, she lost
weight, leading by example as usual, making Pete
eat salads at dinnertime when what he really
wanted was pizza or a burger. As a couple they
were a perfect match.

Helen's normal domain was the office. But, my
god, when she was out on the landing she could
be harsh. She said it how it was, didn't matter
how big or hard you were. From staff or prisoners
she would take no shit. If she was in the prison
service now, where staff shortages mean there's a
lack of control, she'd likely be assaulted. She would
not back down, though, even without support
around. We were all pretty much scared of her at
some point or other.

Pete, like me, was a landing screw at heart, at his happiest unlocking folk, locking them up again, chatting to prisoners, breaking up fights now and then, having the odd brew and a bit of banter. Paperwork? Nah. Leave that to Wainers and the missus. Although he had a temper when pushed, he wasn't particularly tough, Pete, but he was a caring man that the prisoners respected. 'I'm not Johnny Concrete,' he'd say, which made me smile. If inmates had a problem he'd either sort it or say he couldn't, no messing around. In 2008, he actually won the Strangeways' Prison Officer of the Year award and deservedly so. He had integrity, one of those people who bring light into your life.

I never wore a watch in prison, which used to drive Pete mad. It would have been handy, but you'd be asked for the time every five minutes and I'd rather get on Pete's nerves instead. Finally, he got so pissed off he gave me his own expensive timepiece, gold plated, crocodile strap.

'I've had it ten years,' he said. 'Cost me £200 did that.'

I'd only been wearing it two minutes when we were called to a restraint. Soon, shards of glass were all over the floor and all that was left of the watch was the strap.

It was amazing how Tractor and Trailer handled things, together 24/7 with all the stresses and strain that brings. That said, despite being on the same wing, it was rare to find them at the same incident. It did happen once, though, when Helen was in charge of locking-up time on the threes and was putting everyone, including Bertie, in their place. I was on the twos. Hearing a bit of fuss, I looked up to see Pete arguing with a prisoner and Helen going in a cell in front of him and drawing her baton. Screws used to have truncheons, wooden jobs with a leather handle; now they have collapsible batons. With 200 prisoners that's not a deterrent and, for legal reasons, there is an unwillingness to use them. Pete went in after her, someone hit the alarm bell and onto the threes we all went.

It turned out Pete had seen someone cutting himself. I've got my own classification system for self-harmers, on a scale of one to ten. Nine to ten means hard-core. They go to extremes, aren't fearful and know no limits. If they haven't started on healthcare they will end up there. Less than 5 per cent of the prison population are like that. Four to eights are genuine too. They'll have been at it for years, mentally unwell or been abused as a kid. It can be a cry for help. We had a lad once on K Wing who people didn't like. When he cut himself bad, which he did now and then, it was for release. 'Sorry to bother you, Mr Samworth, can you get a nurse to dress this?' He didn't want to be off the wing. Those sorts are few and far between too.

The guy Pete saw was one to three – manipulative. This type could be a druggie who wants moving because he's in debt. He might present staff with a noose saying he's going to hang himself. Among self-harmers in prison, they are the majority. If someone is really going to commit suicide they won't tell you, they will do it quietly.

To cut to the chase, this lad was scratching at his arm with a razor blade and Pete had been trying to talk him down. Until Tractor bumped Trailer out of the way, stormed into the cell and twatted him. The prisoner, that is – not her husband.

Every wing had a little brew room, where officers could use the kettle, eat meals, store stuff in the fridge, microwave food, etc. On K Wing, it was on the fours. At dinnertime, Helen and Pete would share a table. They were the sort of people you'd be happy to have as parents. They weren't that much older than us but, as senior people, they looked after the younger ones. On the landings they were decent role models for lads from broken or dysfunctional homes. Totally different as individuals, if you could blend two people for the perfect officer you'd have him or her right there. You had respect for them. They did the job right.

In K Wing, I was on twos pretty much constantly. It had four gated landings, plus an office and servery in the 'basement', our ones. As the wing was huge, looking after a single landing was a big job in itself. When prisoners were out of their cells during the day, they'd stay on their own patch, as would the staff, two to each landing – in effect, six officers guarding two hundred inmates.

On the twos, effectively the ground floor, the landing was around ten metres wide, maybe less, on which prisoners could stroll up and down. The walkways on threes or fours were only a metre wide. Nor could cons walk circuits, because one end was locked off; they were stuck in a sort of U bend. That's why we also had in-cell association, which meant they could mill about, but we wouldn't have them out on the landing chatting at night. Two hundred lags doing that at once – bedlam. You'd shout, 'Get off the landing' or 'Get behind your door,' and they would.

We were strict though, I'll tell you that. On the twos, there were forty cells, twenty each side. The bottom end had a dozen for the orderlies, or cleaners as we called them, mostly doubled up as they weren't thought a risk. Orderlies are model prisoners. They've got jobs to do in the day so they'd be on the landing cleaning, get a lot of gym, generally be out of your face. Down the wing on the left-hand side was where we kept the basic regime lads.

Prisoners come into jail on the IEP system – incentive-earned privileges. They start on standard regime, are put in a cell, given a TV and away they go. If they manage three months warning-free, they can apply to be an enhanced prisoner, which lets them spend more on their prison canteen every week, i.e. groceries like powdered milk, tea, chocolate and biscuits. They pay for these themselves to a spending limit, out of accounts topped up by their family, perhaps, or with money earned at work. Nine shifts would earn you around £6.50. Once sentenced, a prisoner is obligated to work, and would either apply for a job or get given one, for which they would get paid. But in reality at Strangeways there weren't enough jobs to go round so inmates with money coming in from their family wouldn't have the incentive to apply. We had about 300 spaces in the workshops, and a small number of orderlies on each wing, who'd clean or man the servery. There were also about 80 to 100 spaces in education,

On top of their wages, there was 'bang-up pay', which every prisoner gets whether they are working or not – it used to be around £2.50 a week. As they weren't yet guilty of anything, in Strangeways remand lads could spend £40, sentenced cons £24. An enhanced prisoner had maybe a fiver more. Extra visits too. A standard prisoner got about four visits a month, enhanced prisoners a couple extra. Remand visits could be daily. If you're on a long sentence, two more visits is a big deal. At an hour per visit, instead of four hours in your family's company, you had six.

Enhanced prisoners could also apply to have PlayStations sent in, a reward that would send some newspapers and members of the public crackers – 'Holiday camp, blah blah blah.' Well, they are model prisoners, so if every single prisoner had a PlayStation I'd be content: it would mean my jail was running sweet. No con is on them twenty-four hours a day – a couple of hours at the weekend maybe. It's not the massive issue it's made out to be. They need an incentive to behave, which is better for staff – civil servants remember, average people.

Below standard regime was basic regime: corned beef clobber, no telly, restricted time out of their cell. On K Wing, that meant two hours a day, an hour of which might be on exercise. A standard routine, by comparison, was a couple of hours morning, afternoon and night, though that could vary at weekends, say, and different wings had different times. A normal prisoner got a maximum of two warnings before being reduced to basic. Bertie and Spongebob were very good: if someone got caught eating or drinking on the landing, which was not allowed, only in your cell, they might let him off. If somebody was in a fight, however, or robbed or smashed something, was abusive to staff, they'd be warned.

About forty staff worked with all the alpha males locked up on the wing. We probably had twenty-five really, really good staff and fifteen not so good ones, but it worked. It was a tight-knit team.

Feeding time was a sight to behold. People visited from other jails just to watch. We dished it out on rotation. Monday, we might start with the twos, Tuesday threes and so on. One hundred and fifty portions of sausage and chips, forty curries, twenty vegetarian options, first come, first served. At Strangeways, they'd then eat in their cell.

We unlocked one at a time, half a landing at a time. Prisoners would walk down via the stairs at one end, collect their meal, then come back up the staircase at the other, a one-way circular system we were very strict about. No one came up the wrong way. Two hundred prisoners fed in thirty to forty minutes – we didn't fuck about. With food involved, the servery could be a real flashpoint. Everyone gets the same portion. The lads on there do it fair but if some intimidating gangster comes on – 'Give me more chips . . .' – it can escalate fast. If he gets more chips there's ten lads after him who'll want more as well and then you're fucked. We had situations where lads had to be restrained but it could be fun. At dinnertime you'd get to have conversations with prisoners and rip the piss out of each other.

For lots of officers that sense of organization was important. Not everybody was hoping for drama and excitement. Take my mate Lennie, who'd come in from the ranks of the OSG, control room, ages back. He looked ten years older than me, when he was actually ten years younger. He was one of the chameleon types I referred to at Forest Bank, taking on the work ethic of whoever he worked with. Next to a twat, he'd be a twat.

Somebody good, he'd rise to that level. But he did have a big heart. If a prisoner was aggressive he wasn't the type to dish out orders: what he would do is stand behind anyone taking charge, not cowering but in support. He'd follow you into battle. With staff like that, confrontations either fizzled out or the prisoner got away with it, unless someone was there to provide leadership.

The visits hall in prison is heavily controlled. Lots of fixed tables in rows with a six-inch 'divider' in between – the Berlin Wall, as one wag christened it. At Strangeways the place held 200 visitors and prisoners all told. Visitors – they might be family, friends or a solicitor if the guy is on remand awaiting trial – pass through security, and then wait in the hall for the prisoner they've come to see, to be fetched in by officers. If they're partners or children they can hug at the start of the visit, quick kiss or cuddle, and again when the hour is up. Drinks are sold in lidded cups so nothing is passed by mouth; you can't pop a wrap in a coffee that he'll swallow and get back later. It's all on camera. Officers walk up and down monitoring activity. Security is tight.

Lennie was on duty one time when I brought a prisoner over. In the hall I noticed another lad being visited who I knew well. This lad had been a young offender at Forest Bank: big kid, six foot four, plenty of gym, massive arms on him.

'Samworth, what you doing here? Better go away

or I'll do you in.' It was meant as banter, but he looked shifty.

'Don't be bigging yourself up in front of your family,' I said, 'or I'll sort you out after.' Yeah, yeah . . .

Lennie broke away from his colleagues. He looked nervous. 'Laughing boy there is plugged,' he said. In other words, he'd stuck some sort of package up his jacksie.

Now what should have happened – and would have happened with enough staff on – is that while someone pressed the alarm, the others ought to have approached this kid, told him his visit was over and, if he'd kicked up a fuss, restrained the fucker. So I asked, 'Why has nobody pressed the bell, Lennie?'

'We didn't want to cause a problem.'

'How long ago was this?'

'Fifteen minutes.'

By then, whatever he'd received – drugs, phone, money – would have been lodged right up his arse. I could have rung the bell myself then and taken him away, but there was nothing to be gained. These officers were embarrassed and asked me if I'd do the strip search when his visit was over. If he'd struggled, he would have been dragged off to the seg'.

As it was, he agreed to go downstairs and squat while I looked up his backside. There's a lot of controversy around that, human rights and what have you, but how else are you going to do it? Again, rather than escort him to the little room we used for strip searching, they let him come down on his own. He actually knocked on the fucking door. Normally, being on your own with a prisoner in a situation like that would be a no-no. If the lad was a dickhead he might allege I'd felt his cock or grabbed his arse or something, and then I'd be in bother because it's my word against his. But I guessed the young female officer already down there would prefer not to see this, so asked whether she'd rather wait outside and she did. Again, that didn't say a lot for those middle-aged men upstairs who were supposed to be prison officers, did it?

This con knew I wouldn't find anything, though – it would have been so far up by then as to be tickling his tonsils. So he just lifted up his bollocks, bent over, and proffered his ricker.

'Is that all right, Mr S.?'

Normally when a con received a package and you couldn't get it back, you'd put him in a dry cell where the toilet isn't plumbed, it has a tank. Whatever they flush, staff will find. Problem was the dry cell was in use, so he went back to his wing job done. Or not done, if you know what I mean. Got clean away with it. Not only him, his visitors too. The message it sent is that anyone could get away with passing stuff to this kid. The message ought to have been two years on his sentence and his visitors arrested, charged with trafficking. Prison officers without the courage of their convictions are a problem.

Same area of the prison, a couple of months later: Lennie nodded his head in the direction of another lad. I went over and this brick shithouse got to his feet.

'He's received,' Lennie said – perhaps he'd learned his lesson.

'Right,' I said. 'You're off the visit.'

The guy's fist clenched. 'Fuck off, I'm not going.'

'What've you got in your hand, lad?'

'Nothing.'

Bam! I went for his hand and there we were, fighting. He was a big lad, and it took us a good thirty seconds to grapple him to the floor, while somebody hit the alarm. He'd a parcel all right – a double whammy, phone and drugs – and hadn't had time to plug it. If we got hold of the thing, the likelihood was he'd be busted, in for extra time. His visitor would cop it too. So he fought like fuck, trying to get his hand in his trousers and push it up inside. This time, because I'd initiated, Lennie was straight in, no messing about, although in the end it took eight of us to restrain the bastard.

That's prison officers, you see. Not necessarily gym-heads or Rambos or physically fit, just average Joes doing a job that sometimes suits them and quite often does not.

As it happened, the police later found insufficient

evidence on camera to prove anything had been passed over, so not only did the visitor escape prosecution, the prisoner also couldn't be charged by the police for receiving. We had to make do with putting him on report internally. No pun intended.

CHAPTER 6

ONCE AROUND THE BLOCK

In prison noise is constant. There's a non-stop background hum. You can talk above it, but there's this low-level drone of chat and music from the cells. If it got too loud you'd warn them. From six o'clock in the evening that volume would lift and during association time, after tea, the vibe could be electric. On K Wing, 200 prisoners would be out, locked on their landings. The place buzzed like a giant beehive, and could sting like one too if you weren't careful, which is where dynamic security came in. Those two little words cover a lot of ground, but basically it's about developing staff–prisoner relationships that are built on respect, routine and common sense.

Dynamic security, in my view, is one of the most important aspects of prison life that in recent years has become devalued with disastrous consequences.

Security – physical, procedural and dynamic – was dealt with in training, although none of it means anything until you experience it first-hand. The last category is probably the most instinctive and some people bring little to the buffet. Me, I tried to build good relationships from the start and they stood me in good stead. One of my ex-customers lives less than 100 metres from me now, as the crow flies. Manny, they call him. He was a bad lad, he knows where I live and is no mither. I was known as someone who was firm but fair. I got on with people, treated them with respect.

One lad was an absolute monster; a cage fighter who came into Manchester prison after winning some belts. He was a European champion at some form of mixed martial arts – I don't know what. He'd got a pedigree and weren't happy at being in jail. He came on our wing and there was somebody there who knew him, a Scouse lad from the same sort of arena. He says to me, 'Mr S., he's a bit of a handful. If you want to put him in with me . . .'

Couple of days later we got in a row with him, me and my mate Nobby Nobbler, who you'll meet properly in a bit. We were toe to toe; it began to look dodgy. Reception had taken some rings off him, which he hadn't taken kindly to. Nobby lifted his eyebrows at me, as if to say, *Fuck me, I'm not after fighting this. He's a brute.* Fortunately this Scouse lad then wandered down the landing and took our cage fighter by the arm, leading him away. After a few minutes the new kid came back.

'Sorry, boss,' he said, shaking Nobby and me by the hand. 'I must apologize for my behaviour. I'm out of order,' and off he went with his mate.

Dynamic security infiltrated everything as far as I was concerned. If you worked a lot of overtime, like I did, you might find yourself on reception doing strip searches. I always tried to do that in a proper, appropriate and sympathetic manner, others just used to bark orders. To me, that's counterproductive long term. Without looking soft, you need to respect their dignity a bit and they'll remember that, meaning they might well be less hassle in future. They'll go to G Wing and then maybe move to K Wing where they'll remember you. It's about building a rapport.

Nobby, although he liked to make out he was a badass, he'd do his bit, Trailer Pete the same, one or two others . . . chat to the prisoners, tell them how it is, sort things out. Fantastic. Always remember, as a con, if your money's run out, your mam's ill in hospital, whatever, you have to ask a screw. You can't phone finance yourself – 'Where's my brass?' – they rely on you. And don't forget that prisoners move around, not only on the wings but through prisons too – many of those lads I knew at Forest Bank I bumped into again at Strangeways.

Familiarity, decency, respect . . . all these things come into it.

In a lot of ways, being in prison is like being in a soap opera. Prisoners interact with each other, friendships build, people fall out, all the things you'd expect. I've seen prisoners come in homeless, not a penny to scratch their arse with. You put them in a cell with a lad you know and they'll take them on board, help them get on with it. If someone's been on a wing a long time and been all right, you might put them in with a mate as a favour. There's not a lot of surface bullying, believe it or not, and in fact some lads inside wouldn't allow it of anybody.

Friendships can be formed on the bus, coming away from court. If you've shared a holding cell, there's a face you know to latch on to and it builds from there. Some are quite unlikely. Once, we had the son of one notorious gang leader in the city palling up in a cell with a lad whose dad was very high up in the ranks of their deadly rivals. They got on well. Some time later, on the out, one actually tried to kill the other, who ended up losing his eye.

In every prison on every landing there was a Mr Big, a mover and shaker. Some of the best-behaved lads, who were trusted with jobs like prison cleaners or whatever, were very often candidates for that. They might be running drugs or tobacco, having people beaten up if they stepped out of line, that sort of carry on. They'd take people under their wing too. There was always a hierarchy, sometimes two or three lads living in uneasy alliance, turning a cheek to what the other group was doing. The channels can be quite complex, but someone is always pulling the strings. We officers didn't give anyone special treatment, but we knew the Mr Bigs were there and that underworld could be very scary.

Their reputations can be an extension of what goes on outside, mutual enemies and mutual friends. Even then, though, you could use dynamic security to get what you wanted. You might have a word, 'Look, can you sort this kid of yours out who's kicking off or else he's going on basic,' and they'd nip it in the bud because they wouldn't want to lose a 'soldier'. The haves and have-nots are another hierarchy, as is toughness, though not as much as you'd think. There are plenty of hard bastards, street fighters, inside with fearsome reputations, so it's not as if that's a unique talent. I remember one con, a real hard case, who could beat anyone senseless. He couldn't hold out against four nineteen-year-old kids who battered him and then covered him in sugar and boiling water.

During my early years on K Wing we had this dynamic security aspect down to a fine art. If trouble was brewing, staff–prisoner relationships were key in shutting it down. You could tell instantly. Lads would start looking at each other, look at you; you'd go to a cell and, sure enough, there'd be scrapping. One minute the atmosphere was lively, then there'd be this slight lull – you knew something was up.

Prisoners are not grasses but, when it's in their interest, they'll let you know. 'Mr S., you might want to look in cell seventeen.' He might do that because he likes or gets on with me, but also he won't want banging up. When the alarm rings, the first thing staff coming on to the wing do is stick the prisoners behind their doors. Ideally, as soon as the problem is dealt with, everybody comes back out. More often these days, lack of staff means they are banged up for the night. No time to phone the missus, have a shower or get burn.

In the mornings, your average wing was very subdued. Weekends verged on peaceful given that no one went to work and often stayed in bed all day. No one was in a rush to do anything; it mimicked what happens on the out. With enough staff around they were dull, quite honestly. Standing on a landing from eight until half four . . . you don't want a riot, but fuck me, there are only so many brews you can drink. Then, suddenly, you'd be dashing to the yard as someone had lobbed a bag of drugs over. So yes, shifts might be boring, but they were also unpredictable at any time of day or night. Which is what made the job of a prison officer so unnerving and, now and then at least, exciting.

In my first couple of years on K Wing, when leaders weren't in short supply, we worked a buddy-buddy system, looked out for each other. Often I'd pair with Trailer Pete and other times Nobby Nobbler, who was quite definitely the joker in the pack.

Nobby was a big lad then – around eighteen stone and forty-two years old – though he lost a lot of weight later through illness. Again, he wasn't the hardest man on the planet – not all ex-squaddies are – but he had bottle and a great way with prisoners, a real funny fucker. Anyone who can bring a bit of comedy into jail is going to be popular because there's not a lot else to laugh about. Unless the joke is on you, of course. He'd cause shit on purpose, Nobby, throw in verbal hand grenades. 'Are you going to let them get away with that?' he'd say, winding you up, egging you on. I think the cons admired his troublemaking.

Like everyone else, at first he didn't like me. A man of good taste. Before long we were getting on fine. Better than fine – we had a lot in common, him and me. We didn't socialize, but our shifts were always good craic. If the two of us were on a landing and one went to make a brew, he'd tell the other. If one of us went to make a phone call, you'd say so. Going for a piss, same story. Some used to think that was over the top but we had a volatile population. You'd forty cells to supervise and needed to know where your mates were, eyes on all the time in case someone got ragged into a cell. Out of everybody I ever worked with on K Wing, save perhaps Pete, Nobby was my favourite.

With him it was one-upmanship all the time. We had a guy come in from healthcare around four in the afternoon, a stocky foreign national who we put in the end cell. He'd been cutting himself. On my scale of one to ten, he'd have scored a three. They'd done what they could and he was back with us, where he did not want to be. He was still on an ACCT form (assessment care in custody and teamwork), which officers filled in four or five times a day when a prisoner was deemed at risk, confirming duty of care. The forms marked that prisoner's progress and were given out after an initial face-to-face assessment when a treatment plan was drawn up to keep them safe.

Cell doors have an observation panel – vertical slits behind a metal flap, so you can see what's going on. I had a look in and he was over in the corner, this lad, only been with us half an hour, rocking away and cutting himself with a sharp object he'd found somewhere. Superficial scratches – well, maybe a bit more. There was some claret, but what he was doing – and he'd not seen me – was splashing water on his arm, out of a cup, to make it look like blood was pouring. *Fuck me,* I thought, *there's no way the wing staff will tolerate that. He's going back to healthcare.* But whoever found him would have a lot of paperwork, so I walked back and leaned on the stairs. The guy wasn't dying; I'm not evil. I was just getting one up on my mate. Nobby, who had been making a brew, came and handed me mine.

'Have you checked on this numpty?' he asked, sipping his tea. I shook my head, all innocent like.

97

So over he walked, brew in hand, leaned forward and opened the flap. He must have been stood like that for a good ten seconds before looking around, pulling a face and calling me a twat.

'I beg your pardon,' I said, offended.

'You're a fucking twat. Anyway, I'm having my brew first.'

Moments later, another officer came on the wing escorting a prisoner, as happens in a high-security jail. It's called running. You carry a radio, ask permission to move and have a maximum of eight convicts per officer. She wanted to know if that lad she'd brought on from healthcare earlier – sideburns like Prince Albert – was all right. We assured her he was fine, knowing his cell floor was likely a river of Ribena by now. Sensing that something was up, she went for a look herself.

'Oh my god! Oh my god! He's cut his wrists!' she yelled and hit the bell.

Prisons are like swimming pools, you're not supposed to run in them, but suddenly the place was full of people 'making haste'. Nobby Nobbler looked to the heavens.

'Fucking hell. Don't get the nurse,' he said. 'I'll take him to healthcare.'

So we wrapped a couple of towels around his arms and off we toddled.

It can be a cruel job on everyone – you don't eat well, sleep well, live well and often drink too much. Nobby rarely had anything for dinner. If

I'd a spare buttie I'd give it him, or save him a couple of bangers off the servery. He did though get a sudden urge for orange juice and began bringing a litre in. One day he said, 'Listen, prick, if you want a drink, just ask.'

I told him I didn't know what he was on about.

'It's disappearing from the fridge. I have some, put the carton in, when I come back it's empty.'

I suggested he poured some orange in a little bottle and diluted the rest of the carton with water. He liked the idea but took it a step further. He began to urinate in it. This went on for six months. At some point every single day, usually locking time, we'd look at each other and say, 'I wonder who's drunk the piss today?'

That might not impress some people, but humour was how you got by. If you hadn't taken work too seriously and no one got hurt, that was a good day in Strangeways.

I was on with Nobby Nobbler one morning on K Wing when I saw a prisoner I knew. His name was Johnny Gell, and I'd first met him in the segregation unit at Forest Bank.

Short, stocky, ginger and scruffy, he was assaultative like you don't know. At Forest Bank he actually went to a medium-secure mental health unit for a couple of weeks before being sent back to us. He assaulted three nurses – two males, one female – and hospitalized one of them. He actually floored me at Forest Bank, twatted me good from behind. I was wobbling all over. I'd been unlocking his cell door to let him back in. On a three-officer unlock he still banjoed me. Luckily, the lad I was working with was an absolute giant who'd put him on his arse straight away. In prison from an early age, Gell was a very violent and unpredictable individual. Two weeks of calm, then he'd lamp some fucker without warning. Bash. Straight out. He took some watching all right.

Here he was on K Wing. Only in for a week, he said, out Friday. This was Monday. I warned Nobby, 'Don't put your chin in front of him,' and went to see Bertie.

'We've a lad here who shouldn't be,' I said. 'He should be down the seg'. He's not good with crowds, best confined on a small unit in his own company. He will hurt somebody.'

Bertie got on to security, who confirmed his chequered past. Gell hadn't been in prison for a while, but had a record of dirty protests, cell fires and staff and prisoner assaults. 'Yeah, he's a bad 'un.'

Segregation, though, weren't for having him. Even Bertie couldn't convince them, so he went upstairs to see Captain Hurricane, the governor.

'Stick him behind his door for now and we'll get him moved,' the governor said.

For two more days this lad stayed on K Wing, so we locked him up and got him out like they do on the seg', followed their routine. A couple of times he had to be restrained. He'd far more strength than his size indicated. One morning,

Nobby was talking to Bertie across the landing when who should I see heading towards me but Gell. The situation didn't register at first, but suddenly I realized, 'Who the fuck's let him out?' Instinctively I knew something wasn't right, and as he went by, out of the corner of my eye, I saw his face change. Too late – *bang!* He'd belted me again, right on the jaw, and nearly taken my head off my shoulders.

I stayed on my feet, don't know how, and must have staggered a couple of metres. Gell was behind me now so I wasn't looking at him, I was looking at Bertie. He was in shock. Nobby spun round, I spun round, and Gell glared straight back: it was like *High Noon*, only he was the Clanton–McLaury gang combined and had already fired the first bullet. He must have been thinking, *Why is he still stood up?*

I was quite definitely thinking, *You're fucking dead, you, lad. This is the second time you've caught me unawares.*

For a prop, my nought to ten metres is pretty quick. Gell set off running and I followed him, towards the stairwell at the bottom of the landing. It had a locked gate, barred vertically and horizontally. When I hit him it was with the force of a rugby tackle in his shoulder, and he hit the deck hard. Pretty much as soon as we landed, I felt the force of Nobby – all eighteen stone of him – coming in as well. I was on top of Gell and Nobby was on top of me. We had an ace cleaning warder on K Wing, the floor was like glass, layer upon layer of polish, mint: we slid four or five metres, like a ride at a fairground.

What happened next was a car crash moment, when everything went into slow motion. We built some momentum and I could see what was coming. All three of us slid into the bars. I put my hand over my face, Nobby ducked, and Gell lifted his head just in time to crust a horizontal bar. The thing lifted his fucking scalp like a spoon on a boiled egg.

All hell broke loose now. Alarm bells clanged, and by the time we'd come to a halt, the troops were there. Bertie was back on form, shouting orders, and somebody had dragged me up, slapping either side of my face, which was clever given how my jaw was still ringing. To be honest, I was dazed. Anyway, the melee went on. After the initial impact Gell lay quiet, but then he started fighting again – half his head might be hanging off but he wasn't going to go peacefully. Eventually they got him to his feet, a waterfall of fruity Bordeaux gushing down his face. Blood everywhere.

Gell was stitched up and sent to seg' eventually. The incident was placed on report and went to the police, but nothing happened. Where assaults on prison officers are concerned, it seldom does. In fact, he got out as planned the next day after refusing medical treatment. When he left reception, he was still covered in blood with a massive swelling on his nut. There was little the nurses could do other than suggest he went to casualty.

Bertie told them to take me to hospital. Not only was my jaw throbbing, there was concern I might have dislocated my shoulder. The doc there didn't bother to X-ray me, just got me to pull a few faces, and as the week went on I developed lockjaw. Turned out later that I'd cracked the bastard. It gave me grief for a good six months did that. Nothing was ever made of it. I wasn't the type to put in a complaint anyway.

On the Sunday I rang Spongebob. 'What the fuck are you calling me for?' he said. 'Don't be a hero, phone back in a week.' Then he put the phone down. But them were the good old days.

People do not age well in the prison service. Take the Hat Collector, who was close to retirement. I've no idea how old he was – anywhere between fifty-five and ninety. He was five foot five and seven stone, an officer who organized prisoners' work patterns in the Labour Control Unit, a natty little job in a gated office near the servery, safely out of trouble. That nickname: back when screws wore caps and jackets, hats would fly everywhere during restraints, and our old boy's self-designated role was to gather them up and take them back to the office.

I was on running in the top jail one day, ferrying prisoners back and forth for visits, and as I walked on the twos and started bellowing names I saw the Hat Collector pop out of a cell on the threes. He must have been there on overtime. Anyway, he spotted me and began gesticulating. 'Here! Now!'

Up I went to find Bertie and another officer struggling with a handy-looking lad who was having none of it. As usual it was a wrestling match rather than a fistfight, though you can get punched if you're not smart. Restraints look violent but are usually controlled; people know what they're doing. So in I steamed, third man – we don't fight fair – we got him to the deck, no mither, and he was hauled off to the seg'.

In the office, someone complained that the Hat Collector hadn't got stuck in and that, if he had, there'd have been no need for me to get involved. But as I told them, he was jockey weight – he'd have made no difference. In fact he'd have got in the way. What he did very well was, first, alert me, and then have the presence of mind to undo the gate and hit the alarm. We're not all fighters. Very often you can see why those who aren't stay out of the way.

Reg Urwin was another old-timer among our team on borrowed time. Small in stature and about sixty years old, he'd worked in the prison service since Winston Churchill smoked sweet cigarettes, not cigars. On K Wing, he ran the store. If officers came asking for replacement shorts, shirts, toiletries or whatever for the prisoners, he'd tell them to go and look 'store' up in a dictionary. Stores were for storing things, in his view. If he kept giving stuff out he'd have nothing to store, would he? To get anything, if you could, you went behind his back.

We had a prisoner on basic regime, the Charmer, an arsey little twat five foot tall but as wide as he was long and nasty with it. He'd been on K Wing eight months but didn't have long left. Just as well – he'd threaten staff, that type of carry on. His language was atrocious, especially to women, a non-stop stream of vulgar sexual insults.

One day he was sent down to the stores for clean boxer shorts, because that could happen too. Soon, him and Reg were toe to toe.

'You old twat,' this kid was saying. 'I'll fucking knock you out . . . I'm going to find you, I'm going to kill you, I'm going to kill your wife . . .' I'd been alerted to the commotion at the store by then along with some other staff and we dragged the kid upstairs to his cell, effin' and jeffin' every step. Not that Reg gave a toss, he'd heard it all before. By the look of it, we'd had a run on underpants and Reg was not letting another pair go.

Reg was also a cleaning warder – a job I did from time to time – supervising orderlies. That was important on a wing as big as ours; it took some cleaning. Not easy with so many people around. Clean an empty house – piece of piss. Now try doing a four-storey one with forty overgrown kids on every landing.

Reg took cleaning to a new level. Every day he had a project. He'd pick the biggest badasses you can imagine, lads you wouldn't want to face on the out, tough guys with tough reputations, and put them in greens – trousers, T-shirt, boots, the usual kit for working in – and make them graft. He'd have them stripping and polishing floors, as Gell found out, painting . . . he got a lot of work done.

Cleaning warders run the servery too. They are in charge of all the domestics. Now as I've said, the servery can be a flashpoint. Normally, there'd be a cleaning warder on there, an SO and maybe a couple of other members of staff outside the area, looking on. This day, I was on the servery with Reg and the Charmer came swaggering down the landing. He'd maybe got two days left with us, this obnoxious scrote, and then he'd be out of nick. So he got his dinner, took an apple, and wanged it straight at Officer Urwin. He obviously held a grudge.

Well, it hit Reg hard in the chest. I heard it – a real thud. If it had got him in the face it would have broken the old lad's nose.

Thing is with prisoners, if they know they are going to be in a brawl, when it's pre-meditated, they'll oil up, to make themselves slippery. This lad was greasy as a gigolo's dick, baby oil all over him. We struggled to get locks on, even when four or five more joined in. So I kicked his legs from under him. *Bang!* He hit the deck hard. I went down like a stone too, his skanky breath in my face, and there was this enormous crack as my head bounced off the floor. I felt my eye swell straight away. This prisoner was dragged off again, to seg' this time.

Next morning I walked in the office with a plum on my face. Reg had his back to me, arms wide, and was telling the story of how he'd twatted this con.

As soon as Nobby Nobbler saw me he cottoned on. 'Was it a right or a left?' he asked.

A little shit had tried to knock him out with an apple – but the guy's sixty years old and ready for retirement, so why not have a war story? I went over to the kettle, my back to him, while Nobby still egged him on. Telling his tale Reg got more and more excited. People were laughing by now, the ones who'd clocked my eye. I got my brew and sat down, looking right at him with my good peeper. Mid-flow in *Jackanory*, he did a double take and the room erupted.

'Shit,' he said, head in hands. He apologized every day, did Reg Urwin, and retired three months later.

The Space Cadet was one who came straight through G Wing, the induction unit, so we knew he'd be a handful. I never knew what he got locked up for; he was a remand prisoner, could have been anything. He'd been telling them the aliens in his cell were threatening to beam him up. He came to us one morning on the twos, high as a kite, LSD by the look of it. You couldn't converse with him – he was staring off into the farthest reaches of the universe, *nanu, shazbot*.

At dinnertime, we'd served the fours and threes and then it was the twos' turn. When I looked into the Space Cadet's cell, I saw he'd been cutting.

Also on our landing that day was Dylan, a young officer who'd started when I did, a former marine that I got on very well with. But hey, he'd only just clocked on and I was on an early shift and wanted to get home. This oddball prisoner wasn't dying: he was trying it on and I didn't need delaying with paperwork. So I stepped to the next cell and Dylan, not noticing, unlocked the Space Cadet instead. I'm not proud of that. All I can say is it seemed like a good idea at the time. When the con came out on the landing, arms bloodied, as soon as Dylan touched him that was that. He started flailing and we were at it.

You are taught to restrain prisoners on their feet, but in pretty much every restraint I've been involved with we took them to the floor. It ended up needing six or seven staff to control this lad. We were not getting locks on and he had the uncanny strength prisoners get when they are in that zone – possessed by demons, they'd have said in medieval times. This lad, for example, was tall but not big, no muscularity about him at all.

I tried my best to get the Space Cadet in an arm lock, someone was on his head, people were lying on his legs and he really had it going on. At one point he ripped the shirt off my back. I went to wash the claret off my arms and neck – could have been my claret, could have been his, could have been anyone's – and when I returned they were still at it. I ended up back on top of the lad. Meanwhile the cons behind their doors still wanted feeding, so we bundled him off to healthcare. It was only a hundred metres away, but it took us another twenty minutes to get him less than halfway, and we had him in cuffs by then. With arms behind their back it's usually game over: not this guy.

Eventually we got him into a constant observation cell – no door, just a gate covered by Perspex so you can see through. The nurse manager told us not to leave him, though – he was too dangerous – so we had to lug him a bit further to the seg'. Six or seven of us were still sweating our backs out nearly half an hour after coming in, and off we went again with this lad whirling like a dervish. By then, the entire jail was in lockdown and prisoners in the seg' were cheering him on – 'Go on, lad, give it 'em!'

To get him there took another twenty minutes. Normally their staff then took over, but they saw us covered in claret. The cuts weren't deep, but mixed with sweat, blood is like oil: a little goes a long way. He went in the special cell, where the idea was to do a strip search, common procedure with non-compliant prisoners after relocation. You'd lay them down using a variation on the old wrestling 'figure of four'. Now this can be very painful – I've had it done on me in training – and once again the Space Cadet was having none of it. His legs were like steel: he'd got them straight and they weren't for bending. The seg' staff were outside gazing in.

'Are you giving us a hand or what?' I asked the seg' SO.

In came the troops, eight or nine on him now, and in the end it was decided the best course of action was to get the cuffs off and then, one at a time, as best we could, get the hell out. How we did that wasn't textbook, but somehow we managed it. It was three o'clock when I left the jail, so much for getting off early. Served me right, I suppose.

A couple of days later, I answered the phone on K Wing. 'We've a lad in segregation for you, been here two days . . .' the officer said and I started laughing.

'The Space Cadet,' I said. 'We brought him in . . .'

'Yeah and I heard it took forty of you a couple of hours,' he said.

Anyway, I went down as backup for the Tornado team, one of whom gave me a nudge when I arrived. 'We've got the experts in now, Sammy,' he said. 'This is the A team, not K Wing's shower of shit.'

They opened the cell and out walked the Space Cadet, clearly still tuning into Mars. To their credit, they realized their predicament straight away and tried to guide him back. He'd only stepped out by a metre or so, if that. But guess what? He was having none of it.

Forty minutes later, with a bit of help from yours truly, in he went. Our Tornado team 'expert' meanwhile was on his haunches, helmet off, sweating like a sumo's backside.

I'm not sure how the Space Cadet got back to K Wing. Maybe Scotty beamed him up.

CHAPTER 7

LOCK ALL THE DOORS

I never got calls from work at home, ever. But this Saturday night I'd just cracked open a can of Stones Bitter, my favourite as it's brewed in Sheffield, and 'Strangeways' flashed up on my phone.

'Officer Samworth – Tornado?'

'Yeah. Is it Danny Gee?'

I knew it. I'd had a couple of sips of bitter, and it would've been easy to have put my phone on silent and left them to it. The takeaway I'd ordered got put on hold. But by now I was on the Tornado team myself and this was what I'd done my training for. I put my ale down, went for a nervous shit and got in the car.

Tornado training involves kitting up with protective gear, like shields and helmets, and learning to work in teams on everything from controlling troublesome prisoners like the Space Cadet to putting down a full-scale uprising. In my opinion every jail should have a greater percentage of staff Tornado trained. It's a very good thing: it gives you confidence, especially in potential riot situations, and at Manchester there was no shortage of lads wanting a go.

It had been a tough enough course in Doncaster, lining up with shields at forty-five degrees, three against one, while guys threw stuff at you, and as the week went on, it got tougher. One block of wood hit me in the guts, leaving a six-by-six bruise. Fucking painful, but you got on with it. Us Manchester lads were up for it and got stuck in, breaking down barricades, all the scenarios you'd expect in a prison riot. The guys from other prisons looked terrified – southern softies who don't like chips and gravy, I bet, filing accident forms for stubbed toes. But riot training has to be realistic. People need to know what facing angry nutters who are out to knock your head off will be like, don't they?

We trained as twelve-officer units which, when qualified, were theoretically at the prison service's disposal, primed to be sent to whatever jail had a riot, or 'mutiny' as they now call it, on its hands. But as Manchester is in the high-security estate, we were rarely called out: it's not the sort of jail where you can afford to send, say, twenty-four lads away for three days at HMP Haverigg, a Cat C prison in the Lake District. It used to piss me right off. I'd got the Tornado training and wanted the opportunity to experience a real-life situation, but it didn't happen. Instead our four units, filled by forty to fifty staff, were mainly used in-house, where at least you'd get scenarios that might require such skills.

Normal prisoners would be taken to hospital,

say, on a minibus or van. It would have a cage in, but wasn't bulletproof or anything, just an ordinary Transit with a driver and someone cuffed to the criminal. For taking people to court you had sweat wagons, the white vehicles with little square windows that everyone's seen on the news, mobs of people spitting at them, usually. Cons are locked in little cubicles similar to Catholic confessionals. Cat A transport is different again: they might have up to four mini-cells aboard for fuckers like that, and the vehicle is armoured, with big bumpers, and often has a police escort. They're called heavy vehicle ballistics, or HVB, for good reason: they can go through walls if they have to. Whatever the transport, if someone is non-compliant you go on in your kit, get them out of their box-cell and take them off safely.

I couldn't wait for my first chance to put the Tornado training into action and it came when an HVB was scheduled to arrive at Cat A reception with a Muslim lad on it from Belmarsh. He was a violent extremist, we were told, a lot of staff and prisoner assaults, all sorts flying about, so they wanted six tough guys to greet him. There we all were, fully kitted up, yet when he came off he was about five foot eight and sobbing. What a let-down. Yeah, he was extremist. Yeah, he was a Muslim. But he was not big, not hard and he'd been brought to Manchester because he was on trial in Liverpool and they weren't going to transport him up to Merseyside from the Smoke every day. It was my first taste of Tornado and I was left bitching about it.

Now here was my phone ringing on a Saturday night about Danny Gee.

I knew that going in a cell with that monster was not going to be fun, but also that I couldn't turn the chance down. Something in my personality, I suppose. Anyway, all the old rugby adrenaline began to kick in.

The Gee family are infamous in Liverpool: notorious local gangsters. We had Danny's brother Darren, the brains of the operation, on K Wing for two years on remand. Me and him got on well in the end, though I've no doubt he was a naughty lad. You would not want to cross him. Eventually, Darren Gee was found guilty of conspiracy to murder. No witnesses, but he was caught within a mile and a half of the victim, and it had been common knowledge in the underworld that he was out to get him. The guy had tried to take his own life and killed a friend of Gee in the process. Gee got an eighteen-year sentence, but with time served call it sixteen. With good behaviour and parole, he might be out in eight.

Darren Gee spoke to very few officers; in fact it was six months before he spoke to me. He was a cleaner, not a Jack the Lad type, but quite definitely cool, calculating and devious. I'd sum him up as a brutal, ruthless enforcer.

When he got sentenced he was moved down to C Wing, as a lifer. By time I'd moved on myself, to healthcare, a part of jail there'll be plenty more about anon. For now, all you need to know is that one particular morning we had a kid come on shitting himself, and I don't mean diarrhoea. He was a well-behaved and likeable prisoner normally, so I said, 'What are you doing here?'

'I've done something very stupid, Mr S.'

'What have you done?'

'I didn't know who Darren Gee were and some of the lads paid me to do him in.' Segregation was full; Gee could still have reached him on OP, so he'd come to us for protection.

That tells you something about Darren Gee, the fact that people had wanted him done in but were only brave enough to get someone else to do it.

What had happened was this: Gee had been playing pool when this kid walked up and twatted him with a tin of tuna in a sock. After being knocked to the floor, Gee then got up and chased his attacker back to his cell. Although Gee's not as well known in Manchester as he is in Liverpool, there are plenty of Scousers in Strangeways who were happy to enlighten the kid, so he is now panicking and wanting out of the jail.

I didn't blame him. Security reports came back that if he returned to a normal wing, they were on his trail and he'd get stabbed, so he got his wish.

The concern now, though, was Darren's brother, Danny, who'd been playing up in the seg' special cell. He was here on accumulated visits, back in

116

Manchester from some long-term dispersal prison to be temporarily closer to home. He'd been inside since his youth and battered senseless as a young offender. The system had made this guy: he'd had some hidings. But as a gangster his reputation had grown, and now he was fucking ruthless. He was once shot at point-blank range in the chest with a revolver – it's not an urban myth, this – which had removed a sizeable chunk of his back. When he'd regained consciousness, he'd discharged himself from casualty.

Not only was he tough, he was physically dominating and powerful. American jails have realized that when you have yards full of Olympic weights and get people locked up for twenty years using them every day, they end up huge: not great when battle lines are drawn. Danny Gee's neck measured about twenty inches. He stood six foot one and weighed seventeen stone fit, twenty-one stone unfit. His wrists were like my thighs, tree trunks. Ankles too. He could've bench-pressed an oak tree and squatted nearly 300 kilograms.

Now, I've met people like that on K Wing, and we've restrained them easily. Even with decent muscle mass, when someone puts you in an arm lock it will throb, perhaps even more so. Gee's mentality was something else. He'd been in prison forever, seen and done it all – cell fires, restraint, dirty protests, the lot. He'd fought prisoners, had staff coming at him with shields: the guy knew no fear. He was one in a hundred, him.

The night before, he'd been in a normal cell and threatened to do untold damage, so they'd wanted him shifted. He'd refused to move, and ended up battering eleven staff in full riot gear, a fair few hard nuts among them. He'd not attacked anyone specifically: he'd just stood in his cell and swung them around, like a grizzly bear swatting mosquitos. He got one lad by the back of his helmet and lifted him up and down as if he was sucking his cock. Eleven staff! They were coming out, taking helmets off, wiping away the sweat, putting them back on and going back in. They got nowhere fast. This was one incident that couldn't be de-escalated. He was yanking their chain because he could.

'Why are you being like this, Danny?' I was told the governor had asked him. 'We just want you to move.'

'You want me to move, guv, ask nicely. Get these muppets out.'

So that's what had happened. The staff came out. Gee collected his burn and was led away to the special cell. You couldn't even call it a score draw.

When we assembled it was about nine o'clock that night. There were twelve of us in total. At the briefing, we were told not only had Danny Gee been given tobacco, but he'd also got a lighter, and he was now threatening to set his new cell alight.

'We are taking no shit,' the big daft Scouse PO said. 'We are not having this prick dictate to us.'

He was right about that, the PO. If we backed off, Gee'd take the piss. We had to stand up for the jail. We were going into battle.

Most of us were in our standard PPE gear, but the C&R instructors wore full-on SWAT outfits, like the elite Tornado national squad wear: German helmets, goggles, fitted overalls. Their tactics were impressive too; shame about the execution. The first guy would go in with a small shield a foot and half wide, handy for manoeuvrability. He'd be followed by two more and a fourth German helmet with a large shield – about three foot wide – behind him, two more at the rear. Hands on shoulders. The rest of us were sweeper-uppers, coming in on the tail – two of us literally with brushes to clear any debris so Gee couldn't set it on fire. In we all filed as ordered, me at twelfth man with a broom. I'd been shitting through the eye of a needle for this and missed Ant and Dec, but being professional I took it on the chin.

Now, this special cell was about eight foot wide. But what this strong fucker had done somehow was climb onto the ceiling like Spiderman, an arm on each wall – it wasn't that high, but Christ – and blocked up the observation panels with wet toilet paper, so no one could see him. He'd also blocked the door panel, so we went in blind.

The bolt was cracked, and what a fucking car crash. He'd done the old cons' trick, wet the floor with piss, shite and soapy water, and people were slipping everywhere. While the first through the door were falling arse over tit, the lads behind pushed further in, and the German helmet brigade wasted no more time. They dived on Danny Gee, five of them took his head and upper arms, a fellow Yorkshire lad called Gilly the other end, one or two in between. I'd got my sweeping brush. Here was something else nobody had thought about. The fucking light was out – we were in the dark.

Someone hit the switch and reality dawned. Gee wasn't a normal prisoner. They'd assumed his head was at the top of the bed but it wasn't. It was at the bottom. So actually there were five lads in German helmets on his legs and one lad, Gilly, on his top half. More lads piled on and there were ten people swarming over him now. But guess what? The fucker started to rise. Sod the sweeping up. I threw the brush into the corridor and jumped on his shoulders with Gilly. We were both looking directly in Gee's face.

'You dirty sneaky screw bastards,' he said. 'Coming in here to fucking twist me up when I'm asleep. I'm going to fucking kill you.'

I had a bit of a nervous chuckle because he had the potential to do that, trust me. One or two lads were panicking, and a couple had evacuated the cell already, so the dirty dozen was now ten.

I can't tell you exactly what happened next, it was like when you're a kid with your schoolmates, a copper chases you and you're pissing yourself, pushing each other out the way. You don't want to be at the back. I do know that I was one of the last to get out and that by then Danny Gee was up to his full height and going for it, desperate to have somebody.

You know those old cartoons where the puddy tat passes the bulldog and the dog grabs its collar but the legs keep going round and round? Danny Gee did that with one of our troops, the officer's legs and arms reaching out in vain as he was ragged back into the cell. Shit. So we piled inside again, four of us anyway. Eventually Gee was sent sprawling to the deck – it was only a glancing blow, but the floor was covered with all sorts and he slipped, freeing the lad. This was about survival now. We battered him a few times so he'd stay down and give us time to get out – we had gloves on, but even through padding it would have hurt.

For a moment, he started crying, which is not to knock him. He'd single-handedly fought twelve trained and mostly hardened prison officers and had us on a string. I dare say there'd be some who'd see this as mindless macho brutality on our part, a goon squad mentality. In which case, I'd have been happy to swap places and ask how they saw it then. We were desperate, stretched to the limit. This wasn't about coming out of there saying, 'I've twatted Danny Gee' – we were making sure we could grab his lighter and clear the cell, full stop.

It worked as well. Mostly. We'd got our opportunity, maybe ten seconds, so we got up and rapidly backed out one at a time, keeping our eyes on him. But by the time we'd cleared the cell, he was back on his feet and he still had his lighter.

What I expected when that cell door shut and I took my helmet off was not what I found. Apart from us four, only the governor and the Scouse PO were there. The landing was clear. What if he'd got the better of us and got hold of someone and began to rip their arm from its socket, or worse?

So we walked across to the adjudication room and, fuck me, one of the southern softies already had his overalls off.

'You need to get the nationals in. We're not going back in there,' he said.

I asked another if he was all right. He was in shock. I'm not saying they were cowards; adrenaline got the better of them, that's all. Fight or flight, and they chose the latter. I was pissed off at the time though.

The PO went ballistic, 'If we need you back in that fucking cell, you're going back in.'

'We ain't phoning the nationals,' said the governor. Prisoner kicks off and we can't handle it – how would that make us look as a jail, however big he was? We'd already looked like the Keystone fucking Cops.

Danny Gee then hit his cell bell.

Oh, no – what now? We'd already gone in there mob-handed to get a lighter off him and been lucky to escape with us lives. And when we got back to King Kong's cell, there he was, dancing around in a pair of goggles he'd got from one of the C&R team's precious German helmets.

'Hand them over, Danny,' said the PO, trying not to laugh. 'Let's have the goggles.'

'Nah, fuck off,' he said.

'Danny, please,' and at that point please was appropriate.

'Give me some burn and you can have 'em,' he said.

There were two ways of looking at this. You could give in, but in doing so de-escalate the situation. Or you could resume battle. Having had a breather, four of us would be up for it, but that was all, it seemed. So they gave him his smoke. It was three o'clock in the morning by now, but we'd got the goggles, had a fight and shown him that he couldn't dictate at Strangeways, the best result on offer.

The incident became legendary in the jail, and not everyone's reputation survived intact. I am proud to have got a letter thanking me for my part in the operation from the number-one governor. Otherwise, it was one of them events like the Sex Pistols' gig at Manchester's Lesser Free Trade Hall in 1976, when afterwards everyone swore they were there even though only a handful actually were.

Some years later, when Danny Gee was back in HMP Manchester, this officer I'd never met before started telling me the story, from his own point of view, of how he'd been part of our human centipede. I sat and listened to this lad for twenty minutes, telling me how he went in and fought Danny Gee. It goes on a lot in prison, that. Some people steal your lives.

As distinct from crime families, gang-bangers made up as much as a sixth of the K Wing population; in 2006 we had thirty-five in our total of two hundred. And by gang-bangers I don't mean dodgy parties in suburbia with car keys and fruit bowls, I mean violent gang members drawn from the meanest and toughest Manchester estates.

Who's deadliest, crime families or gangs, because they are two different things? That would be like saying who'd win a fight between a shark and a crocodile.

There's one particular crime family in Manchester and Salford who saw themselves as Robin Hoods. The reality, though, was different.

One of their slogans was 'Keep drugs out of Salford', but what they were really doing – according to the grapevine – was robbing dealers and giving the drugs to someone else to sell on for them. Doing that on the quiet would have been necessary because gang-bangers and crime families operated an uneasy truce. They know each other, have very often been banged up together, but there is hate and distrust there quite definitely. All out war, though, would be in no one's interest.

It's very much like *The Sopranos* or *The Godfather*, with lots of sit-downs refereed by trusted intermediaries. Let's say one family member has been out for a drink on Saturday night and filled in a gang-banger. This third hard bastard will be approached to sort the beef out. There are a lot of peacemakers inside, too, who'll do exactly that job when needed.

Every prison officer knows not to push some of these lads too far or there might very well be repercussions. You can't let them see that you know that, but you'd be daft not to be a bit wary, wouldn't you? That said, what happens in jail tends to stay in jail.

Where you live on an estate dictates the gang you're in. Manchester's gang culture is well publicized; shootings, drugs, lots of pretty hard-core stuff. Most cities have one – Sheffield has at least two gangs based on postcodes. Bottom line is, if your dad was a gang-banger it's odds on you'll be one too. Prisoners with infamous fathers come in with different surnames that their mother gave them in the hope they wouldn't get involved.

A lot of YPs at Forest Bank were gang members, and quite a few ended up dead. One lad I remember really well was Justin Maynard, who came in aged eighteen. Lanky, funny and clueless about prison, he was always getting in trouble, but was a naughty boy really, not a hardened crook. You had to like him. Driving into Strangeways one day, I heard he'd been gunned down; it was quite shocking. You'd have taken him to your grandma's for tea.

The majority of gang-bangers in Strangeways were from Doddington and Gooch Close, the city's most infamous gangs, in Moss Side. A lot of other gangs, Wythenshawe, say, were affiliated to them. I'm not from Manchester, so to find out that they are just named after streets was a surprise. I'd been thinking Crips and Bloods but no, it's really not that complicated.

Gangster life is brutal. If you're from Moss Side and a gang member and go back to that area on release from jail, there's no way you are going straight. Once in you stay in and chances are you won't live through your twenties. Later on at Strangeways, we had a kid on healthcare in the gated cell, face an absolute mess. The police had brought him in for his own protection. I was on nights then and he was under constant watch. He had scars all over his body – stabbings, gunshot wound – and had also been leathered with a baseball bat. He'd a gang tattoo on his arm. We got to talking.

'I've got a missus, two young kids, told them I wanted out,' he said. He'd decided to put his family first and they'd tried to kill him for it.

All the gang-bangers from Moss Side in Strangeways were black – in fact there was only one white lad among them, and it so happened that this single white lad on K Wing in 2006 belonged neither to Gooch or Doddington. Understandably, coming out of his cell he'd always have his back to the wall. We had twenty Gooch lads who outnumbered fifteen or so from Doddington, but there was an unwritten truce. No one wanted to start anything. On the twos, again there were more Gooch than Doddington.

Then Bertie got us in the office, 'Right, security's been on. They said our thirty-five gang-bangers are to be spread around the jail.' Over the next week, we dispersed them and got rid of maybe fifteen. A fortnight later, we had thirty-five again. They'd migrated back: the other wings wouldn't tolerate them. Rarely were there any fights, just the sort of heavy nervy atmosphere that made you twitchy.

One Doddington lad, Mac, was built like a steamroller and must have weighed around twenty-four stone. He could have taken out four or five people on his own. At one stage he'd been number two in the Doddington gang. But a lot of the real hard cases, lads like Mac who'd been in prison before, were respectful of staff to some extent. He knew K Wing was strict. He knew which staff to talk to and understood the routine. He was influential with hotter-headed lads and, in his way, helped keep the peace.

The last time we met inside was 2012. I was in reception doing overtime and he was coming in for another spell, must have been missing the place.

'All right,' I said. 'Looking at a big one?'

'Might be,' he said. 'You all right, boss?'

'I am. Thought you'd be keeping your nose clean . . .'

That's how we'd always been, chatty and cordial.

On that occasion, a pair of Doddington lads had been in a club, someone had spilled champagne on one of them, there'd been an altercation and a young lad got kicked to death outside. Eleven of the gang were arrested, whether they'd been involved or not, and were up for murder, pending investigation, Mac included. They will do that, the police. If they suspect two of them have done it and there's eleven of them there, they'll get arrested and put on remand. It gets them off the streets, doesn't it? Makes it a bit quieter.

He must have got off, though, because I then bumped into him again on the out in Manchester, Shambles Square. I didn't see him, but he saw me and came over for a chat. He could have cracked me, ignored me, anything while I was distracted, but just wanted to catch up. 'Y'all right, boss?' he said, and off we went again.

Anyway, back during this earlier term, this one officer on the threes was getting under his skin. It got to a point where Mac and this lad were arguing, so they tried to restrain him. He had some muscle, Mac, under the fat. It took maybe thirty of our forty staff, swapping over, to get him to segregation, an operation that ended someone's career. A colleague of ours got trapped underneath and was forced to retire with a crush injury. An ex-para, he'd been in the prison service a long time, but twenty-four stone on top of you – dead weight – it's not going to do you any good, is it? It was a real shame. The lad was a good landing screw.

A lot of officers, incidentally, are offended by the word 'screw'. There's no need to be – I looked it up. The old slang word for key was screw; it's as simple as that. When you locked anyone up, you turned the screw.

Why didn't we knock Mac out, as you would a rhinoceros? That's a decent question; I'm glad you're paying attention. There is a 'liquid cosh', Largactil, Acuphase or whatever you want to call it. It tranquilizes people and also stops them harming themselves. Back in the day, if someone was really violent – *bam!* They'd get a jab. Charles Bronson had it used on him. It did save a lot of bother.

I've seen it used three times, but there's an unwillingness to entertain it nowadays. It has to be a last resort, authorized by a doctor. That's because it is quite dangerous, putting antipsychotics in someone out of control. You don't know completely how it's going to affect them. Do they have a heart problem? Will they suffer a stroke? What will be the impact on their mental health? There are times, though, when common sense says it's worth the risk.

Gradually, some gang-bangers went to court, some moved on and it thinned out to around a dozen. One group convicted of an infamous drive-by shooting got around thirty-eight years each. A lad who'd been in the drive-by vehicle got thirty-three years and we had to restrain him more than once, he was so full of testosterone. Two of them,

129

Lee Amos and Colin Joyce, became the unwilling stars of a poster campaign plastered all over what the tabloids were calling 'Gunchester'. Their two families objected but had to lump it. These posters depicted them both at the age they were when they went in, and as what they'd look like when they came out. It was an attempt to deter kids. A couple of others who had been dealing drugs for the gangs and got seven years behaved like the stroppy teenagers they were.

The thing about gang-bangers and crime families, as we've seen, is that they are two sides of the same coin. They like to make threats, intimidate you if they can. It happened a lot inside – some twat threatened us every day and not only gangsters. On the whole I shrugged that off. It was just part of the macho culture. Only two ever unnerved me and the first one had nothing to do with gangbangers or organized crime.

It happened when I was working at the kids' home. I had three young 'uns with me in Bury town centre when I saw a smackhead I remembered from YP at Forest Bank. He saw me an' all, from just across the street.

'Listen,' I told my lot, 'you know how I once worked in a youth prison? Well, there's a lad there and we might end up fighting. If anything happens, all I want you to do is walk up to the police station and wait for me.'

One little shit said he wanted to watch, but I

sent them packing. As they went I got a massive dump of adrenaline, legs shaking: this guy looked like he was going to start. He hadn't really got to me inside, but now here he was in the open air – his big chance.

As I got closer though he just said, 'All right, Mr Samworth?' nice as pie. This is the thing, you see: out of prison he can call me what he likes, just as Mac could have done – dickhead, cock, prick – and what am I going to do about it? Inside, during one particularly rough restraint, he'd threatened to cut my throat.

'I am,' I said. 'How are you?'

'You think I'm going to start, don't you?' he said.

'I do,' I said. 'You always told me you would.'

'I know I gave you a bit of a hard time,' he said, 'but no hard feelings, eh? Can we shake?' So we did that and off he toddled.

That lad is the only prisoner on the out that I have ever been fearful of. I was ready but it never happened. All the others, and I've seen loads – gangsters, the lot – they either avoided you completely or dragged you over to meet their family.

The only mobster who really got to me was also at Forest Bank – Tommy Beveridge, who we'd had on seg'. He was an associate of Curtis Warren, Britain's most notorious drugs trafficker, though not part of his empire. Beveridge was in his forties by then but in his day had been a proper bastard. Famously, around twenty years earlier, he'd fought the heavyweight boxer Paul Sykes in Armley jail

131

and won. He was once recounting his youth and it was a mess – he'd been shot, stabbed and hacked. I asked the question I always did, 'If you could have avoided this life, would you?' Quite definitely, he replied. They always do.

While he was in seg', three members of staff went on the sick due to his threats. Every morning when I came on shift, his bell would go and he'd yell, 'Samworth – get your arse down to my cell!' He'd only ever do it when I was on my own, and how he knew that I couldn't tell you. It was instinct, maybe, or the sound of my feet; he just enjoyed the feeling of frightening people.

He was well connected, this guy. One day he was on the phone when an SO, two staff and myself were there, telling someone on the other end that he had a lad here called Samworth. There aren't a lot of us in Manchester.

'I want you to find his address and kill him,' he said.

I asked the SO, 'Are you going to let him say that on the phone?'

'He's entitled to a phone call.'

Characters like that will get in your head, which is why seg' staff are now monitored psychologically and rotated. It's different to the rest of the jail. After a while, you need moving on.

CHAPTER 8

BLUE CHRISTMAS

Most prison officers worked one in two weekends – Div One and Div Two, as the shifts were traditionally known. Div One was alpha male, Div Two, my shift throughout my time on K Wing, less so. They had a derogatory name for us, but I never cared. We had easy-going staff, as reflected in how the weekends tended to go. Div One had far more incidents than us. We had intelligent people who were able to talk prisoners down.

Tractor and Trailer were in Div Two as well, and Helen used to do the officers' breakfast every Sunday. Without fail, Pete would cart in a load of bacon, sausage and the rest, pre-cooked by his missus at home. The prisoners knew we had it, and nobody complained. Tea, toast, two eggs, rasher, banger and black pudding – quid a pop. Can't go wrong.

If weekends in jail were quiet, Christmas and New Year were even more so. Landings were subdued. You could rely on that. They were missing their friends and family.

Listen to the critics and you'd think prisoners

get fed better than old folk and schoolkids. Well, it's cooked from fresh, so the standard is good, but the amounts are small. Me, I'd be starving. When I started at Manchester, prison food was two hot meals – dinner and tea – and a breakfast variety cereal pack with a small carton of milk. I'd need three packets of that to fill me up, but there you go. It's not Brighouse Holiday Inn. In 2013 a dinnertime hot meal got stopped and they went to sandwiches, noodles, hot dogs now and then. At night they'd have various choices, minced beef and potatoes, lasagne, curries and such, a lot of filling carbs.

For Christmas dinner they got sliced turkey you could see through – it looked like polythene – stuffing, roasties, sprouts and gravy. It wasn't bad. At teatime, they had the cold buffet as that was easy to serve and there was plenty of it for them to take back to their cell to eat while watching the Christmas night film, maybe.

As for decorations, there weren't any, apart from a sad-looking tree near the entrance to the sterile area with a bit of tinsel strung around it. All in all, it was a glum time. Some prisoners made a little tree or stuck Christmas cards up if they had any. There might be some special activity – inter-wing five-a-side football, say – and there'd be church services available for all religions. No one sat in front of a blazing log fire unwrapping presents.

In prison, you are always going to be working

one of the big three. Me, I always did the Christmas morning shift by choice. That way I'd have Christmas night with my family and Boxing Day to sleep off the eggnog. I once did seven nights over Christmas, encompassing New Year's Eve. On the first night the in-cell power went off for a while, meaning no one on K Wing could watch TV. There was hell on. Bedlam. So I went from cell to cell promising everyone that for the rest of the week, if they behaved, I'd bring in DVDs and play them all night, every night. You weren't supposed to bring DVDs in, as it happens, but a blind eye was turned. The prison had a film channel, so everyone would get to see them. The entire wing was watching movies from nine at night until 6 or 7 a.m. and most of them didn't get up the next day – quietest Strangeways Christmas ever. *Jackass* was a big favourite.

Christmas Day with Tractor and Trailer was like Sunday, only with turkey and all the trimmings, not just a fry-up. Helen was helped by an officer called Kate – Pete was just their whipping boy – and the first dinner I had there was a fine sight. We'd cover their jobs while they prepared it. We staff had a trestle table in the brew room, tablecloths, mince pies, three-course meal, soup, bird, veg – the full monty. Three years on that wing Helen did our Christmas, and it was fantastic. After her cooked dinner I didn't want to work; none of us did. It was better than you'd get in a pub.

The first Christmas, though, was significant for one incident. Prisoners got money inside by their families sending them a postal order, if you can remember those. The relatives would address it to the governor, and a correspondence department opened the mail. What should have happened is this: mail comes in, opened, postal order removed, sent off to finance department who would deposit it in the prisoner's account. It would show up, ready to spend. There was a kid who hadn't been in long and wanted this cash so he could phone his kids on Christmas Day. Every single morning he'd been on at me: 'Mr S., it's not in my account. Will you check, will you check, will you check?' I did ask for him now and then, as you would, but come Christmas Eve, the damn thing still hadn't turned up.

Now unfortunately, some aspects of prison aren't run so well. Letters arrive in the mailroom and get lost among the rest, especially at Christmas when it's obviously busy. There ought to have been a rotation system but there wasn't: the staff just kept working from the top. I'd warned the lad: his letter came in early, so was probably bottom of the pile and might not get dealt with in time. So he said, 'Is it possible to sort me a call out, Mr Samworth?' We had that facility.

The phones all worked by PIN. Prisoners would get a secret number connected to their account with which to get a line out. If they had money, there was no problem. But SOs had their own

PIN and could facilitate a call; give them a bit on credit. We did that in genuine cases. So I told Bertie this lad had been good as gold and deserved a call.

'Yeah, but you'll have to tell him it will only be a couple of minutes,' he said. Just about everyone wanted to phone out.

About half past ten that Christmas morning, I'm on twos and this same kid comes walking down the landing with a postal order in his hand. Mail had been delivered that morning, but he shouldn't have had that: it should have gone to finance.

Next minute, there's another lad with another postal order, asking me to take it from him. Then another. And another. Fuck me: they'd all opened their mail, not only on my landing but the other landings too, and we ended up with 220 postal orders. Major stuff-up. Some of them had three, posted weeks ago, and very few had money on their accounts. The others hadn't said anything, just hoped theirs would arrive. Well, here they were, God help us.

I went to Bertie Bassett who, as you can imagine, wasn't too chuffed. I suggested asking security to turn on the phones with our PIN. He told me to crack on, so I did and an OSG officer answered my call in a very curt tone.

I told him we'd a situation and that K Wing needed plenty of credit. Could they add it, please? As things stood, we'd enough for twenty-five calls when we needed a couple of hundred.

'We won't be putting the fucking phones on for K Wing,' the OSG said.

This being the season of goodwill, I asked who he was effin' and jeffin' at, and the bellend put the phone down. I phoned back and another officer answered.

'Who's that?'

'It's Officer Samworth on K Wing. We want the PIN putting on.'

'Yeah, that won't be happening, kid,' and he slammed the phone down too.

When I told Bertie he blew his stack – cartoon style. Wig went up, steam came out his ears. 'Who the fucking hell's there?' He stormed off and I tagged along.

He let this officer have it, did Bertie. Finger-pointing like a piston engine – 'Put me 200 quids' worth of credit on NOW. It's Christmas Fucking Day.'

I went around the cons and told them they had two minutes on the phone each. Prisoners might be bullies or smackheads and all round vicious bastards, but mainly they respect staff, and gestures like that help a wing to work smoothly. They queued peacefully. At teatime, we gave them a bit of a buffet and, as they went behind their doors, they thanked us for it.

That was a good Christmas Day in the prison service, when we did our good deed. It's a good job Bertie Bassett was on, mind, or there would have been a Yuletide riot.

★　　★　　★

An officer called Two Pens almost gave us our noisiest Christmas.

Two Pens let things annoy him, and when they did he'd pursue it. Every day in that job prisoners fuck you off, you need a thick skin. His was like wafer-thin ham. He'd treat the file we made our comments about the inmates in as his own personal diary. Two Pens would chip away, a relentless bureaucrat, hence his nickname.

One lad was on the phone, eating an apple. Prisoners weren't supposed to eat or drink on the landings, though personally I'd have let him finish the call before telling him – he was no bother. Two Pens told him to get rid of it but got no response. The lad wasn't ignoring him, he just didn't hear him as far as I could see. Two Pens told him twice. After a third time, he grabbed the phone, which got a reaction. The kid's eyes came out on stalks. It could have ended in a restraint. I knew the lad really well – dynamic security, good relationship – and calmed him down by putting him behind his door for twenty minutes.

Another prisoner was a wanker and a prolific one at that. He'd been on healthcare and yanked his todger in front of governors and staff – male or female, he wasn't fussed. He did it under the covers, not in the open, but was restrained God knows how many times, the sort of prisoner everyone avoids. Not violent, just odd: he wasn't wanted on any wing. You don't want people tossing themselves off all the time, do you? It's antisocial and the sheets have to be cleaned.

The wanker had been to court the night before, a basic prisoner in his own clothes.

'I want no fuss or alarm bells,' the SO told me quite clearly, 'but here's Ivor Biggun's corned beef.' The maroon combo. 'Tell him to put them back on. If he won't, lock the door. We'll sort it later.'

Standard practice. After court, they get changed.

As soon as I'd left the office, Two Pens whipped this clobber out of my hands and him and his gang of mates 'made haste' to the tosser's cell to deliver their own brand of dynamic security. He cracked the bolt and in they all piled. It was well over the top.

'Put these fucking clothes on!' he yelled. It sounded like an LA drugs bust. When they came back out he said, 'Where's our fucking back-up, you soft Yorkshire twat.'

'You what?' I said. 'There were ten of you, to one prisoner.'

He was at the end of his tether all the time. When a job affects you to such an extent, it's time to pack it in.

Anyway, Ebenezer Two Pens and me shared one job on the K Wing servery, which was to order the following day's hot meal for the prisoners. If you'd sausage, chips and beans on the menu today, you'd request some different scran tomorrow. One hundred and sixty portions of whatever you decided, plus a halal choice for your Muslim prisoners – thirty of that, say – and maybe fifteen butty packs too. Some lads preferred crisps, orange, yoghurt, cereal bar or some other snack food, especially when they'd worked all day. The servery could be stressful, especially if you ran short of food, but Christmas Day was a piece of piss. No thought required.

Lucky for him, Two Pens was on duty Christmas Eve – so, easy. You'd order the full works, wouldn't you? Lashings of turkey followed by Christmas pudding and custard, quite definitely; halal meals and a few butty packs, just in case. Not this clown. He asked them for 170 portions of fish curry. On Christmas Day! No one ate that at any other time of year – it was minging. I only found out when I phoned the kitchens on Christmas morning with my own order for Boxing Day.

'Very funny, Donna,' I said to the lass who answered. 'What's he really ordered?'

'Fish curry.'

I had a Bertie moment. 'You are going to send the biggest wing in the jail 170 portions of fish curry on Christmas Day?'

'It's too late now,' she said. 'I thought it was strange . . .'

Anyway, I told our beloved SO and *boom* – through the fucking ceiling. 'You cannot do this to me! The wing will go bananas. It'll be 1990 all over again with tinsel on.' He told me to get back on to Donna.

'Right,' she said. 'What I'm going to do is send

you the fish curry, which comes with rice. But what about chips as well?'

We were getting somewhere. 'Yeah,' I said. 'Can you do me 200 portions of chips?'

Yes.

'Got anything else?'

'Well, it's pretty tight. I might be able to send you two dozen Christmas dinners, but that will be it.'

'Have you got anything else for a main course?'

'We've got eggs.'

'Eggs?'

'Eggs.'

Now they didn't usually get eggs, the lads. We'd only served them once before on K Wing, when there'd been a food shortage. It's the sort of grub that prisoners love, though. Like toast. They didn't get that at one time, although they do now. Egg and chips, believe me, would be a delicacy, a speciality dish. So I said, 'Can you send me 200 portions of egg and chips, Donna?'

'Yes, I can. I'll also send you the Christmas puddings and fish curry and anything I've got left over. Happy Christmas.'

It was eleven o'clock on Christmas morning now, so I started prepping the cleaners. I sent them out on the landings to tell everybody that Two Pens had stitched me up. I told them I didn't know for sure what would be on offer, definitely egg and chips, and that whatever I got they could eat.

It used to come in on two trollies, but this day the kitchens did us proud. I'd never seen so much grub. Tray after tray of chips, about 360 portions . . . rice . . . more fried eggs than there are chickens in the north west of England, rubbery as fuck but who cared . . . fish curry, which actually wasn't bad as fish curries go . . . and butties galore. A big steaming pile of plum duff too. And custard.

Walking down to the servery, the prisoners were buzzing – 'Oh, chips and egg, man, yeah! Nice one.' Nobody left with an empty belly, and it was another silent night, no thanks to the Grinch who'd tried to ruin Christmas.

New Year's Eve could be a rum one too, though no one inside was ever in the mood for partying. I know I wasn't and nor were the prisoners. Every year it was described as a potential flashpoint. We went on high alert but it never kicked off. Like Christmas itself, it was a melancholy period. On K Wing it was just a normal day. Most of them found something to watch and had a smoke. Or got some shut-eye. As the countdown approached it went quiet very, very quickly. If I were on nights, I'd do my rounds of the landing at eight o'clock, ten o'clock and midnight, by which time pretty much everyone was fast asleep. In prison it didn't pay to look too far ahead.

At Forest Bank, back in 2003, one officer I worked with kept pestering me to take her to this New Year's Eve do she'd been invited to, once we'd banged them up. She was on at me through the shift. I was working New Year's Day though, so knocked her back. I knew from engineering that if you're supposed to work that day you'd best not ring in sick. You don't want to be driving in pissed either.

She carried on mithering and I started to feel shit, thought it might be flu. We'd a lad come on the wing with an arseful of weed; the place stank. The whole wing was stoned, so maybe it was that. I rang the manager, 'Just warning you, I'm doggo.' He wasn't happy, and nor was this lass as she went off to ring in the New Year alone. I couldn't sleep, tossing and turning, shaking like a shiteing dog. My nose ran like a tap, eyes watered, I felt awful. I phoned in poorly and did get a warning when I went back into work two or three days later.

Fast forward to K Wing in 2007. A lad came in who I knew well; I gave him a nod, bit of a cheeky chap – I hadn't seen him since Forest Bank. As we were chatting he chuckled, 'Remember New Year's Eve – were you rough?'

I totally lost it. Ragged him off his feet and into the back of the cell, pinned him up with a forearm, choking him.

'Mr S., Mr S., let me go . . .'

'What did you do?'

'It weren't me – it were her you were working with!'

Now I know he's a con and so hardly the most reliable witness, but as soon as he explained it all made sense. This lad said he'd seen her popping a tablet in my brew, probably to liven me up a bit and go with her to that fucking party. I was fuming. Mind you, as a student of eastern mysticism I knew all about karma, and took comfort in how she'd already had her comeuppance in more ways than one . . .

Some time after that New Year's Eve, while I was still at Forest Bank, an orderly had approached me. He'd told me to check the laundry. He was a good lad, this one, took prisoners' washing and brought it all back ironed, dried, folded, the lot – hard bastard for sure, in for some horrendous crime, but a terrific cleaner.

'Nah, it'll be mint,' I said.

'No, no, Mr S. Check the laundry.'

So I'd had a walk over and found the door ajar by a few inches. I pushed it open and looked in. Guess who was inside? The female officer in question, up on the washing machine and having a party for two with a con, a lifer as it happened. Tits out, head down, both going for it like billy-o.

What the fuck . . . I'd thought, backed out and shut the door.

She started hammering on it. 'What you doing? I'm trapped in here! Help!'

I phoned the security manager, someone I trusted. 'We've got a fucking problem,' which we did, quite literally.

The shagger, once unlocked, said nothing, just skulked off back behind his door. He was on a big sentence, saw a chance and took it. You'd think prisoners would like an officer who did favours, whether like this or by bringing in clothes or drugs or whatever, but funnily enough some have a code of integrity. They view bent officers as weak, a bit of a plague. By the end of the day, he'd been transferred many miles away. As for the shaggee, 'Get your things, hand in your keys,' the manager told her. 'I never want to see you again' – and she was walked to the gate.

For obvious reasons, sexual relations between prisoners and staff were strictly forbidden. There was the usual hypocrisy – she was a slag while he was just doing what came natural – but the bottom line is you can't be having that. It's a clear-cut issue for officers too, so this time no one was accusing me of being a grass. The prison could have called in the police, but in circumstances like that people are often given the opportunity to go of their own accord as it saves embarrassment all round.

The wider issue is the standards we should expect of a prison officer. They're just human beings, they're just civil servants, as I keep saying, and they're not paid very much. But they're in a job where, if they do it badly, the consequences can be extremely serious.

CHAPTER 9

BLACK AND WHITE TOWN

What is quite definitely unacceptable in a prison officer? Let's start with racism.

Tackling racism inside is far from straightforward. Why wouldn't it be? If racism occurs in the outside world then of course it will be an issue in jail. Think about it. Officers, most of them white, guarding a population of inmates of all races and cultures who are guests on account of being liars, cheats and much much worse. The sort of people – criminals in short – who if you give them an inch will steal half of Greater Manchester, the vast majority being completely innocent, or so they'd have you think. Many are plausible in their alibi – might even believe it themselves – charismatic and manipulative. If a prisoner can paint himself as a victim he very much will, especially if there's advantage in doing so. It's obvious really. A prison officer is a handy target, but the scope for him or her to abuse their powerful position is also enormous. It's a potential minefield.

Whenever I was called a racist – which very rarely happened because I am not – I'd walk down to where the incident forms were, write my name on it so they didn't spell Sam wrong and say, 'There you go, lad – fill it in.' Having been an officer myself, I naturally tend to think about these issues from our side of the bars first and foremost, since that's my own experience. I promise you this – my own treatment of prisoners wasn't consciously driven by race, religion or colour, and nor in the vast majority of instances was it different with the screws I worked with. You treat them as criminals, plain and simple, deal with what's in front of you. If a person is polite and well behaved, they'll get that back. If someone is arrogant or takes the piss, plays the victim or thinks of you as their butler, you might adopt a less friendly approach. It's important that they know you are the boss.

I met my fellow officer Raffles on my very first day in Strangeways, and boy, could he be ruthless. The inmates on his strip didn't fuck about because they knew they'd be punished, even the hardest among them. He had his own particular brand of dynamic security. I spent half of my first shift on the twos, where I ended up mainly based, and the other half on his landing. Before he'd so much as said hello, he'd slapped a clipboard in my chest and told me to 'Get the labour out' – i.e. organize the prisoners who were off to work. Then he sauntered back to the office and made himself a brew.

Over time I got to know Raffles better – he had a dry sense of humour and I began to like him

– but he could make you cringe sometimes, the way he spoke to people. He gave it to you straight and talked to everyone that way. He wasn't one for nuance. It was an attitude that could land officers in bother, especially when it came to race. He wasn't a racist, but he wasn't one for backing down either. The majority of prisoners get on with their jail; they know which officers they can push and how far, and won't go beyond that point. A minority can get arsey and their behaviour deteriorates, resulting in confrontation with prison officers. At this point a prisoner might play the race card and you would be informed that someone had put in a complaint. You might be told to go easy or to watch your back. Raffles however would not think about diffusing the situation – convinced he was in the right, he'd still be on the prisoner's case. He was like a dog with a bone! This could lead to further complaints of racism even though that wasn't the cause of his behaviour. He challenged management and fellow officers just as much – he was difficult but he was consistent and I would definitely have him on my team.

I've seen loads of TV programmes and read tons of reports where the prison service is accused of institutional racism. In September 2017, the Labour MP David Lammy said that some prosecutions against black and minority-ethnic suspects ought to be dropped or deferred due to 'bias' in the British criminal justice system. Overt discrimination was in decline, he reckoned, backing up what I've said I suppose, but BAME individuals still had it tougher than anyone else. He said there is 'greater disproportionality' in numbers – 3 per cent of the public is black, rising to 12 per cent inside.

I've no reason to doubt his facts and figures, but I repeat, in the vast majority of cases, once inside, everyone I saw was dealt with the same – unfairly on occasion, but that had nothing to do with race. I've worked with racist officers, quite definitely. I must have, they are human beings and human beings can be racists. How many do you know? They are in every walk of life, have a look on social media. But I can honestly say I never saw any officer abuse their position on the basis of race and only saw one use a racist insult on duty. She was the sort of officer cons don't like: inconsistent with her warnings. When that happens, you can find yourself on basic regime without understanding why. Sometimes, nice as ninepence, she wouldn't even tell them, just add their name to the paperwork.

One black prisoner absolutely hated me – white this, white that – making threats of rape against my family, sticking it in. I treated him professionally, no differently to anyone else, though I admit that was hard. He was overstepping the mark. One day, on the servery, he must have said something to this officer, because when he turned his back she mouthed an insult in return. Now, having worked in engineering amid all the noise and what have you, I can lip read. I know what she said, but had best not repeat it here because it would only be my word against hers. Either way, this lad, in for petty crimes but a lot bigger than I am, very intimidating physically, spun around on her, going ballistic. His plate went in the air. If I hadn't intervened and taken him to the floor he would have filled her in. Our manager had a word and soon afterwards she was moved to the VP wing, though not for that. Was she sanctioned? No. How could she be? Nobody but the con had heard a word.

I don't know what the target is nowadays, but the prison service back then aimed for about 7 per cent of its annual officer intake being from ethnic backgrounds. I get the logic of wanting to have more diverse staff – it's important to mirror inside what's going on outside, then everybody can just get on with the job. But you've got to apply common sense given what a challenging place prison is to work. You can't afford to have weaker staff, which is a risk of employing people by ethnicity alone. What's important is to encourage the right kind of BAME candidates to apply, then you'll get the numbers up naturally over time, won't you? Come to think of it, that's true for candidates across the board anyway. What you should be looking for is the ideal prison officer – honest, firm, fair, courageous, bit of life experience; well-rounded people in other words. Then just look after your staff well, pay them a decent whack and make sure you've enough of them to provide a proper service.

There was a recruitment drive in Birmingham involving role play that new prison officer applicants had to go through. Job Simulation Assessment Centre it was called, or JSAC for short. I had my doubts about it. Being good at role play doesn't mean you'll be any good in real life, does it? It just means you'd do a fair job of locking Cain Dingle up in *Emmerdale*. However, at that time I thought I might one day earn promotion and if you wanted to climb the ladder it would be good to have experience of scoring the assessments. So down to Brum a few of us went, where we found eight rooms with a scenario apiece going on that we had to watch. Mine was called 'Angry Man'. No idea why they gave me that one.

An officer in civvies pretended to be raging. The potential recruit came in and had to deal with it. It was all being filmed for analysis later. I had to watch how the applicant behaved, reacted and spoke. A group from the North West went first and their pass rate was 53 per cent. JSAC wanted 50 per cent, so that was good. People might not say the right things, but you could see their potential. In week two it was the Midlands' turn, and by Wednesday, at dinner, the pass rate was 23 per cent – diabolical.

The eight of us doing the assessments were assessed by three POs ourselves, making sure we scored it right and that the ones we said were suitable candidates actually were. One cockney governor, though, wasn't happy.

'What I want you to do,' he said, 'is go back and pass all the females and anyone from an ethnic background.'

'What?' said one of the POs. 'You can't do that.'

But we had to do as he said. Let me tell you, some of the people we'd seen were clueless. Some will call that positive discrimination, but it's not positive at all, is it? You're giving jobs to people who will be unhappy in them, might get injured and could cause chaos. Why is there pressure to do that? If they'd told us to go back and reassess everyone and pick the best of a bad lot, fine – you've got to get officers from somewhere. But again, you should be taking the best candidates for the job, whatever the race or gender.

A little later we were informed that K Wing was getting a new officer, direct from training. What's more, she had already put in complaints of a racial nature against the instructors. That didn't bode well, did it? We were also told our new recruit had been a copper for ten or twelve years, although when she clocked on it turned out she'd been a clerk in a police station, not an actual officer.

I suppose you could describe her as middle class. Whether she actually was or not, it was certainly there in her attitude – I know the job and you are not telling me how to do it, was the gist of it. You couldn't tell her anything. For my sins I was informed I'd be her mentor.

The first day, in my Yorkshire twang, I said, 'Listen love, what you need to do is open that flap, look in and see what you're unlocking. You need to know there's not someone stood behind there with a table leg ready to bash you on the head.' Normally, I'd have said 'twat you', but thought better of it. As it was, she pulled me up over the 'love'.

'I don't know you well enough for you to call me love,' she said. 'And we will never know each other well enough.'

Yeah, yeah, I thought, *avoid going shopping in Sheffield if you find 'love' offensive – and anyway, what about that table leg?*

The next time I tried she had her hand up again to stop me, 'Don't tell me how to open cells.'

She continued to unlock cells her way, while I was left to work out whether to do my job properly and pull *her* up. Yes, I decided, I would.

'Like I told you before, what you need to do is . . .'

'And like I told you before, don't tell me how to do this job.'

I worked with this officer for a month. Nightmare. Most of the time was spent treading on eggshells. It was like that film with Danny Glover and Mel Gibson, *Lethal Weapon.* Only we didn't end up as pals and it was her who was lethal.

Near the end of her probation, there was a Rastafarian prisoner on the threes. I met a lot of Rastas in the prison service. Usually, they are peace loving and don't give you any strife. This lad wasn't cut from that cloth. Bit of an angle on his language: he began telling me he'd fuck me over, stab me – stuff like that – because he claimed I hadn't come through on a promise to sort something out, can't remember what. Our conversation was lively, although I struggled to grasp much of it due to his half being in patois.

'Bumbo-pussy-rassclaat . . .'

'Listen lad, I can't tell what you are saying.'

'Kiss mi rass . . . liar . . . batty hole,' and he'd start pointing.

'You need to calm down, I can't understand you.'

'I'll cut you up, bloodcleet . . .'

'I've never said I'd do anything . . .' and on it went until I put him behind his door, gentle hand in his back. It had been heading for a restraint.

'Well,' said my mentee, who'd witnessed all this, 'this is why I am here.'

'I don't follow,' I said.

'For people like that.' I'm figuring she meant black people. 'The way you just spoke to him was disgusting.'

'He threatened me with violence,' I said. 'It's been sorted with as little force as possible.'

Not that she was listening: never did. What she did do was walk down the landing, open his door and let him out.

The kid couldn't believe his luck. He walked straight at me and threw a fist. *Bam!* He went for my head but gave me a glancing blow on the collarbone. We were in a restraint situation, as

155

feared. Troops piled in as usual, flooding in from the twos, fours – everywhere. And all the while I'm struggling she's pulling at my shirt collar, shouting, 'Get off him! Get off him!' When the incident was over she went home upset.

She put a complaint in, and before long I was in front of an SO. I didn't pull any punches: the prisoner came at me with urgency and purpose, and I expected a fellow officer to back me up, not take the prisoner's side. Security footage confirmed my account. I was no longer mentoring her when eventually she was moved sideways into an admin role.

I think it was Morgan Freeman who said the best way to do away with racism is to stop going on so much about it – just treat people as people. Or, in jail, treat prisoners as prisoners.

Corruption in prison officers is another big no-no, and again one that tars everyone with the same brush. As with self-harming, I've categories of corruption too. In my view there are three.

One: officers who are weak and vulnerable and may as well have a target on their head.

Two: officers who get off on the risk. The one who was banging a con with the office fifteen metres away knew what she was doing. There's also an element of stupidity to it.

We had another officer who fitted that bill – let's call him Cash4U, another from the OSG ranks. He was on a restraint once and afterwards he told the nurse he'd had hot water thrown at him. She checked his back and it was badly burned and blistered, so she sent him off to the hospital wing. Then he put in a claim for personal injury.

Thing was, the day before he'd been gardening out in the sun, and everyone knew he had because he'd been showing off his back to anyone who'd look. As one of those people who can't keep their own shit, he told me he'd made a good few grand out of that.

Another day he came limping in. 'What's up?' said Bertie. 'What've you done to your fucking leg?'

'Nothing, I'm all right,' he said, bravely soldiering on.

'You're hopping about like a dick.'

Later on, another officer and me were watching the prisoners out in the exercise yard. For some reason, by the way, cons always walk around anti-clockwise – never clockwise: don't ask me why. Like water down a plughole. Maybe in Australia they go the other way? Anyway, a fight erupted – full-on aggro, about twelve of them going at it and only two of us – and I hit the alarm.

I didn't see Cash4U arrive, I was too busy split-ting them all up, but I did see the aftermath. He'd fallen to the floor, knee clutched up by his chest howling, 'Aaagh! My knee!' A sick note went in again.

Later that year – by which time he'd been in three car crashes – he got a letter that he asked me to explain. It said he'd been flagged up by an insurance monitoring service as a likely fraudster: fourteen claims in twelve months – motoring incidents, accidents at work, paint on the carpet ... If this pattern of behaviour continued, it read, he'd be unable to insure his house, car or anything else. He shat blue lights.

The third kind of corruption among screws is opportunists. I worked with a few – basically contraband runners for the cons. One saw it as a business deal, got close to someone and they made him an offer. Later, he tried to portray what he'd done as weakness. Bollocks. His family weren't threatened: he'd seen pound signs. They caught him bringing smack into jail. Seven years.

CHAPTER 10

BORN OF FRUSTRATION

Those first years on K Wing were among my most enjoyable in the prison service, and it was because of the management team. Bertie, ably backed up by PO Pennington, dealt with everything head-on but was also very astute. So many things in the prison service could be sorted in the way he did it.

But in 2007 the time came for Bertie to move on. On K Wing, he'd been a fantastic officer and superb SO, so his promotion came as no surprise to anyone. Good luck to him. He became a principal officer for a while, before ending up a governor. Even then he was exactly the same. He'd swear and shout, bawl you out, rarely using PC language. You'd have a go back and it would be right as rain.

Colin Edwards was our replacement SO. He hadn't done his JSAC nor sat an exam, but was made up anyway as he'd been on the wing a while and was a respected regular officer. Once settled in he did a top-class job and – like Spongebob, who was still with us – he was a Bertie clone. He had lots of bottle and was straight as a die, with great interpersonal skills. Colin did the job like Bertie, having been taught by him, and for a while it carried on being a very disciplined wing. Every prisoner who came on was read the riot act: stay in line, no problem; fuck about and the staff will be all over you. It worked. When a prisoner was in danger of going on basic, he'd have a word: 'Listen lad, wind your neck in.' Perfect.

He went on to do three years as senior officer, Colin, and during that time failed his JSAC three or four times by similar scores. In the end he was demoted back to officer status. Given what I'd seen in Birmingham, if the governors had really wanted him to be an SO they would have passed him. Everyone on the wing signed a letter saying what a top job he'd done, pleading his case. It didn't work.

I did once apply to be an SO myself, but was told by my PO that I couldn't. I complained and a governor told him he had no power to stop me. If I wanted to go for the job I could. So this PO told me he'd reconsidered and would now put me forward. Thanks but no thanks, I said, which is me to a tee. Once I got more experience, I realized I'd had a lucky escape. I'd have been a good SO, I reckon, but would have had to bite my lip too often. Most POs are useless, and I couldn't have been arsed with the politics. No, I was content getting on with the job.

Then a new bunch of staff and managers came on the scene.

The best new bosses in most jobs don't tip things upside down immediately. They get a feel for a place, so that when change does happen it is built on knowledge. Not this time. Our new senior officer was a more guarded personality, quite definitely no Bertie Bassett. Our new PO – Venables – was very well respected at first, but that soon changed, with me anyway. Of the rest of the intake, many were inexperienced or from the ranks of the OSG, so the joint had a different feel. A gigantic broom swept our well-drilled regime away.

All our little routines were gone. Half past seven – get people out for medication; lock them back up. Labour, education, off they'd go at eight o'clock. Quarter past, we'd have a brew and then the rest of the prisoners would be out. Lock them back up at half eleven, then out in the afternoon and out again at night. Suddenly, we were told to unlock everyone at half seven, full stop. We stuck at it for nine months and tried to take this disruption on the chin. We maintained the same volume of staff, and Nobby Nobbler and I would still have a laugh and look out for each other.

Then PO Venables asked me what I thought of the wing now and I made the mistake of telling him.

'You want me to be honest?' I said; the days dragged, there wasn't the same vibe. I wasn't enjoying it as much. It was better with Bertie in charge. I was having problems with his replacement by then too.

Shortly afterwards, a couple of young officers confided in me that a prisoner they'd escorted to this SO's office wasn't bollocked as they'd expected, but clobbered. They were in shock. They said this senior officer – let's call him Clyde – had accused this con of calling one of our female officers – let's call her Bonnie – a slag, and cracked him. Another senior female officer in the room had walked out. I had no idea if any of this was true or not, but it was a shocking allegation.

Not long afterwards, SO Clyde told me and an officer that I got on well with, through our shared love of motorbikes, to bring in a French lad, probably our politest prisoner at the time. He spoke pretty good English and his manners were impeccable. It seemed odd that he should be in for a roasting, but we took him along as ordered. A third officer, female, was already in there.

Our man made as if to sit down.

'On your fucking feet,' Clyde said, and the next moment leapt over the desk and twatted this kid, who went down like a sack of spuds. Bewildered, the biker and me had to drag the SO off. The other officer asked if she should press the alarm and I said no, best leave it.

'Fucking pack it in,' the biker said, with a hand on the SO's chest. The bloke was slavering. He'd completely lost the plot.

I got this French lad up, he was obviously unhappy, and told him to go back to his cell. When he'd gone, Clyde told us that Bonnie had accused the kid of being abusive, which he denied.

Either way, what we'd seen was a sacking offence. We three were in disbelief, as was the SO, Spongebob, when we told him. I asked what he was going to do. If the female officer told a governor she'd seen this SO hit someone and we'd said nothing, the biker and I would be as guilty as he was in the eyes of the prison. Spongebob said he'd have a word.

There are officers – even now – who'll get violent and punch prisoners. It's hard not to when your adrenaline is going and you're being attacked. Some cons deserve it, they're almost begging you to lose control. You are trained, though, to be restrained and proportionate in your response. I've been in restraints when officers were hit and punched back, big style. Down the line, I'd find myself in exactly that situation and I regret it to this day. In the modern era, though, it's not so common. The prison service is more PC, managers more aware of their behaviour. But when anything bad does happen, staff fear speaking out.

A couple of days later, my biker mate collared me. 'We are in bother,' he said. 'The governor knows.'

PO Venables got me in and I ended up having to write a statement. So did the other two officers. In mine, I didn't say Clyde twatted the Frenchman: I tried to be diplomatic for a change

– 'overly aggressive' is what I put, and it went to an investigation.

I don't know for sure who began calling me a grass, but I've a pretty good idea. It swept through that prison quickly. Bear in mind that it's a macho culture and accusations of snitching are hard to shift. As prison officers you are all in it together, which is exactly why I brought it up in the way I did, to avoid that outcome. I just wanted it quietly sorting, in-house.

For six months, I got the cold shoulder treatment, even worse than I'd had at Forest Bank. On one wing, when I was doing an overtime shift, a senior officer said to my face that it would be a good idea if I didn't get involved in any restraints as his staff wouldn't be backing me up. Wherever I went, people turned their back, and all the while the investigation was ongoing. My own union representative was aggressive with me at the hearing, implying that the SO's sacking would be my fault.

'We've never had an officer grass another at Manchester before,' he said. 'All the governors are talking about it.'

I asked what he'd have done; just reckon not to notice?

'Well, you know . . .'

In the end they didn't ask me the questions they should have and I didn't have to lie. Would I have? We'll never know, will we? Clyde ended up getting a warning and moved off the wing, away from

Bonnie. However, I still had a problem because Strangeways as a whole was shunning me. Nobby Nobbler and a mate of his set off on a quest, going around the jail putting people right.

If you're a prison officer, you can be lazy, rubbish, court trouble all your career, but unless you do something really, really stupid like offend a few people on social media, you ain't leaving – it's a job for life. Boy Racer was another officer who didn't have what it takes. He'd not been at Strangeways long when he was spotted in Preston, impressing the ladies by wearing his uniform, epaulettes and key chain – in a boozer! Not only that, he'd been demonstrating C&R techniques with them on the pub floor. He was always either in trouble or on the verge of it.

In August 2007, HMP Manchester joined in a national day of action over pay and management changes. I wasn't there, I was on a day off, but when I put the news on that morning there were my mates. Tractor Helen and others had spoken to the troops and they'd agreed en masse to join their mates protesting around the country. A lot of civilian staff and some officers not in the POA union stayed put. As people came in on late shifts they would see their colleagues. As a union member, if I'd been working I'd have been outside with them. From what I've been told there was friendly banter, nothing too nasty.

Boy Racer was in the POA, I think, but went in anyway. One officer later got touted as the Devil for asking him why. His reply was to the effect of, 'I'm not losing money out here with you muppets.'

Next day I was on shift and so was he – an outcast.

'All right, lad?' I said.

Nothing. Blanked me. Did that with a few others too. A couple of days later, the governor began calling us in. Staff had been abusive: the Boy Racer had written a list.

My turn came. 'Mr Samworth, we meet again.' Wry smile. 'What did you shout at Boy Racer in the picket line?'

'You tell me,' I said, one step ahead for a change.

'He says you called him . . . let's see . . . a "fucking scab".'

'Did I? How many times?' Cat and mouse, like.

'Right, stop fucking about now, what are you smiling at?'

'I'll tell you what I'm smiling at, guv. I was at home. I didn't even know they were out until I saw it on the news. I was on a day off.'

Those were my first dealings with the Boy Racer. Then I was made his mentor!

First shift, off he went at eight o'clock, call of nature, he said. Nine o'clock – not back.

'Where is he?' Nobody knew.

Ten o'clock, I got people out for exercise, locked the rest up, still on my lonesome. Eleven came and went, half eleven we were feeding, serving meals, usual carry on. Finally, he strolled up.

'Where have you been, you prick?'

First line out of his mouth, 'I'm not having you talk to me like that.'

So I threatened to drag him outside. He buggered off home, and you know what's coming next, don't you? Perhaps not. This time I got in first, explaining how he'd gone for a four-hour shite.

'We checked the whole wing to make sure he wasn't held hostage,' I said, which we had.

Enquiries were made. It turned out he'd spent a pleasant morning with friends on G Wing, as I recall, and was moved off K Wing pretty quickly after that. A fair bit later he was in strife again for a rant on social media after some global terrorist atrocity. I'm sure you can imagine the subject matter. He took it down but it was too late; it went to the number-one governor, did that.

The Boy Racer liked his cars – he was the sort to drive into a wet prison car park in his BMW, put his foot down, spin three times and roar off through red lights, as he did one busy teatime while I was there. Nearly hit three motors. One night he came out and was filmed speeding down the A580, the East Lancs Road as it's known locally. He claimed he'd thought someone was on his tail and going to shoot him. They looked at all the CCTV – cities are manned-up now – and tracked him for around twenty miles with nobody threatening him at all.

Bottom line: you had to manoeuvre round people like that, try to keep them pacified or stay out of their way. And that's awkward in an environment where you have to be tough to survive. As an officer, you need to be able to tell it straight, not constantly worry about saying the wrong thing. The place will eat you alive otherwise.

The grievances against me were a worry. Prisons are political places and you get a reputation. There's plenty of opportunity for falling out. As a manager, if you hear a complaint, you should hear both sides of the story before taking it any further, but most often that wasn't how it went. First in was the one believed. If you didn't make a fuss and got on with it, you were at a disadvantage. Stuff that should have been talked through was officially investigated without delay, which led to more grievances and bad feeling.

It also means that when those first complainers get their way, and when the gender or race card has been played, a feeling can grow that some groups are being treated differently to others, whether that is true or not. There's no place for racism or sexism in any organization – but in prison box-ticking too often had the beating of common sense, and blatantly so. That's stupidity. A crap officer is a crap officer.

How about this for an example? I went on I Wing, the detox unit, to fetch a prisoner. HMP Manchester is so big that sometimes you only knew officers to say good morning to, not necessarily their name. Due to shift patterns, you might go months without seeing others. I knew the officer there by sight; there was a slice of cake on the table in front of her, surrounded by crumbs.

'All right, love,' I said. 'I've come for so-and-so.'

'Hello,' she said and offered me what was left of the cake.

Now that's a no-brainer for me, so down the hatch it went.

'It's my birthday,' she said. I wished her a good one, thanked her for the cake and after collecting the prisoner went on my way.

Following week I took this prisoner back and cheekily asked if she had any more cake. No, she said, adding that I'd got her in bother.

'How?' I asked.

'You had the last piece.'

It turned out that when I'd gone, this other officer came in and, spotting the wrapper, asked where his slice was.

'Big Sam, the officer from K Wing, has had it,' she told him.

A couple of days later she was in front of a governor. This lad alleged that by deliberately not saving him a piece of her birthday cake she'd been racist. As embarrassing as that may sound – and she did laugh about it – she was genuinely upset and had also been made to apologize.

Let me tell you, if someone had got a cake out in K Wing with fifteen staff in the office, cut it into ten, there'd have been fighting. If someone could have got hold of three pieces they'd have had three pieces – every bastard for themselves. If I could've put a whole cake in my face, I would have. None left when you got there? Tough shit.

By the time the Bonnie and Clyde investigation ended I was having disagreements with PO Venables on a regular basis. I saw him as interfering and unreasonable; wanted to be left alone to do my job.

I went to see one of the governors who'd been there when I did my training. He knew me as a decent officer, even though he'd once thought me a cunt and bully. We got on well now. He'd been thinking, he said, and asked if I fancied going to work on healthcare.

Now, at that time, healthcare had a terrible reputation. Not only were the prisoners in there climbing up the walls, it was short-staffed – nobody wanted to work on it – and people were also wary of one or two of its officers and nurses. My few remaining K Wing mates like Nobby Nobbler said I was mad.

'Look, just do twelve months for me,' this governor said, 'and then if you want out I will give you any job in the jail, wherever you want.'

It seemed like a good offer, so I went over a couple of times to have a look. It unnerved me. Not the job so much as the staff. They looked tricky to get on with, and I'd had enough of that. A couple of the nurse managers were scary, and I began to have second thoughts. But at the front of my mind was that offer, and there was another incident that swung it.

Again it ended with a complaint, and again the prison eventually saw that there was nothing in it. I was moving prisoners from reception; three were destined for G Wing. It got to eight o'clock and it was noisy, but I picked up the phone to tell them this trio were on their way. These lads would have to wait, the officer on the other end of the line told me, and we got into a bit of a heated discussion, though being deaf in one ear and with everything else going on I only really heard my half of it.

'I need to get them out,' I said. 'It's rammed down here.'

This admissions officer carried on talking, but I couldn't tell what she was saying so put the phone down and set off.

G Wing is very much like K Wing: you walk in on the ones but the office is on the twos. I walked upstairs with this trio, locked them in a room there, and went to the gate. This same officer was sat behind a desk.

'Don't you bring people onto my wing, and don't you put the fucking phone down on me,' she said.

I was annoyed by her attitude. Every new prisoner comes with documents attached, so I put a pile on her desk with a bit of a thud and told her to go fuck herself.

'I beg your pardon?' she said.

'You heard.' As I went out I slammed the gate,

but I soon calmed down. *A storm in a teacup*, I thought: it would soon blow over.

A while later, PO Venables came up to me on K Wing. 'You need to apologize,' he said and read out the grievance. '"On the night of so-and-so, you told officer so-and-so to go fuck herself."'

I laughed.

'What are you laughing at? It's not funny. Did you say that?'

'Yes. I'm not having anyone speaking to me like she did.'

'Well, you're going to be in trouble. You need to say sorry.'

'Don't you want to know what she said to me?'

'It doesn't matter, does it?'

'Of course it matters,' and I told him my side. 'I'm not fucking apologizing; we've had a row she started, that's all. I was just doing my job, running prisoners.' I admit I can be a stubborn twat.

Anyway, to cut a long story short, this latest grievance also went nowhere, as it became obvious that I wasn't bullshitting. By then, though, I wouldn't have cared either way. Frankly, I was plain sick of the place and gagging for a fresh start.

CHAPTER 11

EVERY DAY HURTS

I arrived on Strangeways healthcare in November 2008, and it was a turbulent first year. At the time they had a system of eight managers – farcical for such a small wing – three nurse managers, three prison managers and two POs, one from the prison, one the nursing ranks. Too many chiefs meant they were falling over each other and disagreeing.

Six officers would kick off the shift there, reduced to four when two went downstairs to organize the running at nine o'clock, bringing prisoners on and off. In that first year, we looked after about forty patients on the top floor, a lot. The upper landings were known as X, Y and Z.

To begin with healthcare ran a bit like seg': a strict routine. Get them out for a shower, hour's exercise and ten-minute cell clean. Two meals a day plus breakfast and perhaps a phone call. In a morning we'd two officers on each landing, two prisoners out at a time. Cons on unlocks were left until last, when things had settled down a bit and the remaining four officers could deal with any trouble.

The place had an atmosphere all of its own. Segregation units are intimidating, weird at the best of times, but healthcare is even more unnerving. The inmates are very often mentally incapacitated, which is something for which you don't receive extra training. Many have done dreadful things. Visitors came on the wing – students, solicitors and so on – and were terrified. Prisoners too were put off by the place. Healthcare was an eye-opener even for the hardest; it demolished everyone's comfort zone.

With most seg' prisoners, you knew where you were. On healthcare, absolutely anything could happen and very often did. If seriously ill detox patients came on from I Wing, for example – alcohol or drugs – it could get crazy. With booze, after a couple of days they'd be eating flies, throwing shit out their doors, screaming at night and hallucinating. No one got any kip. It was much worse than the seg', which acted as a pressure valve for us sometimes as we didn't have the staff. When I went in early to let the night staff get off, like I always did, everyone reporting in that day – nurses included – would pull a face. It got you like that.

It was the sort of job that really tested your patience. When we had forty on, all the manipulative bastards took some looking after. Lots of officers couldn't hack it – their stress levels would go through the roof, the pressure got to them. Fair enough. I reached levels of stress on there myself

I hadn't got near before. The threat of violence, difficult people, the horrible atmosphere, constraints of the job – the miseries were endless. At one point we had only two actual prison officers on that unit.

Light was an issue there too. Aside from cell windows, there was no natural light at all, only that artificial glare given off by fluorescent bulbs, humming and fizzing. Leaving the joint, you'd be squinting like a pit pony. The association room wasn't too bad – that was quite spacious, with a pool table, comfy chairs and telly, a bit like a pub lounge. You could get ten or twelve people in, barred windows on all sides, so quite bright, not bad considering.

The noise could be fearsome. If you'd got someone disruptive, kicking and banging doors, it sounded like a Victorian lunatic asylum. When we were short-staffed, people from other wings would come in on overtime, experienced officers some of them, who just didn't want to be there. Understandable. You didn't know how to react sometimes: your usual ways of doing things was no use. A lot of staff would try to be the same with the prisoners on healthcare as they were with prisoners on a wing, which never worked. It's no good shouting at someone with a terminal illness or mental issues to get behind a door. Either they will take no notice, start harming themselves or go berserk.

And there was the smell. Healthcare was very

clean, the orderlies did a good job, but it stank. People weren't necessarily throwing up everywhere or throwing shite around – though that did happen – but the aroma was constant. It wasn't clinical, like you'd get in hospital. Nor did it smell of disinfectant really, though there was plenty of it used. It was a farmyard smell, and I don't mean of fresh-mown hay. It was just the nature of the beast: unwell people have their own body odour. People on medication don't just sweat BO. Quite often the chaplain would bring joss sticks in; you'd light a few if someone was approaching death.

While I was there, we knocked through a couple of cells and had a nice little en-suite room built for the terminal inmates, people on their very last legs. Officially, it was called the enhanced nursing suite; we called it the death cell. Otherwise, if people were no danger to anyone any more they might well go to a hospice, still supervised by staff.

But some cons had spent their life in prison and chose to die there. When Eric died, for example, he was still serving time forty-five years after his original offence, way above your typical life sentence. As prisoners go, he wasn't a bad fella, although back in 1966 he had killed his girlfriend and got locked up for it. For murder, people nowadays do as little as ten to fifteen, but they don't backdate an earlier sentence. Look at the Great Train Robbers. Only one guy did the killing, but they all got thirty years. Eric had only ever been out once when, after starting to see a woman, she'd complained he'd had a drink and swore at her, and he got locked up again after ten months. At one point we had him as an orderly, but he deteriorated. He'd always smoked and eventually got cancer. He was petrified. Those familiar walls and bars were his only reassurance.

Them so poorly they'd be staying a while were kept secure on the landings upstairs, while downstairs in a two-storey building was 'out-patients': podiatry, dentist, doctor and such – basically anything you can get on the NHS. Doctors and nurses are employed by a trust to work there and the dentists, opticians and so on often have their own practices on the out. Most cons recognize they are getting a service, so don't complain or kick off. We'd stand outside the surgeries keeping an eye on them if anyone was worried. Any prisoner could apply for a visit, if they had a lump on a bollock, say, or a dodgy tooth. I've known prisoners to come out with a new set of gnashers they haven't paid for. Anything they can get done, they will.

Two holding cells were also down there in a gated area, with normal location prisoners in the largest. It housed up to thirty-five. The other was for VPs, kept separate. At times it was standing room only in the normal one, and first come, first served. There were three ground-floor entrances and exits: one used to bring VPs in, one for normals and another in a separate stairwell in a gated-off sterile area which took you straight up to the in-patients' unit. The two zones were kept strictly apart. But whenever the shit hit the fan upstairs, the rumpus could be heard through the ceiling.

Prison officers elsewhere in the jail often held healthcare in contempt. A big useless lump on C Wing, small in stature with a neck like an elephant's arse, once gave me a prepared speech I'd heard lots of times before. It got boring.

'Thing is,' he said, 'these nurses need to realize this is a prison.'

My hand shot up. Hold it right there. 'These nurses are in no doubt that this is a prison,' I said, 'but it's the hospital wing of the prison, where inmates are also patients, and I'm happy with that.'

He'd got the hump because they called cons by their first names, and it's true, as a profession they did give prisoners the best care they could. But, believe me, none of those nurses were so naive as to imagine them lads as anything other than dangerous.

Roy Harris came to us from H Wing. He was on a three officer and SO unlock, which was a clue straight away that he was unlikely to be pleasant. At feeding time one day, an officer had chosen to bypass that security protocol, just trying to make things work as we all did, and slid his meal in. To show his gratitude Harris charged the door,

178

jammed it on their arm and broke it very badly. I've said it before and I'll say it again: prison officers are civil servants. Nothing in your contract says you will get punched, kicked, have limbs broken or be strangled. You are in prison, people say: you should expect it. Well, no you shouldn't. Fortunately, the officer made a recovery and came back. Another who witnessed the incident left with PTSD.

As a result of all this, Roy Harris was with us now on healthcare. I'd always check backgrounds so knew what he'd done, and treated him as though he could kick off at any moment. He never assaulted any of us, was rarely out of his cell and a lot of his meals went through the hatch. We had him eight months and I never ever let my guard down with him.

KK, Bradders and Sandy were the nurse managers for the bulk of my time on the unit and each was very different in their way. Those three women ran healthcare and did a cracking job of it. Over the three to five years we worked alongside one another, they had a manager above them too, but on the whole they were left alone and ran it like a hospital, which of course it was. And actually, the governors of the jail put up with that. When stuff kicked off on healthcare you couldn't nudge our leaders in with cattle prods.

I loved those three to bits, forging friendships we still share. Through my time, they were never properly supported from above, however. You don't want interference, but you do want to know that when trouble erupts, the jail is on your side. What we did was support each other. The stuff they saw and sorted every day would make hard men faint. Our nurse managers were very sensitive as well as talented and practical. When they wanted a cry, I was there. I'd get upset too, especially if they were. A normal person would, wouldn't they? True, I can't watch *The Lion King* without blubbing, but who can? It often felt like them against the prison.

Healthcare was a hostile environment and they faced the risks bravely. They were careful; if we had an eighty-year-old, no legs, dying and no danger to anyone any more, they would not go in his cell without consulting me first. 'Can I give Mr So-and-So his meds?' If it was a normal prisoner, there'd always be a prison staff member there. Even governors would spout that 'Nurses need to realize . . .' shite. It wasn't about specific incidents, it was just the general impression. Not 'macho' enough, you see. The criticism was unfair.

KK was what I call a proper nurse. By that I mean RGN – the sort who change bedpans and pat your backside with talc in your average infirmary. It took KK and me a while to become pals, but once we did we really clicked. She was particularly loyal when I had my own psychological battles later on, and is still my best mate today.

Our other RGN, Sandy, was one of those I'd been warned about – stern, vocal and stubborn. She was a royal pain in the arse, they said, who had been on healthcare yonks. In fact she was just strong-minded, which scares a lot of men to death. Sandy said what she thought and did not take any nonsense. When somebody wasn't pulling their weight, she told them. I've seen her row with governors, POs, SOs – anyone trying to put prisoners where she knew they shouldn't be. She would stand nose to nose with anyone. I wasn't quite as close with her as I was KK and Bradders, but we had an understanding and I got to like her a lot. Mutual respect, I suppose. We admired each other's professionalism. So much so that I tended to be her first point of contact. I hope that was because she knew I'd do things right, a big disciplined lad with bottle.

I was on a landing with a couple of orderlies when a lad shouted, 'Mr Samworth! You're in trouble.'

Sure enough, there came the familiar sound of Sandy's clippy-cloppy shoes. I was pretty sure I hadn't done anything wrong so tried not to look guilty. 'Mr Samworth! Would you have a word with Mr Vass.'

No question mark, because really it was an order.

Jonathan Vass was truly horrible. He'd a personality disorder: narcissism.

Personality disorders were among the worst prisoners we had. A bodybuilder and steroid abuser, he murdered a young nurse at Warrington, his fiancée who he'd had a child with. She'd accused him of raping her nine times, and some judge bailed him, so then he'd figured that if he killed her there'd be no evidence and he wouldn't be convicted. It was horrendous: he'd waited for her in a car park, and not only did he have one go at her, he went away, thought better of it and went back to finish her off. The parents of the woman he killed have campaigned for a change in the law and my heart goes out to them. Absolute scum, quite definitely.

At the time, his profile was high and really he should have been in seg', but the fact that he was infamous and on an ACCT form meant we had the nasty piece of shit. A big lad he was, bigger than me, but Sandy had been very unimpressed with his manner of dress. I found him on Y landing, talking to another prisoner outside the office, not far from his cell. He was wearing a checked shirt unbuttoned to his navel.

Believe it or not, sometimes I can be quite subtle. On this occasion I wasn't, 'Who the fuck do you think you are?'

'I beg your pardon?' he said, mock politely.

'Where do you think we are? Fucking Roxy's nightclub?' That was a real place in Sheffield, by the way: hairy chests, medallions. 'Get behind your door. Button your shirt up. Start dressing appropriately.'

If he fancied cracking me, here was his opportunity.

He was a bit of a giant, loved himself. This was his chance to drop a prison officer. How would he react?

It wasn't bravado on my part. The creep would be with us a while, so he was not going to strut about like a peacock. Just as I suspected he would, this big bad hombre wimped away to his cell. I followed him in and told him in no uncertain terms that he'd be there until he left healthcare if he didn't watch his step. After that he was quiet as a mouse – or rat, which seems more appropriate.

Sandy, through all this, had been stood behind me. I'm guessing that was not how she'd have preferred it to be dealt with. A quiet word would have been more to her taste, no doubt. However, she said, 'Thank you, Mr Samworth,' and marched off. That's how our relationship went.

Bradders was lovely. Unlike KK, she is still in the job and has given everything to it. A mental health nurse for over thirty-five years, she taught me and everyone else on the unit a lot. She often knew more than the psychiatrists or doctors who came on there. We had a doctor who was more or less resident to begin with, though later they were brought in from outside when needed. Those experts saw patients for five or ten minutes; she lived with their troubles.

One patient, James Whitehead, had been mentally ill since his teens. In his case it was non-specific, but a terrible affliction nonetheless.

People struggle to live normal lives but can't. He dropped on us after behaving inappropriately. Like a lot of people on medication, he'd begun to feel better and stopped taking his dose. His crimes were petty, but he'd done about five spells inside, in and out of medium- and low-security hospitals as well. Maybe during a psychotic incident he might become violent, but he wasn't getting out and was no risk to the public. He'd play pool and mix, a nice lad. The mentally ill need interaction or they become isolated and unsociable.

Bradders and me took him to a psychiatrist one day, who began examining his meds. 'You've been on these for two years,' he said. 'It's time we changed them.'

This seemed unwise, but what did I know? Only that Whitehead was well behaved, stable and currently under control. He didn't look happy now mind. Yet the psychiatrist persisted.

Now one thing about mental health patients: they might lose touch with reality in all sorts of ways but they know their meds. This lad reeled off a fifteen-year history of different combinations, stuff they no longer make, all sorts. Not only that, he also had a good understanding of how each affected his moods. This shrink wasn't listening, so the kid made a prediction.

'If you change them, I'll stop taking them,' he said, 'and you'll end up sending me to hospital.'

The psychiatrist got the hump and I put James

Whitehead in his cell, while Bradders continued to make his case. I overheard her warning when I came back. If someone's unwell, I need to know.

'Look, I understand why you think changing the meds would be a good idea,' she said, 'but these seem to be working and I believe him when he says he won't take the new pills.' That was his problem, replied the psychiatrist.

Soon there were no more games of pool. Whitehead went from sociable to withdrawn in the space of three days. Bradders and I tried to lure him out, but he wouldn't collect his meals or anything. In prison no one sweated that, he'd have gone hungry. On healthcare, we took it to their cell. Different strategy. By day nine, Bradders asked me to go with her and talk to the lad who by now was in a 'safe cell' and very agitated. (A 'safe cell' or 'anti-ligature cell' has very smooth surfaces, meaning in theory that a prisoner has nothing to fasten any kind of rope to. In reality, no cell is totally safe.)

Whitehead was covered in excrement. He had it in his eyes, ears, up his nose, all over the shop. He was completely naked, had his cock and balls in his hands and was trying to pull them off. It was awful to see. I tried to talk to him but he ignored me – it was impossible to reason with the kid. He was incoherent and deteriorating fast.

'Do you mind opening him up?' said Bradders.

Anywhere else in jail, having so much shit

around is classed as a dirty protest, and you are not unlocking that door. You'd put your PPE on and a team would go in. Bradders wanted to give him diazepam, so I cracked the bolt and went in first. He wasn't showing any violence towards us, just himself. She bent down and spoke to him for ten minutes or so. His hand came out for the meds, which he then poured on the floor, so we came out.

As a rule, a prisoner can refuse treatment. Healthcare staff are only allowed to go against those wishes if they reckon him incapable of making a rational decision himself. In theory, having a mental health condition can fit that bill, but often it's not so simple. For a start, you are supposed to try and discuss the issue with the prisoner's family first and, generally, it's very much a grey area, a legal shitstorm if anything goes wrong. It's also true that this sort of scene wasn't all that rare. The doctors – who have the final say – just like the nursing staff and prison officers, are under pressure from all sides.

Next day, he was in an even worse tangle: on his bed, blood all over. He'd been sticking things up his backside. After that, nothing was left in the cell. We stripped it, apart from the clothing he wasn't for wearing. Watching him was painful; if ever there was a signal for the liquid cosh then that was it. He was still tearing at his bollocks, and had begun sticking his fingers in his eyes, rubbing shit in them. It was now obviously an emergency and one of the doctors arranged for a hospital bed on the out somewhere.

Had the wrong crew come in to move him, they'd have smashed fuck out of the poor sod, knocked him all over. When I was younger I'd have maybe been the same. You're educated by experience, or should be. Bradders, in tears, said please be careful with him. He struggled a bit but, having had nothing to drink or eat for ages, was weak. Eventually, they got a pair of cuffs and a tracksuit on him, wrapped the lad in blankets, and off he went.

Prison can't just be about banging heads. Sometimes it requires a bit of compassion. It was thanks to Bradders that Whitehead lived to see another day.

It was around this time that an ITV production crew came in to make a documentary about Strangeways. The prison service, not the prison, had given permission for them to film on health-care, which put us on our best behaviour. They spent a lot of time with us, filmed more than a hundred hours of footage to fill three hour-long programmes. When the series was shown, the number-one governor at Strangeways, Richard Vince, thanked us all for the part we played, which meant a lot. He said we were a credit to health-care, a credit to Manchester and a credit to the prison service.

CHAPTER 12

I WANNA BE ADORED

A prison officer quite definitely needs a strong stomach. It ought to be in the job description. When people aren't slicing bits off themselves – or others – they can get very creative with stuff best left to U-bends and sewers.

Meds can help mentally ill people sometimes, antipsychotics and the like. But for extreme narcissists like Jonathan Vass, and those with personality disorders in general, they don't work. Such characters might be pacified or subdued for a while, but that's your lot. A common symptom is self-harming, and in healthcare a lot of that went on, more than anywhere in the jail. What personality disorders do need is continuity. They need a regime, too, and that's tough in prison because you can't guarantee similar days.

Thomas Riley, our twisted firestarter, had personality issues of the worst kind, putting him among the most dangerous and disruptive prisoners around. He was nine or ten on the self-harm scale. I saw him try it several times. His behaviour didn't depend on his surroundings. If you'd put Riley in the Savoy, in a luxury suite with champagne and a sauna, had someone pissed him off he would at some point have cracked on with a blade or box of matches.

While I was on healthcare at Strangeways I was Riley's personal officer for a while, and if I was on shift with him all day, that worked. You might get a period of calm. But on this particular day Mr Angry, a healthcare manager from downstairs with no patience at all, had given Riley both barrels and wound him up. Despicable as he was, there was no need for it, not least as Mr Angry then fucked off and left the creature to me.

When his cell door was shut Riley produced a razor blade out of his mouth – I saw it through the hatch. Prisoners do that: they'll carry them under their tongue or under skin flaps . . . up their arse . . . you name it.

'Where've you got that from, Tommy?' I asked, knowing full well he wasn't going to tell me. It would cut off the supply chain, wouldn't it? I was playing for time, trying to settle him down. It didn't work. He started cutting into his left arm and made six cuts. And when I say cuts, I mean cuts – down to the wood. He wasn't doing any arteries or committing suicide, just slicing into himself as a butcher might prepare a sirloin steak.

I could have pressed the bell and called the troops, but it wouldn't have made any difference. I could have gone in myself and tried to take the blade by force; again no point. When he was that way out, you'd only be putting off the inevitable.

I'd get it off him once he'd had enough. If we'd bent him up, taken everything out of his cell, he'd have found some other way, probably just as grisly. He hadn't asked for anything: he was either throwing a paddy or punishing himself. Medically, though, it looked dodgy. I alerted KK.

All the while Riley was talking to me very politely, 'Mr Samworth' – not prick or dickhead – 'please fuck off and let me finish.' The cuts were half an inch wide, bits of flesh protruding.

KK came on. 'Thomas, what are you doing that for?'

'Ms Kenny,' he said, in his croaky alien voice, 'fuck off and leave me alone, please.'

'Press the bell if you need anything,' she said.

In the prison itself, that wouldn't have happened. This guy would have been wrapped up, restrained and carted off. But he was not a normal prisoner and wouldn't have coped on an average wing. He refused treatment and the injuries, though horrible, weren't life threatening. Nothing more could have been done.

Later on, though, he decided these cuts weren't enough and decided to rub shit in them. So he piled one up and did just that, still refusing medical treatment. KK gave him the disclaimer, 'Thomas, if you get septicaemia it can kill you.'

'Yeah, all right Ms Kenny. Fuck off and leave me alone, please.'

So we left him again and three days later these wounds were festering. We got a specialist in from

Wythenshawe, and I eventually persuaded Riley to have a word with the doctor.

'I'm not having any treatment, though, Mr Samworth.'

Out he came. Riley's arm was dripping with clear fluid, and the wounds were full of pus. One officer on overtime threw a whitey, spewed and went off sick. We never saw him again.

'Thomas,' said the specialist. 'What *have* you done to yourself?'

'Quack, quack, quack,' went Riley, like Penguin out of *Batman*.

The doctor told him his arms needed plastic surgery. 'Do you mind if I take some pictures to show my friends?'

'Crack on,' Riley said, 'but you're not giving me any surgery.'

The doc asked if he was on antibiotics.

'Nah. Don't want any.'

Thee, me, anyone else, excrement gets in a small cut and there's a good chance we'd get blood poisoning. Possibly die. Not Thomas Riley. Three weeks later, despite the fact he'd been picking at the scabs non-stop, apart from six huge scars he'd completely healed.

Then there was the time he cut his throat.

By that stage he wanted out of Strangeways, fancied a spell in hospital I expect, so a doctor and the nursing staff discussed shifting him to Rampton in Nottinghamshire. The doc gave Riley a few home truths, told him what they'd do with him and forecast that he would have to comply with treatment. 'No, I won't,' he said, backing himself.

Prisoners are given plastic cutlery to eat their meals with, including a knife that with enough force might jab someone's ribs, but which you'd struggle to slice a loaf with. Anyway, Riley had another temper tantrum, arms like windmills, chucking stuff around his cell. Again, I stood at the door when he started to hack at his neck. In under a minute he was an absolute mess.

KK was on the scene again, mopping it up. It was gruesome. He'd somehow managed to make a considerable wound, and you could see his veins. However, it didn't bleed a lot, weirdly, and thankfully he didn't rub shite in it.

This time, he let her clean it and put a plaster on. Could he have died? Quite definitely he could. Half an inch either way, that would have been that. He'd have severed a major artery. As it was, he was parcelled off to Rampton and lived to croak another day.

You might recall that I'd agreed to come to healthcare on a promise that if, after one year, I wanted out I could move anywhere in the prison I fancied. And I dare say, with the likes of Riley to contend with, you might be wondering why I didn't take the governor who made it up on his offer. Well, the truth is that I was building some great relationships.

In terms of how the place was run, it was a transition period. The original eight-manager system was on its way out and the wing had a buzz about it, a real sense of camaraderie among a much smaller and tighter-knit group of staff.

The thought of whether to enforce it and bugger off did cross my mind, however. Especially when, one day, I saw the governor who made the promise – the guy who'd done a report on me every week in training – coming down the steps in the bottom jail.

'All right, guv,' I said.

'Are you all right, Mr Samworth?' He always called me Mr Samworth.

'I am guv, yeah.' And then I went, 'Can I . . .'

He stopped me with a smirk and a glint in his eye. 'If you want to move anywhere in this jail, Mr Samworth, just come and see me.'

As a standing joke, whenever we bumped into each other and exchanged pleasantries from that moment on, we'd go through the exact same routine.

'All right, guv,' I'd nod. 'Can I . . .'

'If you want to move anywhere in this jail, Mr Samworth, just come and see me.'

Deaths are an occupational hazard in prison, but when I came to healthcare I'd been warned about the bodies. Inmates were usually on some sort of watch. Some of the deaths from that period will haunt me forever.

Early in my time there I was redirected with a fellow officer to Hope Hospital, Salford, for a bed watch – a prisoner so sick he was having to be cared for on the out, but still needed a prison officer at his bedside. The night staff needed to be relieved and although I wasn't keen at first it got us out of jail, so what the hell. It was a hospital I'd been to many times at Forest Bank.

When we arrived, I asked the two Strangeways staff if this guy they'd been supervising, Quiggers, a VP who'd been on healthcare, was going to die. 'Nah, he's just poorly,' they said, before buggering off for their breakfast. It had been a long evening.

Immediately they'd gone there was a high-pitched continuous beep.

'What the—?'

Sure enough, this Quiggers had flat-lined. A nurse confirmed his demise. There was to be no resuscitation attempt. Prisoners can now sign a DNR form – do not resuscitate – to say they don't want it. Quiggers had cancer, made a decision that enough was enough and passed away. I called Strangeways' security. They said they'd get the police to come and take the body off us. 'But when they do,' the lad on the other end said, 'they will need to write you a receipt.'

I thought he was taking the piss but, no, they really did. When two bobbies rocked up, they looked about sixteen, but they do nowadays, don't they? They were sheepish too and as unsure as we were about the procedure. That was how our ex-inmate came to be signed, sealed and delivered. Imagine that, a human life reduced to the sort of slip of paper they give you for a few gallons of petrol or your weekly shop.

Alan Taylor was another lad we had on health-care, about three times in all. He'd been in the army and after leaving ended up on the streets. His offences were nothing – petty crime, public disturbances, smashing windows and robbing bottles of vodka, that sort of caper. He wasn't your usual prisoner, clearly no idiot, but something had gone awry. The detox wing had been concerned about him. He'd gone on an ACCT and then come to us. His dad was named Mulgrew. We'd had two of his sons in prison already and Alan Taylor was another one. Mulgrew was one of Britain's most prolific paedophiles. He'd abused his own half a dozen kids and passed them around. Had this been America, he'd have got twenty-odd years for his first crimes. Our system let him out to reoffend time after time. The sex offenders' treatment programme doesn't work – read the fable of the scorpion and frog.

Alan Taylor was a nice lad. Pleasant, polite, but very disturbed. At one point he started writing scriptures on his cell wall. A governor took me to his cell to highlight something while Taylor was in association and his cell empty. Floor to ceiling were beautifully written passages from the Bible, apparently accurate; chapter, verse and psalm. Why had we allowed a prisoner to do this? he asked. Well, the chaplain had assured us that Taylor had become deeply religious and the verses were genuine. We took the writing material off him, but he managed to find more and it took him a fortnight to repeat it all. Every time we tried to wash it off, he'd just write it back on again.

Prison wasn't the right place for someone like Taylor. We did our best with him but the environment was wrong and we couldn't help. It's just not realistic to put such people in jail and expect them to be cured, they need proper medical intervention. Three times he came to us, and three times we released him back onto the streets. He self-harmed, tried twice to hang himself, and shortly before he went out for the last time the prison's housing guy did his best to find him a place to live, in a hostel or somewhere. When they're freed, prisoners get less than £100 and that's not going to last long, is it? He had no psychological counselling and could have done with it. Months later I read that he'd been found dead, hanging from some viaduct. I still feel sad when I think about the lad.

Tom Smith was less sympathetic. Weedy as fuck and in for disturbances that often spilled over into violence, he was all about shit: unprovoked, he'd throw and smear excrement – no saving graces, just nasty. Bodily fluids and shite are the bane of your life on healthcare. It doesn't stop you dealing with prisoners, just causes inconvenience and is thoroughly unpleasant. He was also vile to nurses, telling them what he'd like to do to them – I don't need to spell it out. He spat in KK's mouth, punched a healthcare assistant in the breast who ended up needing scans and, if that wasn't bad enough, striped a young nurse in a Manchester A & E, which is to say slashed her across the face with a razor blade, ear to chin, and scarred her for life. He was prosecuted for that, but didn't serve anywhere near long enough because people saw his outward elderly appearance and were lenient. This was a villain of the first degree. Sometimes I wished he was my size so I could knock fuck out of him. But he wasn't, so I couldn't, more's the pity.

When I first saw him, he was able-bodied and could walk. Then he had a stroke, and although he was about fifty-five, he looked seventy. Within four years of my first getting to know him he was brown bread. He didn't die in prison; he died in hospital. And during that four-year period, he lost a leg because he was a diabetic on drugs who'd been an alcoholic.

He hadn't been with us long when he staged his first dirty protest. His shite-throwing antics were so bad he'd ended up on seg'. An officer there, working on nights and having been pushed to the limit, gave him a black eye. Despite a previously unblemished record he not only lost his job but also got time in prison for assault, which caused controversy and hurt among staff. In court it was pointed out that this officer had worked on seg' for five consecutive years when the national guidelines say the upper limit is three. His defence barrister called it 'an accident waiting to happen' and he was right. I hope at some point that lad gets to sue the prison service for how he was treated. Shameful.

While all that was going on, Smith came back to healthcare one night at about seven o'clock, and we put him in a cell on Y landing. Twenty minutes later KK popped her head around the office door. 'Mr Samworth, have you got a minute?' Normally she called me Samikins, so I knew she was pissed off about something. Sure enough, the outside of Tom Smith's cell was littered with shitty paper that he'd shoved under the door.

The landing stank like a sewer. Then the threats and abuse began. He'd been on healthcare less than an hour and was going on like this. Other people had to live on that unit. At that point he should have gone straight down the seg' but was never going to, because of the assault. We were stuck with him.

At nine o'clock, the night staff came in and I waited for KK, Bradders and Sandy, so I could toddle off down the drag with them. I always did that. If they were going to be late, I'd wait. It was then that we'd have our bitch for the day, get in our cars and leave it all behind, so that when we got home we could be decent human beings with our families. As KK and me walked past Tom Smith's cell, though, I could smell burning. I didn't bother lifting the flap. I looked at KK and she looked at me. We didn't press the alarm. If we'd done that, they'd have frozen the gate and no one would be leaving. I got the fire hose, had a look in and this creature was sat on the bed in his boxers. He looked like Stig of the Dump. His body and face were covered in hot shit, flames lapped around him. I hosed the sides of the door, washed the shite off the hatch and, just as I'd done with Riley, blasted the little bonfires he'd got going to smithereens.

A guy came up from security and looked in as the rancid old twat swore and cursed and danced about, trying to get out of range. He said I needed to be careful, as the governors were watching like hawks. On camera all they'd see was me dealing with a cell fire, so I carried on for a good five minutes until all that mud was washed off. Dripping wet in his boxers, he was a feeble thing. We got him out – and he came out now because he was cold – and put him on constant watch. Eventually we did clock off, and when I came in next morning the place stank to high heaven again.

The final time this scrote came in I was on with the Stretcher Bearer, an older bloke I got on well with. Lads got called 'stretcher bearer' if they worked in the office, not as infantrymen on the front line. I had one tell me his job was more dangerous because he talked to murderers, terrorists, gangsters and so on face to face, one on one. One on one! When do you get them odds on a landing? Six officers to two hundred! Bollocks to that. The lad was all right – he laughed when I pointed this out where others might have put a grievance in. Anyway, Smith, looking feebler than ever, was put in a 'safe cell'. His leg had gone by then, but he was still abusive, all seven stone of him, especially to women, and still chucking shite around.

Because of his frailty and blood sugar being so low, they were afraid he would have a heart attack. KK said we ought to send him out to get some bloods done. Stretcher Bearer and me were elected his escorts. I wasn't keen on going, but the Stretcher Bearer was up for it. 'We'll be all right, Sam,' he said. 'It'll be a laugh.'

So off we went with the human muck spreader.

At North Manchester casualty the ward sister knew Tom Smith all right. This was the hospital where he'd striped the nurse, so they weren't going to forget him, were they?

While we were talking, a big turd dropped out of his backside. KK had put him in a hospital gown, so we got a full-on view of his bony arse as this dollop of crap landed. The ambulance crew looked at me and I apologized – I don't know why: he was the filthy bastard.

The nurse asked what he'd done that for.

'Fuck off, you slag,' he said, scraping it off the bed and onto the floor. They couldn't get us in a side ward fast enough.

It was boiling hot in there, no air, and we had

a two-hour wait before a doctor arrived. By which point, he'd dropped another turd and the place was stinking. We were directly opposite the main reception desk. Smith tried to spit at the doc, called him a bastard and refused to give any bloods or sign a disclaimer.

'Listen,' the doctor said, after ushering me outside. 'If we get his bloods and he refuses treatment, fair enough. We'd have tried. If we don't try and he leaves here and dies, we are in even more trouble.'

So we went back in and, as the doctor stood out of the way, Stretcher Bearer put a sheet loosely over Smith's head. The git was spitting like a camel while I grabbed a puny arm, put one hand on his chest and pinned him to the bed. Any governor watching would have been aghast, but fuck 'em. The doctor nipped in with his syringe, drew blood and escaped being showered in phlegm.

Tom Smith, though, was now bubbling and gurgling, a regular little poop machine. We'd been in there three and a half hours and I was starting to feel faint. I can still taste the stink now. The Stretcher Bearer had been right. We found ourselves laughing a lot, out of despair. Smith refused to be cleaned up, so same procedure, sheet over his horrible noggin. Four hours in, our relief shift turned up. Never have I been so pleased to finish a shift.

Then there was Crosby, a lad in from A Wing, not a sex offender but an OP, own protection – he'd built up a drug debt on B Wing. We only got him because he had a personality disorder and had been threatening self-harm.

It was a nice sunny day, and we'd taken about thirteen prisoners onto the yard to exercise. They hadn't been out long when I noticed my prisoners cowering and clambering at the fence. 'Mr Samworth! Mr Samworth! Let us out!' On the adjacent yard were the Category A lads, high security; the sort you would not want to meet on the out. They were huddling like kids, clinging to each other in fright.

In the middle of my yard stood Crosby, stark bollock naked. I thought he was covering his modesty at first, but no. He had shat in his hands. He slowly brought them up and began to rub the stuff all over his belly, chest and head. The stench was sick-making.

'Aaagh! Aaagh! Keep him away from us!'

Three hours later, once it had all quietened down and he was changed and freshened up, I asked Crosby what on earth had possessed him.

'Don't know, Mr S.,' he said. 'It just seemed like the right thing to do.'

CHAPTER 13

DRUG SOUP

Drugs find a way into prison. They are everywhere. You can be the most resourceful officer, have the best work ethic and there is still fuck all you can do about that. I could have run around all day trying to take illegal substances off people – end up fighting – but one man on his own wasn't going to win the war. Once the drugs are in there, they are going to get distributed. People are going to receive and take them whichever way they can.

Believe it or not, people will walk past Strangeways, near the middle of town, and chuck parcels in. On K Wing, where there's netting over the yards, in winter they'll throw snowballs with stuff in them that can be collected when they melt. Forest Bank was in a park, so you could walk right up to it with your dog. Prisoners might take an orange out on exercise with them, hoy it over the wall, and a mate on the other side would gauge the trajectory and toss one of his own back, full of drugs. Don't laugh. The fear in Salford was that someone might throw a gun into the yard. While I was there, someone chucked a foot-long machete. The officer didn't see it but the lad who picked it up was caught on camera. It came in like a fucking boomerang – lucky it didn't stick in someone's head. It got picked up and handed to someone else, who walked over to this old fella and started hacking away at him. Sawn-off shotgun? Game over.

It's true that staff corruption can also be a problem. There was that officer I mentioned earlier, for example, who went on to do seven years for bringing drugs in. Another lad at Forest Bank, a fresh-faced nineteen year old – too young to be a prison officer – had prisoners all over him. They badgered him for months . . . bring us a phone . . . you just have to pick it up . . . 600 quid . . . wore him down, befriended him. One day he came into a cell and threw a phone on the bed. 'That's it now, stop mithering me.' So they let him alone for a month and started again. We need a phone . . . get us a phone . . . oh, and some two litre bottles of Coke with Jack Daniels in. No 600 quid on offer this time, just a threat to grass him up. Backed him in a corner. One day this lad rang in sick and never came back, well off out of it.

The officer who did the stretch was in cahoots with a dealer on his wing. He met contacts on the out, brought in the gear and got a tidy wedge for his trouble. Unfortunately, the dealer had a mandatory piss test coming up. He used as well so he got a bag of urine off one of the cleaners. Prisoners try all sorts. They'll blow up a finger on a rubber glove and fill it with piss, fasten it to their balls and when they are told to have a slash squeeze it. We saw bags and pipes attached to their dick, all sorts. Contaminated samples are another trick. One reckoned he could only have a slash sitting down, got his hand in the bowl, scooped mucky water out and weakened his sample with it.

In the case of our bent officer, the dealer hadn't realized that the cleaner was on drugs as well. His piss test still read positive.

He kicked off big time, this lad, furious. He had to be restrained and ended up being carted off to seg'. So our officer decided to find a new source and moneyman and, of course, one wasn't long in making himself known. 'I'll bung you 200 extra a week if you bring in for me instead.' Word reached the first guy, who then grassed the bent officer up.

The problem is worse when dynamic security breaks down. Officers haven't got time to watch prisoners' every step and bullying, mostly driven by drugs, is rife. When you build relationships you can tell if someone is a bit off, and have a word in their cell maybe. Find stuff out. There might be family members threatened unless they bring gear in – we are talking brutal and devious people. You can't just let them get on with it. Cuts and austerity and savings are all very well but, if it hasn't sunk in by now, prison is a place where having too many staff means you've got exactly the right amount.

If politicians are serious about keeping drugs out of prison – and the government tells us it is disgusted with the amount flooding the estate – then get your hand in your pocket and give every jail an airport-style security portal. It's not going to happen, though, is it?

There are lots of mandatory drugs tests inside – 'willy-watching' the cons call it. A certain amount of prisoners per month go through the system as dictated by the Home Office, who give staff a list of names, picked at random I assume. There used to be monthly voluntary ones too, as an encouragement to recovering druggies, but like everything else they get neglected nowadays because there aren't enough officers to do them.

With mandatory tests, a sample was taken, sent off and if it came back positive they got placed on report and had to appear in front of a governor. They could request a back-up test, also completed by the prison service to reinforce the first one. The prisoner, out of his own pocket, could then get their legal team to do an independent test, so that's three. If they all came back positive the case went to a district judge. Governors used to be able to add days to a sentence, sixteen for cannabis, say. Smack, heroin, brown, might get twenty days. The maximum, if you were persistent, was around forty-two. At Forest Bank, we had one young offender and heroin user come in on a three-month sentence and actually serve three and a half years.

He was continually on report for positive tests and physical violence.

For me, the punishments don't fit the crime and, for the amount of routine and palaver involved, the number of prisoners punished for smoking or injecting drugs is very small, nothing like it used to be.

As a prison officer you often hear the general public talking about drugs in jail. They look at you as if you personally dish out little trays of goodies. Students of human anatomy will realize that we are back to cavities.

In Strangeways, when radios or clothes or anything was sent to prisoners, it was checked thoroughly, taken apart and reassembled if necessary. At one time, envelopes were soaked in hallucinogenic drugs that a con could then get at by wetting them – cunning stuff. Acid tabs under postage stamps, all sorts went on. Nowadays, I suspect the stuff is mostly brought in by mules – addicts who, while out on bail, have been effectively given notice to lubricate and widen their back passage for use when they inevitably come back in.

When someone with a drugs record is jailed, a nurse interviews him. One lad who came to us admitted to swallowing twenty-five condoms' worth of 'smash'. He'd done so because he was in debt. Someone said, 'Take this gear in and we'll let you off.' He wasn't the brightest and landed an additional sentence. The heroin was safely removed in hospital.

Prisoners will carry stuff into jail hidden not only up their own arse but also anyone else's back or even front bottom. If a bloke will get his seventy-year-old mother to bring in a phone like that, as happened once, anything is possible. That's why even babies are searched. The OSGs who do that job are great at dealing with a public that gets pissed off, especially on a first visit when they are told they have to put their valuables in a locker, walk through a metal detector and then get patted down. Once they know why it's happening, unless they are up to no good – or 'no good' is up them – they tend to be fine. We've had prisoners who've had a baby on their knee, removed its nappy, taken out a phone, drugs or whatever and shoved it up themselves, or maybe they'd hidden something down a toddler's leggings. Some of them show absolutely no hesitation in using children any way they can.

The effects of smuggling can be pretty horrific. We escorted to hospital once this wimpy Liverpudlian who'd been a victim of 'spooning', which might sound cosy but isn't. In an act of bravado he'd told some other cons that he had a phone about his person. At some point he may have had, but didn't any more. His attackers, as they became, weren't to know that though, were they? Two strapping lads, six feet four or similar, sixteen stone, had gone into his cell and made light work of him. Broke a couple of ribs, two black eyes, gave him a good kicking. Then they'd stripped him, turned him upside down and, while one held him by the ankles, the other got a spoon and shoved it up his backside, trying to scoop this device out. They found nothing, but left him in a state.

Of late, drones look like being a menace and need regulation. Anyone caught flying one within half a mile of a prison should get a twelve-month sentence or a ten grand fine. We need a registration scheme for owners, as with dogs and firearms, to trace them back. Flying stuff over prison walls and fencing, onto exercise yards or wherever, is only a tiny problem at the moment, but it is on the rise.

Manchester, for all its problems, is basically a well-run and disciplined jail, where no one takes drugs openly. Like anywhere, though, they are available to anyone who wants them and that includes recreational drugs – coke, ecstasy – as well as steroids. There are a lot of steroids in jail now, which is problematic given how huge lads on them get. Mood swings just make that problem worse.

What has taken off big-style in prison in the last few years is zombie drugs, or synthetic cannabinoids to give them their proper name: spice, black mamba, Bombay blue – there are loads. It's because the stuff is easy to get hold of on the out. There are some restrictions now but they used to be a legal high, very cheap to buy. The other handy thing inside is that they don't show up in piss tests, which cannabis, heroin and more traditional drugs do. People come into prison with a backside of spice and can make themselves fifteen or twenty grand in two or three months. I've seen it happen.

There are people in prison who can't afford tobacco or drugs of any sort. As a practical joke cons would roll a joint, stick a bit of spice in it and throw it on the floor. Some vagrant type, in prison for three weeks, would leap on it, spark it up and – *bang!* Knocked out cold, before coming around and throwing up everywhere. Jails are harsh.

Cannabinoids are also infamous for unpredictability. There are those who can smoke it all day with little effect other than getting a high or feeling chilled. The wrong blend, though, can be a disaster.

Joseph Holden was a quiet lad, a minor offender. He wasn't violent and his sentences were small, but as soon as spice started to become popular he was drawn under its spell. He was found smoking it and got sent to healthcare on a short overnight stay, then within the day discharged back to K Wing. The following night here he was again, same story, using up staff resources. It had taken a good hour to move him from K Wing, fighting all the way. A real battle, it was not like him at all, so he went straight on an unlock.

I tried talking to him, and he was rambling on about the Devil peeping out of his eyes. Over the coming days his behaviour got even more bizarre, to the point where he'd started banging his head on the wall. He said it had Satan in it and he needed to get him out. If anyone normal tried to do that, their body system wouldn't let them; not with any force anyway. It's a natural in-built mechanism. He was full-on though, and it escalated quickly.

I was on an early shift and this lad's head was covered in lumps and bumps, it was awful. A healthcare manager was called: he'd started sticking his fingers in his eyes. I don't mean poking, I mean having a good delve, gouging them. He ended up throwing himself out of bed at the wall, arms tucked in, absolutely twatted himself. The thud as he nutted it was sickening. From somewhere he'd developed the strength of ten men: another one who needed the liquid cosh.

I didn't like leaving Warren, the young officer who came on, alone with what was now constant supervision: he'd be watching a lad his own age destroying himself. But my shift was up. Later he told me what had happened. In the end a team in full PPE gear had gone in and tried to restrain Holden, but couldn't. So they put him in a cuffed body belt, which took a while, and moved him off to hospital where the kid was confirmed to have lost his eyesight. His eyeballs were still there, but he'd damaged the muscles so badly his vision was ruined. He was a criminal, but not a particularly troublesome one. Somewhere there were people whose son, brother, nephew or grandson had gone into jail and come out blind.

That's spice for you. It is indeed the Devil's work.

Another prisoner on healthcare alleged he'd been made to mule a mobile phone and drugs through gang rape. What they'd done, he said, was ram a toilet brush handle up his arse to make his ring bigger so everything would fit. He'd had the items inside him for days, started bleeding and passed out as medics arrived to save him.

All of this reminds me of a time at Forest Bank, when four or five inmates were running drugs. I watched them all day, handing stuff back and forth on the wing. It became very obvious when you took the time to stop and watch. That night, with everybody dashing around as usual before lock up, I migrated to one particular cell. It belonged to a lad with a fearsome reputation. I was face to face with him while a handful of other lads stood around me, a fact I was very conscious of. He had a bag of powder in his hand that I suspected was heroin. I asked to see it.

'Mr S.,' he'd said, 'I like you and get on with

you. I'm not going to show you what's in my hand, but aren't gonna touch you either. What are you gonna do?'

I knew a couple of these lads and wasn't afraid of them, but one or two were sneaky. Although he'd said he'd not do anything, I couldn't be sure of them. I was outnumbered: had I reached for that bag I'd likely have got a beating. I had no radio, the alarm wasn't within reach. I was weighing up the odds, though, when he gave me a get-out-of-jail card I thanked him for later.

'How about I get behind my door, Mr S., and you can lock me in?'

So whatever he'd got, the rest of them weren't getting tonight. First thing tomorrow, security would be knocking on his door and spinning his cell because by then I'd have put a report in, as he also quite definitely realized.

'You are locked behind your door,' I said, and the others went.

By the time security knocked on his door, strip-searched him and turned his cell upside down, they found nothing. He'd either hid that bag very well or moved it on. He was let out for a brew, good as gold. I'd done my bit reporting it, and he'd done his. It was all in the game.

Which brings us to lines. Staff at both Forest Bank and Strangeways used to go on about them all the time. *What are they on about?* I wondered when I first heard them. Well, what they were on about was thin – very thin – strips of bedding, tied together and made into tiny fishing lines, then 'hooked' with something to give it weight. The first time I saw them in action I was amazed.

Imagine you are in the cell next door to me, and there's a half-inch gap under the doors – they're never flush. This particular night you've run out of cigarette papers.

'Got any skins?'

'Yeah, chuck us a line.'

So you'd have a plastic knife or pen tied to the end of this line, throw it under your door with a jerk and whip it around under my door. I'd fasten one to it, you'd pull it back again, and Bob's yer uncle: you've thrown out a line.

At Forest Bank on the YP there were two landings. On a night, you'd see a line come under a door on the twos, drop to the ground floor, bit of tweaking and it was in a cell. Little stuff – it might be a lighter, matches or bit of burn. It used to fascinate me: they'd sling them across landings while you were walking up and down. I'd turn the lights off and stand in the middle – no one would know you were there – and watch. Out they'd come, a strange little delivery service that might be five cells this way or ten cells that. It was incredible, really, and very skilfully done.

I was on B1 one night when this lad asked his mate across the landing for a light – didn't know I was there. 'Sling us a line,' he called out, and threw one out which I caught. Feeling mischievous, I tied it to the leg of a pool table, and he started tugging at it. 'It's snagged,' he called. These are only very thin strips – you couldn't call them a rope – yet he dragged that fucking pool table several metres. I couldn't believe my eyes. I popped up at the lad's door, looked in and we started laughing.

Prisoners can be ingenious bastards. There's not much else to do, I suppose, but practise their skills. Another time, an officer and I were doing a sweep of the exercise yard and heard something come over the wall. We shone a torch into the shadows and there was this little parcel that jerked and began to move. It had a line attached, and up it slowly climbed, towards a window on the twos. At Forest Bank the windows were made of plastic, so to get a bit of air in the cons used to burn holes in them with fag ends. When the place was new we'd replace them, but over time that tailed off, and the whole wing ended up like that. Now, if you thought chucking a line under a door on twos and dropping it down to the ones was unbelievable, how about this? Someone had clocked the parcel coming in, seen where it landed and somehow thrown a line through one of these holes, snagged it with a fishhook and started dragging it back. It fell off and we took it to security, where we found it contained cannabis resin and a mobile. Suddenly the phone rang.

'You fucking prick, Samworth,' someone said, and the line went dead.

At Strangeways, none of the wings butt up to the wall. The nearest point is about ten metres away. Yet lads have chucked lines out of windows, over razor wire and onto the street. Dog handlers outside, patrolling the jail, have seen them pulling stuff for hours at a time, although obviously once it gets near the walls they put their foot on it. We had people coming up at night to talk to prisoners, but not directly: a couple of them would stand by the wall and converse between themselves, as boyfriend and girlfriend maybe. 'Do you fancy going for a drink?' they would call out as though to each other – code the prisoner would understand. Bletchley Park would have struggled to suss it.

Once I was searching a lad's cell in healthcare and he had three tubes of toothpaste. They use it as adhesive to stick photos to the wall, but he was making a mess so I confiscated a couple. I'm inquisitive, so before I threw them in the bin I had a squeeze. Sure enough, some sort of liquid benzodiazepine. He was on it but hadn't been taking his full dose. Somehow, he'd got the stuff in there and begun selling it. We'd been having a quiet weekend in association with a few lads falling asleep, which suddenly made sense.

The lengths some in jail will go to for their fix . . . A lad I'd known since Forest Bank came to us in healthcare at Strangeways with a dislocated

216

shoulder. It was ugly. He'd done it 'playing pool', he said, straight-faced. His arm was dangling at a hideous angle. Even though he'd dislocated it himself, he was still in agony.

I and two other lads were nominated to escort him to North Manchester casualty. The hospital already knew him and he wasn't their favourite. The ward sister warned us she'd seen it before – a day out to get doped. 'He'll be getting a local in the back of his hand and that's it.'

'I'm in pain, I'm in pain,' he howled. The sister tipped me the wink that I ought to go in and see this.

One officer had him on a closet chain – which allowed for the greater movement he needed given his injury, so named because they also allowed prisoners to go to the toilet on their own – and I sat watching. I'd have had popcorn but they didn't sell it. This nurse and a colleague pinned him back and told him what followed would be incredibly painful. He was still yelling for drugs, but not getting them, when the doctor put his shoulder back in. Oh, it fucking *popped*. I couldn't help but laugh. The officer cuffed to him almost shat himself and the patient actually did, screaming all the while. Very professionally, the nurse retained her composure, and back to jail he went.

Weed is easy to find inside. That's at the lesser end of the scale, with booze and tobacco. The booze, as we know from the hooch saga, is often brewed on site, and burn actually helps the jail to tick over. Weed is a step up from those in that it can – and does – lead to harder shit. As a young 'un, like most people I think, I'd dabbled with grass, but skunk, this new strong cannabis, is not like back in the day when, chilling by a barbecue, all you wanted was a shedload of fried chicken. Kids need to understand the dangers. They put all sorts in it. Too many folk suffer psychotic episodes. If hardened users who have been on heroin for twenty years start smoking a lot more weed it can finish them: their mental health is shot to pieces. It's Class A stuff, and so it should be.

A percentage of prisoners will always use heroin because prison is boring and they will do anything to escape it. If they can't get out physically, they do it in their head. Lads on antipsychotics will be bullied for them, so nurses and officers inspect their mouth to make sure they've actually swallowed the meds and aren't 'cheeking' them. And actually, most prisoners rely on that so they've then got an excuse to take them and not pass them on. If the medics aren't on the ball, already unwell inmates are the ones to suffer.

One drug for stomach upsets is very popular because crushing and smoking it gets you high. Subutex, an alternative to methadone, is also in demand. It's supposed to work on receptors in the brain. Painkillers, tramadol, anything opiate-based, benzodiazepines . . . prisoners are mad for them.

I saw one who'd took twenty-five diazepines in one go. They destroy people – out of their head, spewing. But while they're in that state, they are somewhere else. It helps them forget.

Addicts is the politically correct term for drug users with a dependency, but for me that implies someone who may be working or holding their life together to some extent, but who has an addiction. Everybody is addicted to something. I'm partial to motorbikes, Stones Bitter and trifle. A smackhead or baghead, call them what you will, is something else. I wouldn't call it a lifestyle choice exactly but for some it can end up that way – lots of prison sentences for burglaries and muggings.

At Forest Bank we had a smackhead who went in for an eye operation. At the hospital the doctor briefed me, 'I'll take his eye out, have a look inside and bob it back.' There was a waiting room with a TV screen to watch it on, if we liked. *I'm having some of that*, I thought, *our own episode of* Casualty. 'Thing is, though,' he went on. 'I'll need your help, twice. Have you seen a heavy user go under with general anaesthetic?'

We hadn't.

'He'll fight. I'll give him a local, then gas and air. Countdown of ten, he'll be lucky to reach six.' As he breathed it in, the doctor told us, we'd have to restrain him. He'd tense up, kick out for a few seconds and then be zonked.

Sure enough, that's what happened. I'd seen

nothing like it. He must have risen two foot off the bed. I'd got my eighteen-plus stone on his arms, the doctors and nurses also struggling when – *bam!* Out he went. The doc asked us to come in at the end of the op, when he gave the signal, to put the cuffs back on.

I watched the operation and it was fascinating. For some reason my colleague had gone outside to take the air. The doc clamped our bloke's head back and had a nice gory rummage around, producing an eye from its socket like a pickled onion on a string. Then, when he'd finished and pushed it back in, he indicated via the screen for us to return. The cuffs went on and he made another prediction.

'We would be knocked out for an hour,' the doc told us. 'Not this guy. He will—' when suddenly One-Eyed Jack jerked back to life, bolt upright. It was like something out of *The Walking Dead*. Shit a brick, it made us jump. They build a tolerance, do these lads.

At Forest Bank, we'd had a detox wing. When an addict arrived at the prison, they had a five- to seven-day course of DF118 tablets and would then rattle for a few days, a couple of weeks for a heavy user. But what you found with lads who were on a six-month sentence, say, was that afterwards they would start using the gym, put a bit of weight on and begin to look quite healthy. They left jail, a lot of them, drug-free, or as near as possible, with a chance of getting on with their lives and going straight.

Then, in 2003, came methadone – and almost overnight hundreds of prisoners were presented with a new pathway to hell. Are you an addict? Yeah. On you go. In the medical world it was the fashionable thing, but for us it was a nightmare.

In Strangeways and elsewhere, it was a similar story, although the public sector didn't start using it until maybe five years later. Instead of prisoners being released relatively fit and healthy – the best time for drugs counsellors to get hold of them, incidentally – they would come in as skinny little fuckers and go out as skinny little fuckers. There are fat addicts – maybe they smoke weed and eat fried chicken – but most of them do have the appearance and charisma of scuffed pipe cleaners. They maintain that look and lifestyle on methadone.

One or two might come in on it, get a reduced dose, come off it and then start using smack. The cycle begins. They detox again, use smack again. The prison has to keep offering its detox programme – human rights – so on it continues for ten years or more if that's the length of their sentence . . . methadone, smack, methadone, smack, methadone, smack. You ended up with an army of prisoners queuing every day for the stuff. You couldn't fit all the addicts on Detox, so the meth heads were spread out over the prison and they'd queue one wing at a time in the top jail, five or six people a go. They'd have a drink of water, stand in front of a retina scanner, hand their ID card to a nurse who'd pass it to another, be given a plastic cup of water to drink from, before and after taking their fifty mil or whatever, so they couldn't regurgitate this 'cure' and sell it on later.

It was very controlled in the top jail, in the bottom jail not so much. There was no working retina scan there at the time and fewer staff. The ID-card process was less strict: sometimes there'd be water, sometimes not – two different methods in the same prison. One lad, talking to a mate, handed his ID card over and the nurses did the usual. The mate also gave them his card, but when his dose was put on the hatch the first lad necked that as well, double-dosed. They'll try anything. This kid was just an opportunist who got carted off to healthcare. He slept for eight hours and that was that.

So being on methadone means prisoners stop using other drugs, right? Wrong. They still take heroin. They'll take tramadol. They'll take anti-psychotics. They'll snort 'subbies' and anything else they can get hold of. So all you've really done is add an extra course to the menu. Methadone saturates the body, so every time you have a tug, a bit is left behind. You end up permanently sedated by this nasty green stinky liquid that isn't doing you any good.

There are lots of methadone-related deaths in

prison, certainly in Manchester. Over the time I was there we must have had at least a dozen in around a decade, although I dare say you'd get no one in officialdom to admit that. It can lower your blood pressure incredibly, the heart rate too, which is why its effects are monitored by nursing staff. We've had brothers die on it, two or three in the same jail. One lad came into healthcare with an arseful of drugs and on a methadone programme as well. He got moved to a normal wing and died, effectively of an overdose. He'd been on an ACCT form and they still hadn't noticed his extra drug taking. It caused a real shitstorm.

I hated the detox wing. It stank, and was full of people trying to scrounge stuff – people that had been in and out of there twenty times. There were fifty-year-old addicts who'd had thirty sentences, so they weren't learning, were they? A single big stretch was needed, not being let out every six months to rob a few more tellies worth £500 to sell for £30 and get a fix. It's crazy. You've a captive audience inside too, if you are really serious about treating drug addiction. All the programmes on the out are voluntary.

In prison there are doctors and nurses working specifically on detox, in a drug rehabilitation programme called CARAT – counselling, assessment, referral, advice and throughcare. It's a worthwhile project. But I was once talking about drugs with a nurse on healthcare who'd worked in Manchester prisons over ten years.

'If one of your patients is an addict,' I asked her, 'what's the best-case scenario?'

'Needle exchange,' she replied.

What she meant was that anyone who comes out of jail as an addict tends to stay that way.

Methadone is dodgy stuff, and for what? It serves no purpose. It costs a supposedly skint prison service a fortune that could be spent elsewhere, and all because some do-gooder namby-pamby twat didn't like prisoners on the rattle. Help them get clean, and help them again when they come out of prison so they stay that way.

The subject of drugs hits close to home. Just after my first marriage broke down I used to socialize with a couple through rugby in Sheffield: a middle-class pair with a detached house, two good jobs. One day they casually dropped it into conversation that they were on heroin – 'We like a dabble, but only use it Saturdays.'

I told them they were fucking bonkers, and over the course of a couple of years saw them become smackheads. They lost everything, eventually split up – fortunately they'd no kids – and died within six months of each other.

Then there was a mate's brother, a married university lecturer in his late twenties, with two six-year-old twin boys. A top lad, but he went down the same route. On crack as a youth, a decade later he began scoring again. He was found with a needle in his arm having overdosed in his bathroom.

A fourth friend was hooked, and we all told him it would kill him. He locked himself in his flat for two weeks eating chicken soup and came out clean, so far never going back. That's rare.

Getting into the psyche of addicts is notoriously tough. The drugs take them over and the strategies in this country aren't good enough: when customs seize £40 million-worth of heroin it's headline news, but I'll bet for every £40 million found there's over £400 million out there.

We need to educate our children. A huge proportion of the prison population is in for drug-related offences, and our kids are the next generation. If my daughter and her pals were educated to know what harm drugs cause, there'd be no one to buy them. Start talking to them at school.

We should tell them about 'stinky legs', a not very nice name for a horrendous condition. A lot of prisoners inject there, and the result is gangrene. Gangrene smells to high heaven. If you could bottle it and give schoolchildren a whiff, it would do more long-term good than a hundred methadone courses combined. Show them pictures of the ulcers. They would be revolted, but learn. I knew one pin-eyed lad who lost one leg to gangrene, then came into Strangeways healthcare and lost the other.

'At what point are you going to stop?' I asked him.

'Well, I'm not, am I, Mr S.?'

If he'd lost his arms he'd have carried on, getting someone to inject for him, dirty needles into the groin. These prisoners are often diseased too, carrying strains of hepatitis or AIDS, another hazard for nurses, prison officers and anyone they come into contact with.

Let's not be worried about scary stories or unpleasant films: that's exactly what schoolkids should be seeing – shock them into realization. Some parents wouldn't like it, I'm sure, but ask the parents of kids who are addicted or went on to die. Ask those who haven't seen their children in years.

It's got to the stage where drugs in prison are the norm, and that can't be right, can it? If one thing comes from this book, I hope it's that someone in authority takes this message on board. They can ignore everything else if they want: just recognize how the solution to drugs starts young. We need a new approach.

CHAPTER 14

COULD IT BE MAGIC

My first date with Amy was officially on 15 February 2010 – around two years after I began on Strangeways' health-care. Three days later, I bought the best ring I could afford and asked her to marry me.

I'd actually met Amy over a decade before, in a hairdressing salon in Sheffield. That's hardly my natural environment, is it? Why would it be, with a head like a billiard ball? No, a lass on the aroma-therapy course owned the joint, and offered me a spare room upstairs to do my massages in – it was part of how I was scratching a living back then. Amy seemed like a nice kid, but no more than that, given our twenty-year age difference. Fast forward twelve years, though, and when by chance we met again it was love at second sight. My old aromatherapy mate's other half, a friend on Facebook, had suggested we meet up when I was next back in town, and who should be there but Amy? She was now twenty-seven; I was forty-seven. We just clicked.

At the time I was in another relationship, so went straight home and told my then girlfriend that this was all totally my fault, but I needed out. Within days I'd seen a solicitor, signed the house over, taken the worst of the two cars and left everything else behind. Smitten.

Getting engaged so fast might strike some as a bit rash, in which case we've made up for it since. Here we are over eight years later and she's still my fiancée, not yet my wife. When that happens, it quite definitely won't be bridal gowns, wedding favours and fancy hats, though. It'll more likely be a knees-up in Gretna, in rugby shirts and Doc Martens, with a few mates. Spontaneity is more our style.

Amy was and is stunning to look at. Her fashion sense is unique: she's someone who'll wear dresses and Docs, go skinhead or grow her hair long – a loveable individual who does her own thing. Only once did I make the mistake of taking the mickey out of an outfit – never again!

In some ways we are completely different. If we went on one of those dating sites where you get asked thousands of questions, they'd say we were mismatched. She likes her stuff and I like mine. Yet psychologically we are on the same wavelength. I'm good at talking; she's good at listening. If we have rows, no sooner have they blown up than they are forgotten. All our friends confide their problems in her – she'd make a cracking counsellor. We're soulmates, I suppose.

But what has really bound us together is laughter. We share the same warped sense of humour. And that, let me tell you, has come in handy. For our first six months of courting, I drove back and forth from Manchester to Sheffield, a monumental ball-ache of nothing but early shifts, travel and not enough kip. I put 25,000 miles on my car and was knackered all the time, until finally a Salford housing association found me a pad that I invited her to share. Leaving Yorkshire was a big decision for her to make – it would be for anyone – but on the spur of the moment she took the plunge and moved in. To begin with, she must have wondered what the hell she had done. I know I did.

The thing is, the house I'd been offered wasn't just in Salford but in Blackleach, on one of the roughest estates in the city. Not being locals, neither of us knew its reputation – it was near a country park, for goodness sake – but we soon got educated. Fuck me, what a dump.

On paper it looked like home sweet home: nothing could have been further from the truth. When we pulled up in our rented Transit, heads popped up like meerkats. I had to back right up to the door. Eventually, we got everything in, by which time, this being the height of summer, the neighbours either side were in their backyards throwing down the high-strength cider and firing up their barbecues. As the day rolled on they got more and more pissed – or worse – and that night, as we lay goggle-eyed in bed, there was a racket like you've never heard. Next morning, the bloke next door had a face like a butcher's apron. He'd been leathered by three lads five doors down.

The fighting and noise were endless, day and night. Folk had doors cleaved in with sledgehammers, windows were always being smashed. One house was set alight with petrol because the dog barked. And with me being a screw there was always a risk of recognition. We'd rush in and lock the door: you wouldn't want to hang about outside.

One day, a bloke wandered up, staring right into my face.

'I know you, don't I?' he said, and my heart hit my boots.

Here we go, I thought. 'I don't know, kid. Do you?'

'Yeah. Strangeways, isn't it?'

I wasn't going to lie to him, was I? 'Yeah,' I nodded, fists clenched in my pockets.

'What landing were you on?' he said, and then I twigged. He thought I was a fucking con.

'Twos,' I said. 'How about you?'

'Threes, me,' he said, and actually mentioned Trailer Pete. 'I were on there for three or four months. You?'

'Oh, a long time,' I said. 'Fucking hell, small world, eh?'

Not long afterwards, I had my tyres slashed. Nothing personal. It happened to everybody, that.

Amy and me stuck Blackleach for six months, and the only reason we lasted that long was by laughing at how horrendous it was.

When we moved out in February 2011, it was

only a mile down the road to Walkden. No sooner had we come back from dropping off the first load than we discovered somebody had crowbarred the back door and nicked a load of electrical stuff like the telly and what have you. They were welcome to it.

The new house was *so* peaceful. I could even wear my uniform. We couldn't really afford it, though, and that was something else Amy had to get used to from the start. Life was always a financial struggle.

I suppose a fussy person might conclude that I didn't have a lot to offer, and wonder what the hell Amy saw in a big ugly Yorkshire bastard like yours truly, who didn't have two ha'pennies to rub together. Well, according to my good friend KK, I've got something more valuable than money or good looks, and that's charm.

Charm is a rare quality among prison officers, not so much among prisoners. Sometimes it's harmless, often not. Even in jail, male–female romances blossom; it's not all man-on-man action. At Forest Bank, there was a nurse we'd best call the Coffee Shop Queen, who I got on with really well. Cracking lass, trustworthy as they come. One day, in the staff car park, I saw her being dropped off by an ex-con who'd been released from prison the day before. I could not believe my eyes. He was a decent lad, not a hard-core thug, so I said nothing.

Somebody else must have seen her though, because at the end of the day I got a call from security. 'Did she get out of a car in front of you this morning, and was so-and-so driving?' I'd no option but to say yes. 'Why haven't you reported it?'

I told them I was in shock. Relationships between prisoners and staff are not tolerated – and there are good reasons for that, remember Bonnie and Clyde? You could take a harsher view – many do: another lass fell for a smackhead. They found all sorts of messages to him on her phone. She tried to block his prison transfer and only got discovered when she went to visit him in Risley and someone recognized her. But it's best to know the personal situation before condemning somebody to hell.

The Coffee Shop Queen got walked to the gate and I didn't see her for two years after that, the usual embarrassment-avoidance technique. The next time I met the lass, and the reason I call her the Coffee Shop Queen, was over a coffee in a supermarket in Bury. I'd seen her and she'd seen me, and at first I thought she was going to blank me. She didn't, though. Two cappuccinos and the story came out.

This lad had come down to her clinic for some dressing or other and the spark ignited. 'Me and you are going to be together,' he told her. She was married but said she could feel it same as him. There'd been no hanky-panky, she hadn't even kissed the guy, but they decided there and then that they were meant for each other. A week later, she'd told her husband she wanted a divorce.

When this lad got out of jail, they went out for a meal, and had been together ever since. 'The only thing I did wrong,' she said, 'was not leaving the job. I don't know why I turned up that morning.' The lad had told her it was a bad idea but she hadn't wanted to let anyone down – usual prison story.

In 2017, I saw her again, a good decade later, also in Bury, and we had another coffee. Now she was back in nursing somewhere else, a good job, and the two of them were still together with a pair of kids, aged five and six. But the Coffee Shop Queen and her boyfriend were above board and never looked back. I totally relate to the Coffee Shop Queen.

You were in little danger of being charmed by some of the staff in Strangeways, and healthcare had its own share of numpties, ranging from the useless to the lazy to the downright immoral; a few had the ethics of an alley cat.

We had a lad, Jamie Hargreaves, who'd come to healthcare in need of a safe unit: he'd been assaulted on A Wing with a tin of tuna in a sock after being accused of taking another con's mobile. He'd been beaten so badly he'd spent ages in a coma. Jamie became one of the orderlies in the servery: being a small unit, we'd get all sorts in close proximity – mentally ill, detoxers, paedophiles, rapists, the lot – so it was important that the prisoners doing that job could be trusted not to do them harm. I was juggling oranges there one day, as you do, and, messing about, I pretended to throw one at Hargreaves. He winced – and I mean winced, the way a mistreated dog might do.

'What's that about?' I asked the other orderly, but he just put his head down.

'What's going on, Jamie?'

But he wasn't for saying anything either.

Eventually the other orderly told me to look at Jamie's arms. I've had dead legs, when your muscle bleeds out, but I'd never seen anything like this. Jamie's arm was not just bruised, it was black – all the way down below his elbow – and going yellow.

'What the fucking hell is that?' I said.

The story unfolded. It turned out that Biffo Bacon – an officer who hadn't spoken a word to me for months when I started on healthcare – had been going into Jamie's cell and giving him a dead arm. He'd been doing this pretty much every day since Hargreaves came in.

I asked the other orderly why he hadn't told me.

'He asked me not to, I don't want no trouble, Mr Samworth.'

I was furious. It got worse. The other day this Biffo Bacon twat had taken off a shoe and chucked it at Jamie's head – and this is a lad who'd been in a coma . . . No one had reported it. In fact, said the other orderly, the staff that saw it had laughed.

So I went to see KK and put something at her door she didn't want. She came to have a look and was as horrified as me. Had I seen Biffo doing it? No, I hadn't. KK went and had a word with her manager, so it got investigated, if not seriously. It was kept in-house and people began calling me a grass again.

I was on a landing with an officer who'd done thirty-five years and was about to retire, someone I liked, when out of the blue he said, 'We don't do that.' This was a month after the incident and I knew what he meant. So I took him to Hargreave's cell. It wasn't easy, but I got Jamie to take his shirt off and his arm was still purple and yellow. I asked this bloke if he was happy for a colleague to do that, and he couldn't answer. Imagine that was one of your kids. Things were frosty for a bit, and the culprit got moved on.

CHAPTER 15

THE AIR THAT I BREATHE

Funerals are never pleasant, but going to one with a prisoner is worse than on your own. You're not wanted. You are the enemy. I've been to four. Lucky officers don't do any. Only the death of an immediate family member will get a prisoner to a farewell do – child, parent, spouse or sibling: taking prisoners to a funeral is a security risk that the Home Office would rather avoid. We had one lad who'd been brought up by his grandparents from the age of two, and still wasn't allowed to see his grandad off, even with the chaplain in his corner. That seemed harsh and I felt sorry for him, but I suppose you do have to draw the line somewhere. Some of these kids have a lot of grandads!

My first such escort was at Forest Bank, just after I'd joined the prison service. We'd an Asian lad with us, very upset because his dad had died. I didn't know what he was in for or what to expect and, to be honest, the idea was a buzz – I was eager for adventure. Three of us set off with him: one driving, another, Tall Lad, on cuffs, leaving me in charge despite having next to no experience, either in prison or on an escort. We were in a minibus with 'UKDS' – UK Detention Services – plastered all over it. Why you'd advertise yourself like that I don't know.

We arrived on this street, cars double-parked, up on the kerb, loads of Mercs about. Victorian semi-detached houses loomed over us with their bay windows, pointy roofs, typical of that part of Salford. The driver counted house numbers, found the place and, fuck me! The deceased must have been popular. There was a crowd and a half, most of them in robes, Muslim. Most of them were pointing and shouting at us, and not in English so far as I could tell. The atmosphere was hostile, and there was lots of emotion. I wasn't enthusiastic any more; this wasn't a place I wanted to be. One guy began shouting in my face.

'Who's in charge here?' I asked – that was all I could think of to say. After a minute or two I thought, *I've had enough of this*, and went back to the van to say, 'Let's fuck off.'

Then a lad appeared, aged about sixteen, wiry and thin. He had a robe on too and a prayer cap.

'Excuse me,' he said, polite as you like. 'Can I help you?'

He looked at the van and nodded at the prisoner. 'I apologize for all this,' he said. 'Thank you for bringing him.'

Then he started speaking to everyone around him. By the sound of it he was trying to calm them down. Whatever language it was, it amused me to hear 'fuck' translated as 'fuck' as he sprinkled that word in here and there. The garden had about fifty men in it – all men, there wasn't a woman in sight. He invited us into the house. The crowd had spilled out onto the road and was now surrounding the van.

Our hero cleared a passage through – pushing up the path was like running the gauntlet. When we got to the front door, a guy put a hand on my chest, which I didn't take too kindly to. 'You need to remove your shoes,' he said.

'This is my uniform,' I said. 'If you want me to remove my shoes, we are not coming in.'

Again this lad intervened, the voice of common sense, and we went into the front room. The hallway was packed and the lounge was too, standing room only, except for the late father, centre of attention in an open coffin on the table. He'd have probably been buried by now if his son hadn't been coming as, I now know, Muslims choose to do that quickly. The prisoner was upset, bawling his eyes out.

The voice of reason asked if they were all okay to pray. What am I going to say? It was a culture shock for Tall Lad and me. They got down on their mats and my six-foot-four colleague had no choice but to kneel with them. As our prisoner leaned forward, so did Tall Lad. They all prayed together, so every time they prostrated themselves, he had to too. It had its comical side, did that, but I managed to keep my amusement in check.

Despite his grief the prisoner had been very well behaved. The wiry lad gave him a hug, as did the others, sharing brief conversations. He looked at his dad for the last time and we left before the burial.

As soon as we stepped outside, hostility raged again. The windscreen of the van was dripping in phlegm and the driver didn't look too bright either. The scene was grim. People had been kicking the vehicle, spitting and hurling abuse, the longest twenty minutes of his life, he said. When the three of us climbed aboard, it was, 'Ladies and Gentlemen, start your engines!' And off we went, Indy 500 style, without delay.

On my second funeral outing we had another youngster on our wing, David Caplan. He was in with a kid called Bobby Templeton, who'd become a young offender at sixteen. In fact they were just two of half a dozen very clever armed robbers, although thinking about it they can't have been that clever, can they, because they got caught. What they'd been doing was hitting supermarkets in isolated places, where a crook can rob as much money as at a bank with a lot less risk.

Templeton was on his second sentence – he'd started going out armed aged thirteen. When he came to us he was eighteen, so his first sentence hadn't been very big. Over the eighteen months they were on remand these two kids had a massive influence: lads in for minor offences like fighting or taking cars without consent began to model themselves on this little gang with pictures of the latest expensive trainers and other fashionable clobber on their walls.

Another of the group, Fatso, was twenty stone and looked about thirty, yet was only eighteen and driving a Porsche Carrera 4. They'd wealth, prestige, birds, bikes . . . the lot. The wannabes' heads were turned. A lot of those juveniles became major criminals. We'd see them in the years ahead as Cat As at Strangeways.

David Caplan's dad, a well-known gangland figure, had died and the family asked if officers he knew could take him to the burial. His older brother was also going, but he was at HMP Manchester. We picked him up – and another officer, which made four – on the way.

This one was in Salford too. I was cuffed to David, and when we arrived we were surrounded by around forty youths, intimidating once again. One slid the van door open and a few climbed aboard, shaking hands with the brothers – 'Awright, our kid, how's it going? Nice one . . .' – your typical Manc scallies, jibbing about as if we weren't there. We could do fuck all about it, which was exactly the message they were getting across.

Again, I wasn't having good feelings. We got off the van and a horse-drawn black carriage went past, pulled by two mares with the coffin and flowers inside. Then we met the rest of the family.

His mum and dad were separated I believe,

though she was there, sobbing away, as were Caplan's girlfriend and all the cousins, aunties, uncles and everyone else queuing up to hug our prisoners. When they gave David a squeeze they were in my face – I got the full perfume, aftershave and tears effect. It was uncomfortable. David himself was upset, his brother too. Yes they were criminals, but it still sends a shiver up your spine, does all that open grief.

The service was in a chapel in a graveyard. We sat towards the front, just behind the mother. David's brother and his officer sat at the side of us. The other officers were at the back – we couldn't see them. Service over, I thought we were done for the day, but no. The chapel cleared and the SO said we were going to the graveside. *Fucking hell*, I thought: I did not want to be there. But out of the back entrance we went. There were about 200 people in the entourage, all dressed in black, and we had to walk through a crowd containing some very big guys in Crombies, wrap-around shades, beards, the works. It was as if they were there to see off Tony Soprano. We were not only outnumbered but also surrounded.

The coffin was lowered into the grave, flowers were thrown in and I started looking around me. Your mind plays tricks in scary situations like that, but I was convinced weapons were on display, I'm sure I saw a revolver tucked in trousers. I thought I saw bolt croppers, though could have imagined that too. It felt obvious to me that these two were planning on doing a bunk. There were bodies everywhere; we could no longer see the van. I asked David what was going on. 'Nothing, S.,' he assured me. He used to call me S.

The kid kept looking at his brother and so did I. The other lad at least was prepared to leg it; that was clear. The officer cuffed to him, from Strangeways, looked mortified, and I dare say I was white too. I'd never known tension like it. People were waiting for the nod. I do know that for several minutes there was expectation.

David looked at his brother again. The lad was nodding, but David shook his head. It felt like an out-of-body experience. 'Come on, let's go, S.,' he said.

When he hugged his mum, some of the tension evaporated. I glanced at his brother, who looked really disappointed. One wasn't going to go without the other. We walked back to the van, where the other officers were reading the paper and munching chocolate as if waiting to pick us up from the bingo.

Funeral number three was very sad. I was on healthcare at Strangeways by then, and this time it weren't the guests who were the problem, it was the officers handling the escort, the main culprit being an obnoxious sod from the OSG ranks on the van.

Nor did our little outing get off to the brightest of starts. 'Oh, that fucking dick,' said Mr Empathy, the officer on the wing, when I went on to ask for the prisoner. 'He's been banging on his door two days, kicking off and threatening to kill himself.'

When I found the kid he was down in the chapel with Henry, the prison chaplain. Around six foot three, a gentle man with glasses and white hair, Henry looked like Captain Birdseye, only not as weathered. In the nick, as with the IMB, a lot of screws doubt the value of the various religious types who, without exception, don't think badly of people and just try to do things for them. On K Wing, we saw Henry and the rest of the God squad as interfering, maybe. On healthcare, I came to see him from a different angle. He was fantastic, a genuine resource with a good work ethic, who'd really help us out. Sister Mary, the nun, did likewise, as did the imams.

Anyway, Henry told me the tale. This lad had been in jail a week and was only due to do one more. It was his first time inside, two-week sentence, obviously not such a bad lad. He'd no money, this kid, nor had he had a first night induction, which was well dodgy, especially if a coroners' court got involved. Two days earlier, his baby daughter had died, only six months' old. Why hadn't they just released him for the funeral – he'd only four days to go?

Henry went to see him when the news came in and told him if he needed to talk again he should just ask the staff. When he did, Mr Empathy told him to fuck off, so he threw a chair, for which he got locked behind his door until the chaplain found out. Now Henry had brought him down to the chapel for a bit of peace.

When I met this lad, wow: unassuming, polite and respectful. But he was in bits. Then dipstick number two turned up, another officer with an attitude problem. He'd be in charge while I was cuffed to the young lad. We'd got a driver and a third officer too: why the job needed four of us I don't know. He was hardly the Yorkshire Ripper, was he?

The driver warned us we were going to hit traffic and might be late.

'Fuck it,' said our second empathy-bypass. 'If we're late, we're late. It's not my funeral.'

Why would you say that? The lad was sobbing. Thankfully, we arrived on time and this dick stayed in his seat.

The minister introduced himself and we walked to the grave. There was a girl there, his partner. You could tell they were in love. However, the sadness – fewer than a dozen people, including us. There was a bit of a sermon, and the coffin brought tears to my eyes. So small and fragile, it was a very sad sight. In my right ear, though, I could hear this knobhead in the van, having a fag and laughing as loud as you like. The coffin went in the ground, no embrace between this lad and lass, a very solemn affair. We went back to prison, the silence broken constantly by Mr Gobshite.

It was dinnertime when the SO on reception told me the lad needed to go back to the wing for the roll count. 'Listen,' I said, 'he's just buried his six-month-old daughter. Let's put him in a holding cell, get him a brew and give him half an hour down here.' So that's what we did.

By the time the fourth one came around I was an expert on funeral escorts. The officer in charge was the lad who'd handed Quiggers, the flatliner, over at the hospital and then gone for a full English. A kid on his first escort was on cuffs and behind the wheel was Jerky Bob, the driver. The prisoner was a wiry bastard, someone I'd restrained four times at Forest Bank and Manchester. A repeat offender baghead, he'd thirty sentences under his belt by the time he was fifty, a real problem causer, so Full English wanted my hands free just in case. The prisoner was quiet now mind. The funeral was his dad's.

There was nothing much said on the way over. He just sat there nervous, grateful, I suppose, that we were taking him. There'd just been a nod of mutual acknowledgement and that was that. No jollity, no chit-chat, no nothing. No one was in the mood.

We drove up a big semicircular drive and parked in between the two chapels. A pleasant scene: a grass bank with roses and trees – but the funeral was to be filmed by plain-clothes coppers: there'd be people there they were after.

If I'd thought the other occasions were hostile, they had nothing on this. As we arrived, it seemed

another funeral was about to happen simultaneously, big turnout at both. When we got off the
van, these two crowds became one, with us slap
bang in the middle.

The prisoner and our funeral virgin sat at the
back of the chapel and I stood behind them. With
people either side of us, we were crammed in, not
enough room to pick your nose. It would kick off,
I could tell. The atmosphere was electric.

'Don't leave me, Sammy,' the raw officer said.
Terrified.

The service seemed to go on forever, but when
it was finally done we started to move and Full
English slotted in as we went up the aisle. As did
this prisoner's ma, pointing with her spiny fingers.

'Let him go, you dirty bastards!' She wasn't far
off seventy. 'Arseholes! He's not going anywhere!'

There was a big gang of youths behind her,
teenagers mostly, scallies of a certain nature,
bagheads themselves. Game on. Giving it the
eyeball, they sprayed as much abuse as the old
lass had. Then, to our surprise, the prisoner spoke
up.

'Don't be calling these lads dirty bastards, Mam,'
he said. 'They didn't have to bring me. You're
upset, I'm upset, leave it.' He nodded towards the
van. 'Come on, Mr Samworth.'

I took that as our cue, the crowd parted and we
climbed back aboard. Jerky Bob had been watching
in the rear-view mirror, so the engine was running.
I half-expected a sucker punch – they were right

behind us, less than a metre away – but none came. As soon as that door shut, *bang! bang! bang!* Kicked at and hammered, the thing was rocking. There was no reversing: the only way out was up and over that grass bank, so that's the route Jerky Bob took. Rose bushes were flattened, but what can you do? He floored it out of that cemetery.

Again, the lad thanked us for bringing him. I was thinking better of him now, and after that day, his attitude altered too. Our relationship changed. Up to that point all we'd done is battle. Afterwards, we had each other's corner.

CHAPTER 16

ISOLATION

The beginning of the end for me at Strangeways came in 2011, when I'd been on healthcare three years. I say that in hindsight. It wasn't until well in the future that I recognized its lasting impact.

It was one of the worst days of my prison career. Not only for the horror of the incident itself, but as usual for how people were treated, how others behaved. But first I need to return to Forest Bank and tell you another story.

It was the last death in custody I was involved with there, and the way it was dealt with by the really good manager who was on shift that day ought to be incorporated into prison protocol, because it was genius.

I was on a wing with a new officer when a prisoner who'd gone for a brew came back to his cell and began shouting for help. We thought at first someone was being assaulted. He'd found his cellmate hanging.

'Listen, lads,' I told the other prisoners, 'we've got a serious incident. You are going to have to go behind your doors.'

It's not always easy at that time in a morning – they all want to be out – but they did as they were told and we pressed the alarm. Tony, the manager, came on the scene, a straight-talking Scouser and big personality.

First, an officer was posted at the end of the wing – there was only one entry and exit. He was told the only people allowed on were those who needed to be: medical staff, Oscar One and that's all, minimum fuss and interference. They even printed a note out asking prisoners to be patient. The cons weren't happy, but appreciated knowing what was going on. Somebody made sure the young officer and her car got home. She was given counselling but left soon after, very sad. There is nothing pleasant about a death in custody, but that was how they ought to be handled.

Fast forward to Strangeways healthcare. I was in early, usual handover with the night officer, half six, roll call. It was wintertime, so the light wasn't great. Y1 held a Polish prisoner, Pawel Nicpon. He didn't speak very good English and had been with us three months. His original offence, I believe, was carrying a knife, for which you are looking at about three months. But in court, despite having interpreters there, he wouldn't co-operate with the judge so he was sent back to us, still on remand.

He was horrendously difficult to control. He'd kicked off coming into jail and had been restrained straight away in reception. His behaviour was so odd he was sent to seg' where he got diarrhoea, or so they thought – shite all over the cell. The nursing staff and doctor came to see him and decided on hospitalization. In hospital, he wanted to fight, wouldn't lie in bed and refused all food. He was on a six-officer bed watch – that's a lot of staff. With civilians about, it was a dodgy situation – at one stage he'd been trying to smear crap on staff, as well as himself. The doctors, though, diagnosed no mental health issues: he was physically and psychologically fine, they said. Deemed bad behaviour, he came back into Strangeways.

Another off-putting aspect of this guy that attracted constant complaints whether he was in segregation, hospital or our cells on healthcare was his stench. I've never smelt body odour like it. The nearest thing to it is the soluble oil you get in engineering that's used as a cutting agent. The stuff goes off badly and after a month hums something putrid. That was close to it, but Nicpon's aroma was worse – it was rancid. You had to sniff it to believe it. We'd have this lad out and showered as best we could, but even in clean clothes after a proper scrub, within half an hour the stink would be back.

For me, he should have gone back to seg', where they had two dirty protest cells that are easy to clean. He wasn't put on an ACCT form – no one saw the need.

I looked in that morning and I could see his

silhouette by the window: nothing new there – when he wasn't sat at the end of his bed he'd do that. I wished him good morning, but he didn't answer. Again, that wasn't unusual. I finished the count and went to the office.

It got to a quarter past eight and one of the orderlies who took the prisoners' dinner requests asked if I'd accompany him to Pawel Nicpon's cell – sometimes Nicpon came out for dinner and other times refused. He might be aggressive with you or stand still like a crash-test dummy: you never knew what to expect.

I dropped his hatch. It still wasn't properly light, so my eyes took time to adjust. I gawped at his silhouette for a good while.

'What's up, Mr S.?' the orderly asked.

'He's dead, kid. Go back to your cell, please.'

Nikki was just down the landing – like me, a strawberry blonde from Sheffield. Slightly built but tall, she was someone who'd say it as it was. She could be confrontational, and surprisingly enough many prisoner officers would rather avoid confrontation. Nikki didn't hold back, but after a dodgy start we couldn't have got on any better, and she became one of my favourite people to work with. Behind those specs of hers lurked a fierce willpower and intellect. She was also as tough as old boots. I called her over and got my fish knife out because I thought Nicpon was hanging.

When I got to him there was a ligature, which

I cut, but something about this didn't compute. Then I realized he wasn't hanging at all. He was stood, feet flat on the floor, arms by his side, body at an angle of forty-five degrees, neck back and jaw fully extended. This ligature – it was more like a washing line – wasn't tied to his neck: it was wrapped around the bars furthest apart on the window, forming a big loop. He'd leaned forward into it like a ski-jumper on *Ski Sunday*. His neck and jaw pushed out like that: garrotted. It put me in mind of that painting by Munch: *The Scream*. He was fucking *purple*. It was a ghastly sight: the worst body I'd seen. Nikki was in the cell now too. He was rigid, dead quite definitely, and with the line cut he became a dead weight. I'd managed to lift him – thanks to the adrenaline – but when I put him down his legs got tangled in the table. I couldn't shift him again.

'Fuck's sake,' said Nikki, and we had a dark little laugh. Together we got him up, shifted his legs and laid him back on the floor. I cannot find words to describe accurately the smell of that corpse and the look on its face.

Nikki ran her fish knife down his shirt and I started doing CPR. There was no point, but we were taught to do it anyway. 'Who did the early start this morning?' she asked.

'That would be me.'

'You'll be in coroners' court, then.'

The alarm bell went; the defibrillator was fetched, as per protocol, and Hotel One, the nursing equivalent to Oscar One, bustled in and put a tube down Nicpon's throat – again, no point but she had to try. The defibrillator read: don't bother.

This is where events started to diverge from the proper management of a death in custody I've just told you about, and badly. By now we were being watched by a small crowd of officers, a few of them larking around and talking football. Steadily the numbers grew, until all manner of folk had piled on the landing. That happens for an incident, but this was a death in custody, not a restraint. It didn't need an army of soldiers.

I asked Bradders to take over because with these clowns outside the door I could feel my anger rising. CPR continued until a doctor came upstairs and confirmed Nicpon had died. The Hotel One was very supportive. She asked if we were all right before leaving, no criticism there. The group of officers had moved off a little down the landing. Amid all the chat about City and United, one lad had actually asked what the smell was. I think that's why they moved away.

The next twenty minutes were a blur as it got even more like Wakes Week in Cleethorpes, a social event. Brews all round: appalling. Two overtime lads who'd seen it unfold were in shock. Not only at Nicpon's body but also by the behaviour. 'How can staff do that?' one said. 'It's disgusting.' He was off for two weeks.

I went in the office where these six or seven lads were supping tea and still gassing. 'What's up with him?' 'Ought to grow a set.' 'It's a dead con – what's his problem?' The standard macho bollocks.

I'd been angry before, but now I was steaming. Bradders told me to take a break, get myself some air.

For everyone doing something useful there were at least three hangers-on milling about, including big daft Mr Gobshite from the funeral escort who was announcing a 'hot debrief'. Then an admin manager brought three office lasses up to have a neb at Nicpon – fortunately he'd been covered up by now. All it needed was a red rope and we could have charged for entry. Nikki and I gave each other a hug and went into a side room where she had a cry. I had tears in my own eyes.

Fuck me if the IMB – the Board of Visitors as was – didn't rock up now, three of them. When they stuck their noses around the door, Nikki's shoulders were heaving and I must have looked upset myself.

'Can we use the office?' They'd come for a gander, that's all.

'No, you fucking can't,' I said and kicked the door shut.

Nikki and I looked at one another and laughed. By this point I'd have bollocked Prince Charles.

I'd a stinking headache and felt like shit, but things never stopped. There was still a three-hour police interview for me to get through in the association room in which they wanted to know everything: the events leading up to the incident, the incident itself, Nicpon's background, every last detail. The policeman was brilliant, very thorough. Even then, though, we must have been interrupted a dozen times.

When I finally left the jail it was half past four in the afternoon, by which time only the health-care staff and Hotel One nurse had asked how I was. I hadn't wanted people I didn't know hugging me, but it would have been good if someone in authority had acknowledged that I might be feeling a bit fragile.

It was a very strange feeling leaving Strangeways that day. I left the healthcare unit, walked down the main drag, went through a couple of gates, handed my keys in and stood shell-shocked in the car park. The nights were drawing in.

As soon as I'd opened the door of my car and slid inside, my senses reeled. I stank. I sat there for a moment, got out, took my shirt off and threw it in the boot. The car park was busy at this time but I wasn't fussed. I unfastened my belt, dropped my trousers and in they went too. Boots n' all, everything down to my boxers. Some clown wolf-whistled. I got back in the car and drove home like that.

I'd already phoned Amy to say I'd need a bit of space. In the driveway, I binned my clothes. I must have been in the shower for forty minutes and gone through a full bottle of body wash – scrubbed myself all over with a loofah, red raw. But I still couldn't get rid of the smell. Amy brought me a cup of tea and asked if I wanted anything to eat. No. She went back downstairs to the little 'un. I was in work as usual the next day; so was Bradders, and Nikki too later on. It's what you did: got on with it.

From then on, every time I got in my car that smell just enveloped me. I couldn't explain it, and I didn't want to tell anyone. I spent sixty quid having it fully valeted at a time when we didn't have a lot of money. Our lass, who didn't know why I'd done that, went ballistic. I hung three air fresheners up in it – red, white and blue – it knocked Amy sick. I'd be sneezing constantly too. I'd drive with the windows down, whatever the weather. But nothing shifted the smell of Nicpon. I was driving home down the A580 about ten o'clock one night and it was more powerful than ever – it put me right back in that cell. I turned off the main road and pulled up at the kerb. It was pissing down. I loved that little Peugeot 406: it cost me 1,500 quid, the most I've spent on a car. But I got out and left it there. I had no coat, I was a mile and a half from home, all uphill, but, tired and cold, I walked.

When I got home Amy asked where the car was. As usual by now, she copped a blast. That's how I was with her after Nicpon. I apologized later, when she admitted she'd known something was wrong. I couldn't tell her I'd left it in the road because it stank of a guy who'd died three months earlier. A long time afterwards a psychologist would explain to me how smell is a big part of memory. People buy perfume their mum used to wear; it puts you right back in a moment. On a rare day off I sold the car for fifty-six quid, less than it cost to valet. Fortunately, Amy's mother lent us some money to buy another.

Several months later, one fine spring day, I bumped into one of the lads who'd been on overtime that terrible night. He was standing outside the jail with his Alsatian.

'All right?' I said.

'Yeah,' he replied. But the way he said it suggested he wasn't. 'You? You know that . . . thing?' He went on, 'Do you have nightmares?'

'Yeah, I've had nightmares,' I said. 'Have you?'

'Yeah,' he said. This guy had been in the job nigh on forty years. 'I've never seen anything like that in my life, Sam, and I don't want to see it again. It's bothered me. I can't get it out of my head.'

CHAPTER 17

THIS CHARMING MAN

From 2012, I really began to struggle with my right shoulder. Playing rugby at tight-head prop, I led with that side and paid for it now. The joint throbbed like toothache. I couldn't sleep and, after a while, I'd no choice but to have an operation. A superstitious person might call it an omen for what I was starting to feel mentally. I tried to push the Nicpon saga to the back of my mind but, in hindsight, it's easy to see that signs of stress were starting to show.

Anyway, I'd been off four weeks, arm in a sling, when I had a call from a manager, who said I had to come in for an interview. For once, it wasn't a disciplinary.

As healthcare was desperate for staff they had decided on a recruitment drive. Twelve officers were required, not four. Fair dos, quite right too, but those of us already in the job had to apply again. I was narked about that, as you would be, but went to the interview and passed, along with Nikki. Ten new staff came to join us and the unit went on to run as professionally as before. The patients, however, were as challenging as ever.

Bobby was quite intimidating, six foot three and I'd guess around sixteen stone. In his early forties, he was coming to us from Monster Mansion, Wakefield, as a kiddie killer bound for a mental hospital.

This guy had been ill from childhood. He'd never come under mental health services, never been in hospital, never been diagnosed and held down a job. He had a normal family life with a wife and two young children. His missus went out one day and left him with the kids, as you do. When she came home, he was watching television.

'Where are the children,' she said. 'In bed?'

No, he told her, they were in the bathroom.

When she went to see, he'd strangled them both to death, an unimaginable horror.

Bobby's issues were clearly medical. Once, when he hadn't yet been on an unlock, he'd come out on the landing with a TV and held it over Bradders' head while she was talking to someone. If he'd hit her with it, or dropped it, there'd have been nothing I could do.

'Bobby,' I said, as quietly and reasonably as I could manage, 'what's up, lad?'

Bradders turned around to see what was going on and you could see the fear in her, as you can imagine. He was a big lad. That telly was heavy and he could have killed her.

'The voices,' he said.

The couple of minutes he stood there seemed to last an hour. Bradders backed off and people had their hands on the bells, ready.

'The voices,' he repeated.

'Do you not want the TV, lad?'

'No, boss,' he said, bringing it down and giving it me.

'Do you want to go back behind your door?'

'Yes, boss. I do.'

Wow. That was some moment. On the out, incidents like that would leave people traumatized. On healthcare, they happened with such regularity that it almost became normal.

Bobby was genuinely unwell. Not so Cliff, who had also killed his children. He'd moved on and his ex-partner found someone else, which he didn't like. That's quite often the case, isn't it? He took his revenge on her via the kids, a two year old and four year old, strangled brutally. What's more, he had them record a message to their mother saying goodbye.

It's hard not to take such things to heart when a prisoner like that comes into jail. Especially when, like him, they then fake mental illness. You might want to throttle him in turn, but have to stay calm. Maybe he thought that acting crazy would get him an easier time. He sat behind his door, rocking, all very pre-meditated and phoney. He was even talking to the birds, like the Birdman of Alcatraz. He kept it up for a couple of months, before running out of steam as they always do. If you aren't mentally ill you can't blag it forever. He 'came round' and decided to go after a degree.

The woman who came in to tell him about education had no idea why he was in healthcare. We shot the bolt, so the door couldn't be locked when she'd entered, and waited outside. 'What a nice young man!' she said when she came out – she was clearly impressed. I let that ride. Then she started telling me about his ambitions and how it would be a pleasure to teach him.

'Even though he's killed his kids,' I muttered.

KK threw me a look and asked me to leave the office, but honestly . . . the tutor left and never came back.

And then there was Mark Bridger. In early October 2012 I was watching the news at home with Amy, getting ready to go on afternoon shift, when the breaking news had come on that a man had been arrested in Machynlleth in Wales for the abduction and murder of April Jones, the five-year-old girl who had been out playing with friends near her home. He'd lured her into his car and then killed her. Our lass asked if we'd be getting him in Strangeways. I thought so, I told her. When I get there he'll be on healthcare, I predicted, and I wasn't far wrong. An hour after I arrived, Bridger did too.

He was with us ten months, and I spent a lot of time with him, far too much. High-profile prisoners weren't unusual in healthcare: we had murderers, child killers . . . all the scum we could handle. But out of everyone I've ever worked with, Pawel Nicpon apart, only one prisoner ever really got inside my head and stayed there.

Bridger was all over the press, and there were only two places he could be located: seg' and healthcare. Such a high-profile child killer couldn't go in the VP units, whether it be opposite the Cat A prisoners on A Wing or E Wing, because the cons in both would have either cut his throat or strung him up, perhaps both. If you ask me, seg' wouldn't have him because he was on an ACCT form and threatening to kill himself, so that would be too much mither. So healthcare it was.

A big part of the hatred I came to feel for Bridger was fired by how the service reacted to such an individual. The first three days knocked me sick, 'Are you all right, Mark?' 'How are you doing?'

The IMB matrons were all over him like a rash. I don't want to broad-brush everyone. The two ladies we usually saw always tried to find the good in people and help, while also appreciating that some of the characters we had were beyond redemption. The three IMBs who came on for Bridger, though, gave you the impression they wanted something to boast about at a dinner party – 'Oh, you'll never guess who I saw today' – a thrilling little tale to dish out with the French onion soup. 'Mark has had a letter from his mother and father,' one said. 'He is very upset because his dog is getting old and will have to be put down.'

People were constantly coming on to interview him. We had one officer who dealt with veterans in custody: fair enough – lots of ex-squaddies suffer PTSD, leave the armed forces and turn to crime. One thing police were worried about in Bridger's case was weakness of evidence: they wanted as full a picture as possible of his words and actions, however trivial they might seem, and we'd been told that anything Bridger came out with should be documented and a report filed. We'd also been told that Bridger had been in the army, although when the case came to court he admitted that was a lie because he hadn't wanted people in Machynlleth 'to know about his past problems'. This veterans officer, who like the rest of us at that time still thought Bridger had been trained by the SAS, visited him in his cell. On leaving, the officer said he must speak to security immediately: he'd been given a map. Him and everyone else: the police had been dicked about with five different locations for April's burial. The officer went off excitedly with his confessional 'map', only to be disappointed like all the rest. He was a really manipulative sod, Bridger.

A psychologist came to see him too. Psychological input is very limited in prison; there's not a lot of it in there. As a psychologist, you're not fussed about having Joe Bloggs, a smack-addicted cat burglar off Moss Side, on your CV, are you? It's not a feather in your professional cap, that. Of the hundreds of inmates to cross my path down the years that needed such treatment, Bridger was the only prisoner I knew who got it before sentencing. Normally, the psychologists worked solely with the SIU (special intervention unit) which I'll come to later, and seg', and dealt almost exclusively with terrorism, violent offenders, and personality disorders.

In healthcare, Bridger was out a lot more than he would have been elsewhere in the jail, so he had a lot of interactions where that charm I am on about kicked in. Staff would go starry-eyed and take every word he said as gospel. I found it sickening. He was a sneaky, despicable creature. Later, I read the psychologists' reports. One described him as one of the worst killers of the last century, quite a claim when you think of all the serial killers and their like in the hit parade.

Physically, he was around the same height as me and of similar build, six foot, fifteen stone, so maybe not quite as heavy. I expect he could have been intimidating to lads who didn't have that presence. If he thought someone was weak he would quite definitely take advantage, although at heart he was a coward. There was no way he was ever going to be restrained or anything like that.

Every patient had a named nurse on healthcare, including Mark Bridger. Each nurse would have a couple of patients they'd have one-to-ones with, like a personal officer. We called his named nurse the Princess (in a lovely, not sarcastic way) and she had been on a long weekend. I remember her coming in, Tuesday it was, and I was sat with KK.

She took her job seriously, as they all did, and told us that Mark – the nurses always used first names – had been self-harming in her absence. We'd both been working, so it seemed unlikely. 'Do you want a look?' she said, and we went along to his cell.

We grabbed a couple more officers – he was on an unlock – and KK went in.

'What have you been doing, Mark? Why didn't you mention this to us? Why have you waited until Tuesday morning? Let's have a look at what you've done.'

So he rolled up his sleeve and showed her these pathetic superficial scratches. The sort you might get on a twig while gardening, only not as deep.

KK, being very astute, turned to me, 'Don't say a word, Mr Samworth.'

She asked him why he'd done it. 'Oh, I've been feeling down all weekend.'

I wanted to strangle the fucking prick. That's how he was, pathetic to the core.

One lad, Billy Thorpe, had AIDS and the reason I'm telling you that is because he told everyone himself. He was getting on a bit, poor at coping, and I felt sorry for him. He came in to us a few times, largely due to talking about having AIDS on K Wing or wherever. You can imagine how that must have gone down. He didn't need to be on healthcare, could have been handled perfectly well elsewhere, but his openness made him vulnerable.

Billy was an easy-going bloke who'd chat with anyone, including Mark Bridger, despite getting a bit frail and suffering the onset of Alzheimer's. This particular day he was crying.

'What's up, Billy?'

'I don't know what to do . . . I can't speak . . . I don't . . .' sobbing away.

'What's up?'

'Can we go in the office?'

So I took him in the office and enlisted the services of KK. I can do tears, but she did them better. 'What's wrong, Billy? Has something upset you?'

'Mark Bridger killed a child. It's been on telly.'

'Has it? And what did you think he'd done?'

'He told me he were in for armed robbery.'

That was Bridger through and through. He spun lies to everyone.

Bridger was taken off unlock for a while but then, as his trial approached, I put him back on one. By then, everyone in healthcare knew what he'd done and it was for his own protection. If your cell was on X landing, an outside wall, your window faced K Wing, whose prisoners, overlooking, could see in. Until we moved him to Y landing, within the unit, all sorts was shouted across – 'You're dead, Bridger!' and worse. It was continuous.

On healthcare we had some real hard cases in,

as always – heavy-duty murderers and all sorts. So why nobody there had a go at damaging him, I can't tell you. Perhaps they liked the wing and didn't want moving off, or were won over by his greasy charm, I don't know.

Bridger wasn't stupid. He knew I were no muppet and wasn't for wearing his shite. I made him wary. I wouldn't sit and talk to him about anything. Normally I was quite sociable. I'd sit in association and talk to James Whitehead for two and a half hours. This dick? No. But every day I'd see him, creepy as fuck with the nurses.

'Samikins,' said KK one morning, 'could you have a word with Mark Bridger?' Pouting face on, not happy. She held out her hand to reveal a ball of tissue. I unwrapped it and inside was a razor with no blade. A prisoner having a shave would be locked behind their door, and we'd put a little sign on saying a razor was in there. We'd then take that razor back, in case they removed the blade to harm themselves. 'This is how he gave me it,' she said, riled that this dickhead thought she wouldn't check before throwing it in the bin.

I got up, instantly in Jonathan Vass mode. Bridger was disrespecting this unit. The politicians and governor wouldn't be happy with what I was about to do, but I didn't give a fuck. He was a prisoner like any other, in fact far worse than many, and needed putting in his place.

He was in the cell on the end of the landing,

left-hand side, Y11. I shot the bolt and sat on his bed. 'Now listen, you prick,' I said, keeping my voice low for added menace. 'If you ever try to take any of us for clowns again, hide razors, look at someone funny, whatever, I will make your life hell.'

I've got quite a physical presence, and when I'm in that mood few are going to argue, even a bloke with such a violent past. In 2004, he'd been convicted of threatening a police officer with a machete and, three years later, received a suspended sentence for punching someone in an argument over a boiler. Well, he was nearly crying by the time I finished laying down the law. I got the blade back, slammed the door and stomped away down to the office. When KK walked in I was doing my ACCT forms.

'Thanks for that, Mr Samworth,' she said, a resigned look on her face.

Mark Bridger realized very early on that coming straight into Manchester healthcare meant he was in deep shit – the rest of prison must be out to get him. So he dreamed up a new line of defence. He started acting strange, embarrassing, playing the mental health card. Bradders knew what he was up to, but played along.

'What's up, Mark? Can we help?'

'It's April,' he said, 'she's visiting me every night.'

He was at it about a month. The police called a specialist doctor out. If he went to court and was judged mentally unwell it would damage the case. At the very worst he'd get a life sentence with diminished responsibility.

One dinnertime I was on the servery with two orderlies. Sandy would normally have been there, but she was in a cell with one of the nursing assistants. I noticed that something was missing from the hot plate. Spaghetti hoops, I was told.

Had we run out? Had they found a way to smoke or inject them?

'They're under the servery, Mr S.,' said the orderly. Sandy had told him to put them there or our infamous resident wouldn't come out. 'Bridger says it was April's favourite meal.'

I wasn't having him taking the piss to I went to his cell and tore into him again. 'Get your dinner!' As he neared the hot plate, he stopped and turned away, as if in fright. So I took him back to his cell and slammed him back behind his door. Sandy and me had a ding-dong about that but it was soon over.

We had an orderly, let's call him 'J'. He was on an IPP sentence – inside probation as opposed to outside probation – and I was his personal officer. I saw him through a good couple of years and actually spoke at a couple of parole board meetings, which I hadn't done before. He was a Londoner, been up to no good, armed robberies, but polite as you like, especially with female staff, which was very welcome on healthcare. Model prisoner.

One day I was stood talking to Bridger, a rare event, and he was having a bit of a whinge when J walked up. Now, I thought Mark Bridger was Welsh; probably people still think he is. But J overheard and said to him, 'What part of London are you from?'

I thought J had gone mad, but Bridger comes out with the name of an estate that our orderly immediately recognized. 'Fucking hell, do you know so-and-so . . .' J said, and named one of his cousins.

'Yeah,' said Bridger. 'My sister's married to his brother,' or similar. Anyhow, they'd got some sort of shared relationship and Bridger, Jack the Lad, deceitful, then thinks they've got a bond.

Not long after this, J came to me. 'Mr S., can I have a word?'

'What's up?' I said. He looked perturbed.

'I've just had a chat with Mark Bridger.'

'Go on.'

'He told me what he's done to that girl.'

I went, 'Right?'

'Yeah. I've got to tell someone.' So he told me something that, other than writing it on a report to security, I've never repeated. It was very disturbing indeed, so I asked J if he needed some counselling; if so we'd sort him out.

Almost immediately the police wanted J moving, at least off the wing. He was like a one-man cleaning army, him, so I was pissed off about that, but the police believed that what Bridger told J was the closest description of what actually happened as had so far come to light. If the trial wasn't going well, they may well call upon him as a witness, so they had to be separated.

The day Bridger left, within an hour I had J back on healthcare as an orderly. Given the amount of bodily fluids we had to deal with, the nurses needed him.

I could deal with prisoners getting angry or in my face. When a fight looked likely, I could handle it. I had boundaries, knew what I was dealing with. But when someone's just mooching along, trying it on, slimy as a slug that needs salt, I found that so much harder to deal with. I did a lot of overtime, so could be around him six or seven days a week, twelve hours a day. 'Oh, Mr Samworth, can I have a shower? Oh, Mr Samworth, can I do this or that?' All that airy-fairy politeness was nauseating. I wanted to smash him in his face. He drove me absolutely bonkers.

Healthcare staff were offered the chance to attend his trial, to help deal with any demons I suppose. I turned down the opportunity. I didn't want to spend another moment in that monster's company, and certainly didn't want to hear any of his lying and wheedling while giving evidence. To him, people were just pieces in a sick game, waiting to be played.

What I did enjoy about Mark Bridger was his sentencing. He was given a whole of life term, and rightly so. While at Strangeways he'd lived in relative comfort, knew the staff and was high profile, people sniffing around him all the time. Now he was sent to Wakefield prison – Monster Mansion. When the Wakefield staff came to pick him up from our Cat A reception, I smiled to see him shaking, white with dread.

In July 2013, when driving into work, I heard on the radio he'd been slashed. A violent rapist got hold of him and that's prisoner retribution for you. He'd cut Bridger's throat and scarred him for life.

I've thought about capital punishment a lot; prison officers do talk about it. When you move among murderers and the very lowest forms of human life it would be odd if you didn't. There are some very unpleasant people inside that civilized folk would be better off without.

I've come to the view, though, that it's not so simple. Prison can be a far worse punishment. Every time Mark Bridger looks in a mirror he'll see that scar and fear for his life, won't he? Maybe it's better that him, Dale Cregan and others like them live a hundred years, every single day of it in suffering and fear, the drawn-out death they deserve.

On the other hand, for the families of victims, execution would at least ensure those killers are no longer a threat, physically or emotionally. Their photos won't be in the media constantly, as Ian

Brady and Myra Hindley's were, churning up terrible memories.

When push comes to shove, I'd go with the wishes of the people affected.

CHAPTER 18

DAMAGED GOODS

The worst prisoners in Strangeways were put in the challenging behaviour programme, housed in a special intervention unit with four or five cells, like the SIU above seg' in E Wing. Stricter security, less association, a far tougher regime. It's intended to address their behaviour or even rehabilitate them. Counselling is available, and psychiatric help, with a view to getting them back into the prison population at large. It's a worthy idea, but it doesn't always work.

Some religious extremists are dealt with under that scheme and, let me tell you, having met many of them, they are not going to change. They might be under tighter security restrictions, but at some point when people's guards are down and they are back on normal location, years in the future perhaps, they will take someone out, a prison officer perhaps.

We had one guy on healthcare who had ill health; in his fifties most likely but he looked about sixty-five or seventy. Eventually he went to Belmarsh as a Cat A prisoner. He was a hate preacher, essentially, like Abu Hamza, the guy with the hook. Yet with us he just acted like an old man. Because of his unpredictability and influence, though, we had him on an unlock. You don't have to let these people mingle with other inmates. Some of the female staff said they found him creepy, but he never professed his religious views to us.

Harry Mack was a muppet, a repeat offender who was not violent, only stupid. You could never educate him. At Forest Bank, he would often end up on the VP wing – not a sex offender or rapist, just vulnerable in such a tough environment. He'd offend people he shouldn't and was weak and easily influenced. Around 2012, he came on healthcare with a bum-fluff beard. I hadn't seen him for yonks.

'Changed your religion, kid?' I asked.

'Yes,' he said. 'I have.'

That wasn't so unusual. The con who lives 100 metres from me, Manny, one day decided he was Mormon. When you come in, on reception, one of the questions you are asked is, 'What is your religion?' But you can change your initial answer as many times as you want. Manny did that, not through any sense of born-again divinity, but because he could then get six ounces of drinking chocolate every Sunday from the kitchen. Mormons aren't allowed caffeine, you see, so get given that instead.

Anyway, Harry Mack. 'Let me guess,' I said. 'You're a Muslim.' Then he started preaching. 'Whoa, whoa, whoa!' I said. But on he went telling me about the glory of Allah and all of that.

Someone had obviously radicalized him. He came to us as a self-harmer, the type who'd get cutting or produce a noose if someone threatened him, a one to three on the Samworth scale.

His claim to fame, though, had been on A Wing where, one day, he pressed his cell bell. 'I need a nurse,' he told the officer who responded, though wouldn't say what was up at first. 'If I show you, you'll laugh,' he said. The screw just shrugged, so he let the blanket around him fall. There on his dick was a shampoo bottle with his bellend inside, the size of a boiled egg, and the situation was very dangerous because he was still semi-erect.

He was sent out to hospital where the doctors tried everything, with no luck. They had a ring-cutter on it, used to remove jewellery when someone crushes their hand or fingers, but this bottle wouldn't shift. The kid was in agony. He went on a drip, was given some drug and, over the course of about an hour, his mammoth erection subsided and they managed to pull the thing off.

I only heard about that, thank goodness, but another time I was called to a restraint on E Wing where one of our C&R instructors was involved. They'd got a lad who'd been creating all night, keeping everyone awake, they said, and wanted him removed. It would be a Tornado job and, as the biggest there, I got the shield. Finally, some action! I'll give the instructor his due – he did a belting job of getting us wound up. Adrenaline was pumping. We were going to monster this cock, rag him off the wing and make him scream as a lesson to the others. A bit over the top perhaps and not to be taken literally but, as we've seen, you need to be ready for anything. When we got there, I opened the flap, slammed the shield against the door and shouted a warning: 'Back of the cell!'

It was dark inside, so I couldn't see anyone. Whoever was in there could be hiding, ready to use a weapon. It couldn't be helped: we steamed in to find Harry Mack sat there, blubbing on his cot.

I stopped. The other lads stopped. He had his head in his hands, wracked with sobs. Behind us the instructor was shouting, 'Fucking smash him!' He wasn't happy, but we asked the kid what was up and took him calmly off to seg'. They didn't want him though, he was mithersome, so away he came to healthcare, where the first thing I did on removing my helmet, so to speak, was confiscate his shampoos and shower gels.

'What you doing that for?' he said.

'You've got form,' I replied.

He had all these religious ideas though, and wasn't shy in sharing them. Most of the patients on there told him to fuck off.

'Can you tell this muppet,' said one rapist and murderer, 'I don't want him talking to me on association about Islam. I'll fill him in if he keeps going on.'

I had a word and the preaching stopped.

In many ways, though, Mack was the tip of the iceberg. He had the fervour of a convert and was annoying but radicalization was causing worse problems under the surface, as a couple of other stories should illustrate.

One relates to Adz, an Asian lad I'd shared friends and associates with in Sheffield. We weren't pals but our paths had crossed. In fact he'd been part of a crew who turned up with shooters at a nightclub when I was on the door – the second time I had a gun stuck in my face. I ran into him again while doing overtime on B Wing, where he'd been blamed for sending a message threatening to behead someone and was sent to the seg' as punishment. By now, we were 'friendly, not friends', as they say in the service. I used to enjoy chatting with Adz; it gave you a different perspective. It was far more interesting than listening to some old bore witter on in the office, that's for sure. A good Muslim, he swore innocence over the threat, especially as he was coming towards the end of his sentence.

'I've a beautiful wife and kids, and parents who say that if I commit another crime they will disown me . . .' he told me. So what, I asked, had gone on?

'It's just bad blood,' he said. 'I know who was behind it' – and he confirmed there was an Islamic fundamentalist gang culture building in the high-security estate and long-term prisons. Lads who came in were encouraged to join; say no and that pressure would increase until you got hurt. It was a growing problem nationally, he insisted. Adz told me about two guys who had been covered in hot cooking oil at Whitemoor, a high-security prison in Cambridgeshire, where around a third of the prisoners were Muslim and exerted an iron grip. That's a horrendous assault however you look at it, yet it hadn't made the headlines. Checking that online, though, I did read a related report in the *Daily Telegraph* in 2012, which reported prison officers from Whitemoor admitting that they had a policy of 'appeasement' towards the 'powerful and growing population'. They had communal kitchens there, where curries and such could be prepared but in which no one dared cook pork or bacon. It sounded worrying and intimidating.

Another, white, lad I knew from Salford, real hard bastard, landed on K Wing on accumulated visits from another high-security prison. I was on the K Wing servery, doing overtime from health-care, and noticed that as he came past he took the halal option. Later I checked his religion on the computer and, sure enough, there it was.

'What's with the Muslim thing?' I asked.

'It's not about religion,' he said. 'When I landed, I'd heard the stories. It was friendly banter at first. I can fight, me, but I can't fight thirty people.'

It had taken them three months to get through to him, ended by a scrap he'd gone on basic regime for. 'I can't do it any more, banged up all day,' he said. 'I'm too old. I go to prayers and am seen to be learning the Koran. I just need to finish my time and I'm out. It's about survival, boss. There's a lot of it going on.'

He predicted that the next people I'd see in the news, blowing people up and driving into pedestrians, would be white kids like him – John Smith from Salford or Leeds or Rochdale or wherever: people with no family – druggies, maybe – who were just trying to get by.

'They're vulnerable, them,' he said. 'They get sucked up and taken in.'

There is a definite threat bubbling in prisons that won't be stopped by tiptoeing around for fear of Islamophobia. It's a similar story with sex crimes, as we saw with those poor girls in Rotherham the other year. It used to be that when you went on a wing, the vast majority of sex offenders were white. The idea of the dirty old man in a raincoat, always a cliché, is gone. When I left Manchester, it was maybe fifty-fifty, white and Asian.

I don't know the exact figures or how many of those have been radicalized, but that's how it is at the sharp end. If the security forces want to counter it, they should have someone undercover in every high-security jail, where most prisoners are currently free to associate with whoever they like, unmonitored. Maybe we need a terrorist-only prison where such activities can be isolated and contained. It would be a dangerous place to work.

★   ★   ★

Radicalization operates like gang culture, and is about power and control, not religion. We had imams working in the prison and they were good men. But one of them – in a roundabout way – was responsible for a sight that still makes me shudder.

Max Haslam was just a young lad who'd found himself in the wrong place, only twenty-one and a victim of gang crime. He'd had a normal life up to then: girlfriend, small child and a mother who loved him. In a case of mistaken identity gang-bangers had set about him, and the attack left him brain-damaged. People like that should not be in prison. He should have stayed with his mum until they found a place in a brain unit for him.

Brain-damaged people can become disinhibited and act inappropriately. Their injuries sometimes lead to them finding it difficult to distinguish between right and wrong. Max was like a child, which left him better around women at Strangeways than men, because they dealt with him that way. 'Max, you need to be in your cell,' they'd say. 'You need to get a shower.' And he'd do it. He was in for rape, having got into bed with his mate's girl-friend. In the end the allegation never went to trial, due to his condition I assume.

But he was a lump physically and could also act like a stroppy teenager. Showing off one day, as he saw it, he told some other prisoners what he was in for. In healthcare we let the VPs mix with the normal location prisoners because it was well monitored, even though in the prison rulebook that shouldn't have happened. It worked fine usually, but if someone starts boasting about being a rapist it's a different situation. We had to put him on a three-officer unlock for his own safety.

I then went away on my annual leave. I'm not knocking those who were on while I was away but, because he was so awkward, they didn't get him out. He spent more and more time behind his door, in a cell the size of a bathroom. He smashed his TV. That meant he was locked up, brain-damaged with no telly, for twenty-three hours a day. By the time I came back, he'd deteriorated.

Many screws, perhaps, would have tried to stay professionally aloof and detached but my emotional guard was slipping by now and I couldn't help feeling it personally. During his stay on healthcare I met his mother three times. Due to his circumstances, she'd see him in normal visits in the out-patients unit downstairs. She was lovely, worried about her lad. She'd watched him gradually go downhill.

When eventually a place on a brain unit was found, it didn't seem like a day too soon. He'd pissed all over the floor and blocked the toilet, flooding his cell. There was shit everywhere. He'd thrown his canteen – crisps, noodles and biscuits – around; it was floating in an inch of mucky water. The smell was ghastly.

I looked in and there he stood, like some sickening Statue of Liberty, holding up a Koran and ramming big handfuls of mulched-up paper into his mouth. It was doubly bizarre because he wasn't a Muslim – an imam must have given him it, they would if you asked. He then washed it all down with bog water scooped up in his blue prison plastic cup.

I went into the office. 'Haven't you seen this guy? Have you seen what he's doing?' People were quite laid-back about it. He was going to hospital the next day and that would be the best place for him. I'm not sure they took in what I'd said. Eating a Koran. I've seen some horrible things in prison but, boy, did that stay with me.

CHAPTER 19

OUT OF CONTROL

I recently read a report that said on average prison officers are expected to live two years after retirement. Two years! What the prison service is really doing therefore is ensuring its staff will not be alive to collect the pension they've earned. And, don't forget, it has since been decided that they should stay in the job until they're sixty-eight. Scandalous. Here's an example of the sort of thing we in healthcare faced all the time.

I was on with the Stretcher Bearer and Nikki, the other officer who passed the interview with me when the changes came in.

'Samikins,' our nurse manager said, 'we've got a lad in the gated cell. He's been sent on an ACCT form from reception. Can you check his background, please?'

I didn't always do that in the rest of the prison, as we've seen. Very often it didn't matter. On healthcare, though, there were nurses and vulnerable people around, so if prisoners were rapists, racists or terrorists it paid to be aware. We often did it. I had a look on the computer and the first thing I noticed was that he'd been in Liverpool prison, in segregation, for six years solid. That was enough. Whatever he'd been sentenced for, he was either fucked in the head or dangerous. Shortly after arrival, he rang his bell, asking to use the phone. Nobody else was unlocked at the time, so I agreed to his request. Mistake number one.

Out he came, squaring up to me straight away. He wasn't big but he was fit, young too, in his mid-twenties. He looked me right in the eye. Cockfight. No messing. 'Get me down to seg', now.' He didn't care for his new accommodation.

'You're not going to seg', lad,' I said. 'You're on healthcare. When the nursing staff say you can leave, then off you go.'

'Get me down to seg',' he said again, in a very threatening manner, fists clenched.

Adrenaline kicked in, the knees began shaking. Nikki took off her glasses and put them to one side. I pushed the lad behind his door and suddenly we were in a restraint. By now I'd had my fiftieth birthday, Nikki was the wrong side of forty-five, and the Stretcher Bearer was sixty and built like it, little pot belly: not exactly Conor McGregor.

Nikki, as ever, followed us into battle. It took my full weight to drag this kid to the floor, where all four of us ended up. I got him in a neck lock, not textbook but it was doing the job until he shook it off, wriggling like a conger eel. One very long minute and a half later, the cavalry arrived and we were only struggling to pin him down then, nothing else. A minute later, with the extra muscle and weight, we had this limpet in restraint. He carried on struggling though.

'You fat Yorkshire prick!' he said, giving it the mouth. 'You've eaten too many fucking pies.'

He was going back to seg' now, this dick. He'd got his wish. Getting him back was a struggle – he was fighting all the way.

'You need more cardio, you fat fuck.'

'Listen, lad,' I said, 'I'm not the one puffing and blowing.'

As soon as we handed him over to the segregation unit he changed. Compliant. He was where he wanted to be. And that wasn't healthcare.

Back in the office, the Stretcher Bearer had a whitey on. A pensioner almost, he'd just been grappling with a lad nearly three times younger and deserved a sit-down. Nikki was crying, hurt as well, knocked around. But she was upset because the three of us – combined age nearing a top score in darts – hadn't got a lock on: we'd only just restrained him.

'I'm no good to you, am I?' she said.

For prison staff, such physical demands aren't unusual. I'm sure the fun will only increase the closer you get to sixty-eight years old!

Over the coming weeks, I did a couple of shifts in seg' and supervising the exercise yard I saw the Limpet and he saw me. Did he call me a fat Yorkshire prick again? No, he did not.

'All right, Mr S.?' He now knew my name.

'Yeah, I am, how are you?'

'Good.'

'Good.'

'No hard feelings?'

'No hard feelings. What you doing?'

'I'm on my regime. Doing an hour, I kill it.' And he did. Press-ups, burpees . . . he went at it non-stop.

'You need more of this, Mr S.,' he laughed.

'You'll not be so keen when you get to my age,' I told him.

He was quite a long time at HMP Manchester, the Limpet, and I saw him again at least a dozen times. He went out of his way to speak to me and me to him. That's what prisoners tend to be like. They are not all badasses and don't hold grudges. We'd had a bit of a grapple and then moved on: dynamic security and all that.

Nikki ended up getting hurt another time we had a prisoner who didn't want to be on healthcare, and it was all down to the smoking ban.

Healthcare was funded by an NHS Trust and ran to their rules, hospitals of course having been non-smoking for years. Hospital patients are allowed a fag, but only if they exit the main building, and you aren't going to do that in prison. Other parts of the jail would have that familiar tobacco aroma, but not ours, after 2011 anyway. That was when the NHS began to insist we followed suit. Staff in healthcare could then be disciplined for smoking on site. I've never smoked, so I didn't mind. Healthcare was only a small area and the smell was nasty enough as it was. Another plus was that offenders who fancied blagging a break with us, seeing it as easier time, suddenly decided otherwise when they couldn't have their tabs.

It wasn't great when smokers with mental illnesses came on, though. Taking their burn off them was cruel. They were addicted to it. That's all they'd got to live for. We would check their property, strip search them and put their lighter and tobacco in storage. They were offered patches or counselling but basically went cold turkey. It caused real problems. We had loads of restraints, plenty of issues. At least, though, it was only in healthcare.

Then, on 1 September 2017, the service introduced a trial smoking ban right across all high-security and long-term prisons in England and Wales and every other wing followed suit. Soon afterwards, riots erupted in HMP Birmingham, where prisoners could be heard chanting, 'We – want – burn!' before Tornado teams were sent in. This was after massive riots there the previous December.

But let's suppose that in the end this blanket smoking ban goes peacefully. It won't stop people doing it. Around 80 per cent of the prison population smokes. All it will do is create a new prison economy. Burn is cheap compared to heroin. Lighters and matches will be sought after too, smuggled in the back way as usual. A new black market will be born. The bullied will get battered for something else, and a breed of tobacco barons will emerge. The structure for that is already in place. If you borrow burn it's double bubble: I lend you half an ounce and want an ounce back. They already make money; it will just get worse. Yet more hassle and grief for the staff.

In fact, it's already happening. The other day, while out walking my dog, I bumped into Manny. Having just come out again, he told me it was indeed all going to pot, literally. According to him, the burn barons are on the rise, lots of bullying, everyone still smoking. What's more, prisoners are now allowed to use 'vapes', to wean them off cigs. Only what the cons are doing is taking the battery out and using the things like bongs, puffing weed through them instead.

Meanwhile, back on healthcare, a prisoner came to us late one night having tried to punch a member of staff and been bent up. Six foot one, thin as a rake, curly black hair and scruffy as fuck: the entire prison was waiting for us to get him behind his door so they could clock off their shifts. He started giving me lip. 'I'm not stopping on this unit.'

What had upset him all over again was having his burn removed. I gave him the spiel: 'You're here for the night, there's nowhere else in jail.

Tomorrow you can go to a wing and smoke your tits off.'

He wasn't having it. As Nikki and I went to unlock the cell to put him in, I took my eye off the ball. Before I knew it, he'd taken a huge swing. If I'd had hair it would have rustled like hay in a breeze. He missed but caught Nikki, behind me, with a forearm. Thankfully, not full in the face, but he did knock her glasses off. I got him in a headlock while Nikki, although shocked, carried on struggling with him gamely. Eventually we got him to the floor and backup arrived to take him back to seg', where he'd be allowed his tobacco.

My fellow officer was shaken up and again sported bruises I'd have been proud to wear. She had a bit of whiplash too. But the thing that really pissed her off was that in such situations I'd try to push her to one side. 'I'm a prison officer too,' she'd say.

'Yeah, you are love, but I'm from Yorkshire, and if anyone's getting brayed around here it's me, not you.'

I couldn't help but admire her, though. She was far braver than a lot of blokes in there. The administrators and politicians take advantage of officers like Nikki and the Stretcher Bearer. They put them in more danger than they ought to be facing. Older staff and the majority of women shouldn't be placed in such brutal situations and very often wouldn't be if officer numbers were high enough. I dare say some will call that ageist and sexist; for me it's just common sense. What are they arguing for? The right to be battered senseless? Handy for the bean counters and politicians that, isn't it?

Spare a thought too for the young officers just starting out on what they hope will be a fulfilling career in the prison service. Some of the things they are forced to see and deal with will haunt them for most of their lives.

Jimmy Makin was only in HMP Manchester four days, that's all, when he arrived on healthcare. Ten staff brought him up from reception. He'd not been restrained but wasn't right – you could see it. He looked through you. He was a lost soul really, not eating, drinking or communicating: he'd got nothing. He wouldn't talk to Bradders, and neither would he engage with a psychiatrist we brought in. Emergency section if ever I saw one. He'd be off as soon as a bed became available, which might be days or weeks given all the papers that needed signing by doctors, judges, psychiatrists or whoever. An immediate decision was made to put him on constant watch, behind the Perspex shield. I wasn't on that weekend, but Warren was – the young officer, you'll remember, who'd already had to watch Holden gouging his own eyes until he'd blinded himself.

On the Saturday, Jimmy had begun to punch the iron bars, each one an inch in diameter. It's not like punching plaster. By close of play Sunday his forearms were just dangling from the elbows down, jelly. Nurses were crying. He'd broken both hands and his wrists were smashed to fuck. Surely he was a worthy candidate for the liquid cosh? Once he's smashed himself to bits you can't put cuffs on him. A body belt would have been no good, it's a belt around your waist with cuffs. The physical damage was done. Lack of intervention comes back to docs having to make decisions and all the potential legal ramifications. By Monday, when I came back, he'd finally gone to hospital on an emergency section.

Warren spent all weekend watching Makin destroy himself, it's got to be traumatic that. Like me, he might well have been parking what he saw in a box in his mind that one day he would have to gaze into.

On healthcare, a quiet week is as dull as anywhere else in Strangeways. And the ratio of boring days to eventful ones? Boredom was unusual, especially when we were short of staff. On a peaceful weekend, with them all in their cells, you might be eight hours on your feet, leaning on railings. Backache was an occupational hazard. In some areas of the jail, where prisoners spend more time in their cells, you might be sat in the sterile area, but on healthcare you spent the bulk of your time on the landings. There was always a potential ding-dong. You had to stay alert.

It was a really dull Sunday in 2015. There'd been an alarm bell on outer E Wing but it appeared to have been attended to, done and dusted.

Then another voice came over the radio: '*All out stations, E Wing Outer.*' It was a chilling message, rare then, not so much now. What it meant was: anyone available needed to get there fast.

Healthcare could spare four of us: two jockey-weight female officers, one of them an SO, Chris, a male officer with little physical presence, and me. Being younger than me and not carrying eighteen stone, Chris set off like a gazelle.

'Whoa! Slow down!' I shouted. 'You don't know what you're going into. You might need some fight.'

E Wing held over one hundred prisoners on two landings – the threes and fours – and the rumpus covered half of it. On the top deck was a lad who'd taken spice, begun choking and was now unconscious. Paramedics were already there, as were a few nurses, so our SO ran up to join them. Meanwhile, the call had gone out for inmates to get behind their doors and, on such a sunny Sunday, they hadn't liked that one bit. They wanted to be on the yard. The mood turned ugly and now there was more trouble brewing on the threes, so I stayed put.

One guy terrorized the place, a well-known member of the Mancunian gangster clan that used to do the doors on the Haçienda. He was up on a pool table giving it the old, 'We're not going to take it anymore,' as an audience of around seventy warmed to the theme. Ring-pieces were twitching, full-on adrenaline dump. I was on a landing ten metres wide and thought it best not to hang around, so I drew my baton and others followed suit.

These fuckers were out of control and needed telling who was in charge; our officers had needed someone to step up. A couple of dogs were on hand too, snarling and slavering. A dozen screws now had batons drawn. If I needed to use this thing, I would be willing to do so. We were heavily outnumbered but ready to wade in. The prisoners saw we meant business and stepped back.

There was a governor there now to negotiate, and the Manc gangster came forward. 'We are not going behind us doors unless we get us exercise.' Personally, I'd have just twatted him. Against a background of shouts and barking the two of them started talking, but to begin with the tension increased.

A thousand different governors would've dealt with this a thousand different ways; you do the best you can. This one tried to be reasonable and said that if we could get them out, we would. The chaos and noise continued for a while but the prisoners did eventually agree to back down. Rather than move to the end of the landing, however, where we could put them away in a controlled manner, they were allowed to make their own way to their cells.

That seemed unnecessary to me and dangerous too. We had officers with batons out – the cons would have done as they were told – but all the same here they were, walking among the staff, many of whom were terrified. Fortunately, the plan passed without further incident and the chief troublemakers were later dispatched to the segregation unit.

Afterwards, I asked another officer why he hadn't drawn his baton.

'You can get in trouble for that,' he said.

That landing, seventy prisoners, a potential riot on our hands – when is there a better time to get your baton out? Interpersonal skills aren't going to stand you in good stead with five thugs stamping on you. Apart from those dogs, batons were the only protection we had. We'd been in a riot situation, and an officer was worried about self-defence and enforcing discipline in the jail!

Now, as I write this in 2017, there seems to be incidents like it every week. It's the norm. In October, ten Tornado teams went to Long Lartin in Worcestershire, where the likes of Abu Hamza and murderer Christopher Halliwell have been held. Riots have also been reported in Swaleside, Bedford and Lewes.

But don't expect to read many factual accounts of prison riots. When I was on K Wing, Strangeways had some lads arrive from another jail where they'd wrecked a wing, injured staff. They were all looking at ten years. On segregation units, governors do rounds every day, though, and one of them opened the door of one of these kids and told him, 'I know who you are' – this governor had just completed an investigation into the mutiny these lads had come from.

The prison service being what it is, the investigation had been so secret even this prisoner hadn't been aware of it. But now he told his solicitor, who got a copy from the Ministry of Justice. This report apparently confirmed concerted indiscipline and damage to prison property, but said that nobody was injured. When their case got to court, his solicitor produced the report as evidence and the expected ten years was reduced to nil.

Long Lartin, by the way, which needed the ten Tornado teams, has lost a fifth of its staff in recent years, and isn't alone in that. When I first joined, the prison population was 72,000, and when I left, around two years ago, it was 83,000. It's currently approaching 90,000. At the same time, staffing levels have dropped by about 6,000. So the system is crumbling. Under a government recruitment drive, they hope to employ another 2,500 staff by 2018. There's just under 500 prisons in the UK, so if that seems like a useful amount, do the maths. They are talking about putting four or five new staff in each prison – Manchester alone could do with another forty or fifty. It's a drop in the ocean. I am fearful that the entire estate is about to erupt. And when that happens people will get hurt, prisoners and staff, my friends among them. I hope that someone somewhere sees sense.

CHAPTER 20

STEP ON

On 1 March 2015 everything came to a head at Strangeways.

Government cost-cutting had been going on for a while and this was the latest and most revolutionary round. Budgets were sliced, which as ever meant fewer staff. There were horror stories elsewhere in the prison estate so we'd known what was coming to HMP Manchester. The buzzword was modernization. We would have new ways of working, different shift patterns leading to a more economical and strategic use of human resources.

As usual it was all based on theory; there was no appreciation of the practical realities for those on the frontline. I hear now that postgraduates are to be employed to re-think how the prison service might be improved. Supposedly they'll be treating prisoners as customers? Be as polite as you like, you quite definitely will not change a criminal's essential nature. What if a customer tells one of these bright young things to get the fuck out of their cell? You're not selling package holidays.

Prison is not like other jobs. As we've seen, in jail too many staff is the right amount, because you never know what kind of extreme event you might have to deal with. Teams of staff develop, get used to working together over many years. D Wing – like K Wing, in that it held disruptive prisoners nobody else wanted – had an eight-person team formed over a decade. Their understanding was instinctive. It ran like clockwork. The new idea was that staff should be kept moving or they would become demotivated. Dynamic security hadn't crossed the bureaucrats' radar.

But one of our governors was touting this reorganization as the best thing since porridge. He 'profiled' healthcare, which is to say looked at maximum hours and staff needed to cover that unit and came up with four officers on thirty-nine hour weeks, far too low in our view. He actually asked, 'Why do we need prison officers on healthcare?' Well, where do you start? Nurses aren't trained in restraint, for one thing.

Imagine this is Wednesday afternoon at the supermarket. It's quiet, and eight people are running the store really well. Someone comes around with a clipboard and asks, 'So why do we have more than eight on the payroll? Get rid of the rest!' Come Saturday morning, the store is rammed: these eight staff can barely cope, someone knocks over a jar of pickles and, before you know it, the queues for the tills are around the block.

In a supermarket, people would shop elsewhere. In prison you can't do that, and it's not just eggs being broken.

The number of shifts was cut to the bone, especially on weekends. But they hadn't allowed for officers being called away to escort prisoners to hospital, for example, or to rush off to a restraint. Through the week you'd be locking down entire wings so staff could be used elsewhere.

The first day of the new system, I got sent to D Wing to get labour out. That done, I'm off to get exercisers out for B Wing. Staff looking after the visits area were moved, meaning visits ran late, which in turn impacted back on the jail. The whole prison was like that – officers were just moving about, task orientated, and the place never settled down.

A couple of other ideas turned this into a car crash. They set about moving the prison population geographically. Cat A prisoners stayed put but the rest – VP prisoners, rapists, paedophiles, remand – all these groups would be shunted to different parts of the jail. The reception wing would be moved too, as would 150 officers – and all of this simultaneously. If you are moving, say, twenty VPs you've got to lock them up somewhere while you bring other prisoners out of the cells they will now be taking – and then put *them* somewhere else. A logistical nightmare, right across Strangeways: chaos guaranteed.

On top of that, staff were worried there'd no

longer be as much, if any, overtime, which was relied upon to top up salaries. But did overtime go? Did it hell. On 28 February, HMP Manchester was short of eighty officers. On 1 March, according to official figures, we had fifteen more than we needed. Same number of people actually working, mind, just a different calculation. No redundancies either. Jobs had been 're-profiled'.

As new staff came out of training they'd leave virtually straight away. It was, and still is, a revolving door. The depth of the mess would be difficult to exaggerate. Just employ the amount of people in every prison needed to do the job properly. It was an absolute farce.

Twenty-five years earlier the Manchester riot had made people realize that keeping prisoners locked up for twenty-three hours a day was counter-productive. Now the service had gone back to doing just that. Staff–prisoner relationships broke down; dynamic security was consigned to history. When I turned up in the morning to do a job on B Wing, for example, I didn't have time to talk to anyone: I had to get to A Wing, then K Wing, and go back to healthcare for dinner. It got so stressful it was unbelievable, not just for me, but for everyone. It started getting dangerous. The fallout is still being felt, I'm told.

Although working on healthcare was getting to me by now, the odd nice moment did still come along. Towards the end of my time there I was walking through the visits area when someone shouted, 'Boss!'

I recognized him straight away. It was the young Asian lad whose father's funeral we'd gone to in Salford. He was sitting with two women in burkas. He beckoned me over, and I asked how he was.

'I've been great, but I've slipped up and I'm in here for two weeks' – a tax thing, he said, and introduced me to his mum and sister. 'I've told them how you took me to see Dad off.'

The two of them stood up and hugged me. The entire room was watching. 'Ay ay,' the prisoners would have been thinking, 'what's Mr S. doing now?' Officers were staring too. But what can you do? It's your dynamic security again. I was polite and wished him and them well.

This being prison, though, a report went to security. Hugging visitors!

Healthcare was always tough, but with enough staff on to support one another in a well-organized team it could also be interesting. On the whole, the first years I'd been there were fine. But when the smoke of all the reorganization cleared, the prison management took back control of healthcare from nurse managers, and we went back to having too many chiefs. I found that I was the only original officer left; Nikki was moved to K Wing.

I'm best working on my own initiative, yet the new managers had other ideas, rarely based on healthcare principles. I had a barney with an SO on the servery because I was letting out six or seven prisoners at a time. That wasn't how we did it anymore, this SO said – two at a time, max.

'Well, they're out now anyway,' I said, and he spat his dummy. If he was going to introduce changes he ought to have let people know first.

Since I – the only experienced officer in the unit – was most often elsewhere, there was no one around to help new staff settle in. Remarkably, they didn't even have to be interviewed as we'd been: they were just employed on the unit ad hoc. Crazy. We had one naive officer from the OSG ranks who very early on had to deal with a prisoner smashing his TV. Glass everywhere. She sailed straight in. The SO and me had to tell her to come out and shut the door – she could have been assaulted, flying solo. It wasn't long before I had to suffer the consequences of untrained, inexperienced new staff at first hand.

I'd first met Charlie Horner on the seg' at Forest Bank. He was white but had a spectacular Afro. We were warned he was violent. I remember looking at his record to see what we'd got. Although he was just seventeen and only had a couple of chin whiskers, in the juvenile estate, which is how lads between fifteen and eighteen are classed, he'd been assaulting staff and other children. He'd therefore been reclassified as a young offender, a term usually for eighteen to twenty-one year olds.

He had no size or presence – other than that

perm – but his record spoke for itself, and though he'd been on a three-officer unlock for two and a half months without incident, you treat these people with caution. He was also a scruffy toad who refused to clean his cell. Unless you intended to spin him upside down and use his head as a mop, it was a lost cause. Ten weeks in and he had neither cracked a smile nor spoken to anyone. He refused exercise and didn't want to use the phone. So eventually he came off his unlock.

He'd been out and about for a couple of weeks by the time we came to this boring Sunday. As usual it was quiet, and I was on with an officer, Geordie, a big lad, heavier than me with a very dry sense of humour. We'd opened Horner up to take him to the showers, Geordie walking in front, when the Afro looked over his shoulder at me, and the expression on his face was satanic. 'Watch this,' it said. I'd no time to react or warn anyone when – *bam!* – Geordie was cracked on the chin from behind. He fell like a great oak, knocked clean out.

I shouted a warning and the big SO and me rugby tackled this kid, or tried. Our combined thirty-odd stone couldn't put him down. This lad was butting me with the back of his head, and it took nine or ten staff, big lads among them, to get him behind his door. He'd bust my lip and Geordie had a headache for days.

In 2015, Horner landed in Strangeways one night, on healthcare. New sentence, I didn't bother to see what for, but he'd still got a bit of a perm.

I knew his form, though, and next morning in the briefing explained how he was violent and unpredictable: a three-officer unlock minimum. One of the new staff was a know-all, 'I think he needs to come off unlock.'

I disagreed. For me, he was as dangerous as he'd been ten years ago.

For a while I got my way. I told Horner about the unlock myself and as he sat on his bed and looked up, there was a sigh of recognition. As usual, though, he didn't really engage, with me or anyone else. Then I had a rare weekend off and when I came in on the Monday that was no longer the case. 'Why is he off the unlock?' I asked.

I was told he hadn't done anything in two weeks.

Here we go, I thought.

That morning, he wouldn't come out of his cell when I unlocked it and he wouldn't talk to me. It got to dinnertime, and Officer Know-All pointed out that only Horner hadn't eaten, so he went to his door to find out why, and did persuade him, still silent, to go to the servery.

The orderly there was piling his plate with spaghetti when over his shoulder I saw that demonic smile again. Suddenly Horner blew. Let out a roar. His plate hit the ceiling, his body stiffened, and both Officer Know-All and the SO shat themselves. Hand on his back, I ushered Horner behind his door – down the years he'd obviously chilled a bit – and walked away with a spring in my step.

Afternoon briefing: 'Does anybody have anything to say?'

Senior officer: 'Horner needs to be on an unlock.'

In my seven years on healthcare I had seen it all: deaths in custody, people cutting, hanging, the lot. Most of my fellow officers and nurses were great but, boy, did it get stressful. You had to be strong between the ears, quite definitely. I'd be out of the house at six o'clock and come home at half nine at night sometimes, with overtime. If I was at work for sixty hours including travel, Amy spent the same amount of time on her own at home and then, when I came through the door, I was like a bear with a sore arse. She was a prison widow.

For years I hardly saw my daughter Billie at all, and when I did we'd argue. When I did get a day off, I was just interrupting their routine. My unhappiness had been brewing for a while, but the changes that came in on 1 March put the tin hat on it. Strangeways had changed beyond recognition. I wanted out. I asked a PO I got on with for a move.

The exit strategy was supposed to be my gradual removal from an area that was tense and demanding to one that was maybe less so. A Wing seemed like the perfect place. But a bit like soldiers who dodge bombs and bullets one minute and then dodge depression the next, leaving a war zone and settling back into civilian ranks can be tough . . .

CHAPTER 21

HOLLOW INSIDE

The transition did not go well.

From day one on A Wing – 13 August 2015 – it felt like a lifetime, like being in limbo. The officers weren't the issue. One was a miserable bastard, so we hit it off straight away. My other favourite, a cleaning warder like me, was rough as toast and grafted hard, salt of the earth. Let's call them Jack and Vera.

There were other decent officers, but by that time staff right across Strangeways were demotivated, sick of being dicked about. I won't knock them. By and large, screws are ordinary people. Think of the nicest wedding reception you've been to and look around: everyone over eighteen and under sixty-eight is a potential prison officer – your favourite auntie, funny uncle, scrawny cousin and bolshie niece. But now there was a growing unwillingness to get involved. You got no thanks for putting yourself in the line of fire. People were dawdling on incidents, and I could see them praying that storms would blow out with no repercussions. It was in their eyes: *Please, please, please.*

Under this new regime the admin was all over

the place too. On A Wing we had a big turnover of prisoners – a hundred a week – because it's the induction wing. When they came on you'd have to give them a bedding pack: two cotton sheets and a couple of woollen yellow blankets in winter – the sort your grandma might crochet. (Nowadays every inmate can have bedding brought in from home, which is cheaper for the jail and another way to keep them settled and in line.) They were also due two clean towels a week – though they're not much bigger than flannels, for big lads about enough to dry one leg.

Whether through disorganization or lack of funding, from the start it was obvious we were going to struggle. I begged and borrowed – didn't steal – from other wings and it still wasn't enough. Understandably, the prisoners got pissed off. And this was the induction wing, which is supposed to have everything. I despaired.

I had one lad on remand, so by rights he could have as many visitors as he wanted. The computer, though, said he'd been sentenced, which stuffed him up completely. I phoned admin every day for two weeks and spoke to the same lass to try and get something done. It would have taken the click of a mouse. After I'd badgered her for a fortnight, an office manager accused me of harassment. I had to take it all the way to the governor before it got altered. But for me all this was the least of my troubles.

It all kicked off at dinnertime, no more than

a week and half into my time on A Wing. The servery was split, the two parts separated by a gate that was locked manually and electronically. I fed the prisoners on one half while Vera fed hers on the other.

It was all going along efficiently when a con started shouting.

'Are you all right?' I called across to Vera, and she nodded, yeah.

The yelling carried on, though, and I caught sight of this prisoner who was about to kick-off big style. While I got on the radio, a cleaner came up to talk to me – I remember that. I also recall the anxious look on Vera's face and an SO coming down the landing. Much of what came next is blank.

This prisoner knocked the SO clean off his feet. Lamped him one, full on. He then cracked Vera, but luckily didn't catch her as hard as he'd hoped.

'Open the gate!' I roared at the OSG. I'm told that's how it was; I honestly can't bring the actual memory back. Even now, I never stop trying to conjure it up in the hope it might provide vindication for what I did next.

I don't know how I got to this lad, but I did. I had him on the other side of the landing, pinned in his cell doorway. I got him to the floor and cracked him in the face, maybe as much as four times, hard.

Eventually I began to hear voices, 'Sam! Sam! Sam!' People were grabbing my arms.

'You are out of order,' said the PO who'd witnessed what happened. 'I'm not happy with that.'

Red mist, operational stress – whatever you want to call it, I could have killed him too. Jack led him away.

Walking back to our wing, I realized my keys were gone. Bad news. In the past, that's led to new locks for the entire jail at a cost of a quarter of a million quid. I had to buzz the gate to get back on the landing, where a governor was waiting with the missing bunch in his hand. By then I was beyond caring.

The next day my right fist was in a mess – punch someone properly and you get a displaced knuckle – and my knees were bruised to fuck. The prisoner was in a right state. His eye was swollen and he had a broken nose, bumps and bruises all over his face. He was in a special cell for three days, so he must have carried on playing up, threatening staff there. That did me a favour. As he was such a cock, few people on seg' were fussed about how he arrived. He got six added months on his sentence. Plenty would say that wasn't enough – he'd hammered two officers, one of them a woman, our mates. If the prisoners had got hold of him they'd have filled him in for cracking a female officer: you can twat a man, but don't hit a woman, that's their code. In fact, he was under threat in that respect for a while.

But what I'd done wasn't professional. I'd

smashed a prisoner, the first time in eighteen years' service. Blood pressure pumping, my head had all but exploded. There are instances when you lose it, but being a prison officer is not a licence to punch fuck out of people, as I've said. That my emotions had got unmanageable, that I couldn't keep out of conflict – it felt like a terrible defeat. This wasn't the person I wanted to be. When I was young, scrapping just came to be how we ended the night. I know now it's all about adrenaline dumps – fight or flight – and in the prison service I'd learned how to control those bursts of adrenaline and put them to good use. I'd lost my self-control, and with it my prison career.

It was a while before I found out that none of this was on camera. If my mates hadn't blocked the view – not deliberately, they were trying to pull me off him – the best defence lawyer in the world couldn't have got me off.

To add to my misery, a few weeks later I badly injured my shoulder in a restraint on D Wing. He was a stocky lad this con, around twenty-five, and he'd spent a lot of time in the gym. My mate was forty-something and overweight. We struggled to get him to the deck, but another officer, a former soldier, got involved, and the con had hit the concrete four or five times when I felt my shoulder go, with a sound like you get when you twist a drumstick off a chicken.

By the time we handed this character over, my

mate was sweating buckets, grey as a corpse and in danger of a heart attack. The ex-army officer had thrown a whitey, in agony with a bad back, and my shoulder felt like it was hanging out of its socket. The three of us stood there, injured and ignored. Nobody said fuck all. A few days before I'd had a word with my mate and he'd broken down in tears. That wasn't unusual now. During my last six months in that job I saw four officers crying in frustration, all of them male.

At home, Amy sent me to the doctor, who signed me off for a month. I needed it: my blood pressure was through the roof – 185 over 135. At my age, normal is 120–140 over 70–80. Even my resting pulse was 113, still sky-high, which put me at risk of a stroke. Within a few days I was on a high-dose blood pressure medication and high-dose statin for cholesterol.

'What you've got to ask yourself,' said the doctor, 'is: in that job, can you adapt how you live?' If I wouldn't or couldn't change my lifestyle, I was going to be on tablets for the rest of my life.

There was no way. Long hours, terrible shifts . . . There were a few lads and lasses who went to the gym, but not many. On the whole, the prison officer population drinks too much, eats too much and is unfit.

At the end of the month, with my blood pressure not improving, the doctor wrote me another sick note and gave me different medication. Meanwhile, the shoulder injury was agonizing. It was the opposite shoulder to the one I'd had rebuilt in 2012 after the rugby wear and tear. This side was diagnosed as bursitis – inflammation of the fluid sac, a sort of cushion between the tendon and bones, over the joint. When it presses on nerves you get pain. It wasn't dislocated, but I couldn't move it, which didn't help my psychological state either. They gave me a cortisone injection that made me sick as a dog and put me in bed for two days.

I wasn't sleeping properly. In prison on a morning shift, my routine had always been the same – bed at twelve, up at five. Now I was all over the place. I tried every trick: lavender, cherry juice, herbal, counting sheep, everything apart from drugs. I just couldn't switch off.

I am walking through a wood without a care in the world. Sunshine is breaking through the trees and warming my face; it's a beautiful day. With me is Steve, my black Labrador, and while I'm throwing him a stick we stumble across a little house in a clearing.

In an instant, the sun goes in, the world is in shadow and I get a knot in my stomach. I recognize this house immediately. It is Mark Bridger's cottage.

Light glints on a top-window pane, where a figure catches my eye. It is Billie, my daughter. My sweet little thing is inside. Forget all the horrible things I've seen in my life: they don't come close to this.

I push aside the branches and step closer, desperate now to gain entry. But all the cottage doors and windows are barred. In a rising panic, I tear around the lower walls, but can't get in. Upstairs, behind glass, Billie is crying, terrified. She wants me to get her out. I look up at her, heart racing, but can do nothing. Another face forms in a downstairs window, also familiar, staring out through dust. It is Bridger himself. I can't tell you . . . I'd go through a wall to get at him but I can't. I can't.

And then I'd wake up, shaking and sobbing, inconsolable.

It was a regular occurrence, this dream, and it left me a wreck. I'd be distressed, spaced out for two, three days afterwards. It was so vivid I couldn't eat or sleep. Gradually, it came to me less and less, although I still catch myself thinking about it now and then, when I'm half-awake maybe, in that semiconscious state when you don't know if you're asleep or not.

But mainly the nightmares were things I'd actually seen in prison: horrible thoughts, gruesome images swam to the surface, stuff long since buried. Forgotten faces and voices crowded in on me. Miseries I'd endured and watched others endure flooded my mind as I tossed and turned. I'd lie there in the darkness, stuck in this mental House of Wax, head spinning. It had all happened, though, and now I had to live with it. I realized how those old soldiers feel who don't want to talk about what they did in the war. It hangs on your soul and won't shift. You can't scrub it clean.

Awake wasn't much better. I'd take Steve out for a walk at dawn, this torment festering in my brain. I began to picture myself hitting the con, but what I could never see was him twatting my mates. He'd laid one of them out and almost broken the other's jaw – could have killed her. The rest of the scene was soon on a permanent loop – but those two assaults wouldn't come. It was driving me insane.

As if life wasn't tough enough already, in the October my cousin died of alcoholism. That knocked my head around even more.

I started losing it. I stormed out of a super-market because a customer was holding me up by arsing about on her phone. When an ex-con I recognized carved me up in his Audi I exploded with road rage – nearly pulled the steering wheel off imagining jumping up and down on his head, even though I had the missus and little 'un in with me.

I lost all interest in hygiene – so much so that I developed sores under my arms and in my groin. Amy would shove me in the shower, put my clothes out every day – she even had to squeeze the tooth-paste on my toothbrush. At eight o'clock she'd kick me out of the house, and to try and work out my anger I went to the gym every day. I'd do far too much, two hours at a time on the weights until I made myself ill, throwing up outside in the bushes. I'd leave the gym at ten and then suffer a massive emotional release in the car – tears, thoughts swirling – a relentless wave of grief.

Then I had my first panic attack. I didn't know what was happening. It was scary. My chest tightened and for ten minutes I thought I was off to the great segregation unit in the sky. The doctor offered me more drugs: didn't want them. Nor was my shoulder getting better. And still everything kept coming in my head: ghosts like Pawel Nicpon and Alan Taylor.

'You don't sound right, you,' said a friend, and suggested some counselling. I was in a very bad way.

As Christmas drew closer, Amy was getting really concerned. My blood pressure was still going up. I kept losing my rag and had a terrible temper. My missus and daughter were on eggshells. I knew how badly I was behaving, yet couldn't do anything about it. I was a ticking time bomb.

CHAPTER 22

TRAGEDY

Christmas Day was one big panic attack.

I did the dinner as always – Amy had offered but she's an awful cook. She and Billie had been on edge for weeks, doing their best to ignore my outbursts, and now we were all in the kitchen, music on, trying for a nice chilled atmosphere. I must have drifted off peeling the potatoes and vegetables, though, because when Amy noticed what I'd been doing she began to laugh. I'd prepared a shit-houseful of parsnips, carrots and 'taties – we do it right, bubble and squeak next day, chips and pickles – and the result was in a huge pile in front of me. Peelings, that is: all the actual vegetables were in the bin at my feet. I just broke down in tears.

That was soul-destroying; yet more tragedy was around the corner.

New Year had hardly dawned when, on 6 January 2016, Raffles, the officer at Strangeways, phoned me with shocking news. My old mate Pete, one half of K Wing's Tractor and Trailer double act, was dead. He'd only just retired. He was fifty-six.

He'd left on the back of an incident in the jail, too, on the SIU, special interventions unit. He was among the first on the scene and saw it all, blood everywhere. Pete was diagnosed with post-traumatic stress disorder, PTSD, from that one incident, and after a short while went off sick. The longer he was off the worse he got, replaying the event in his head. Disappointed by people he'd thought of as mates, who hadn't contacted him, he also had a downer on himself for being unable to cope. He began to imagine himself as a forgotten man. The nightmares began and the stress got worse: I'd been there myself.

He was off for a total of six months, and some of that absence ran parallel to my own, so we saw each other plenty. After I'd been on sick leave a while, I'd discovered I wasn't bothered what people said about me. They could call me soft or a skiver, I no longer cared. But Pete had been in the job twenty-five years, and the reason he was so respected wasn't because he was hard, it was because he was a decent person. The idea they might be judging him bit him deep.

He'd eventually retired on Bonfire Night, 5 November 2015. The prison service had paid him compensation for the trauma, but then he got a letter saying they wanted some of it back. That was salt in the wound. He hadn't been spraying it around on cars and champagne. He'd used it to pay off his mortgage.

The top governor decides on compensatory

amounts and there'd been a precedent. One lad, on the sick, had set up his own internet business and had to argue the toss, ending up with 50 per cent of what he could have had. Pete originally got 100 per cent because he had been a long-standing officer of good service. Once out, though, he refused to see anyone, doctor, psychiatrist, and someone told the prison. When they asked him about it, he said he didn't feel comfortable speaking to a stranger. So on those grounds they decided that he hadn't helped himself enough and took 25 per cent back.

The last time we'd met was a week or so before Christmas, when he took Amy and me out for a meal after I'd helped him move stuff from his caravan in Wales to his daughter-in-law's. All we talked about was how bad he felt. I tried to re-assure him he'd done his bit and needed to let the job go, but he couldn't. It had got to him.

Like me, he wasn't good over the so-called festive period, and when Helen found him, the day before Raffles called, poor old Pete had died of a massive stroke.

The crematorium was rammed. Helen was over-whelmed by the turnout. Pete was a popular guy, though as usual not enough of us had thought to tell him so while he was here. I went in shorts and a rugby shirt, which Pete would have liked – my usual clobber when not in uniform. Henry, the Strangeways chaplain, delivered a beautiful service. Even the inmates had been shocked and upset, he said. As funerals go, it was a good one. Afterwards, we all went on to a working men's club in St Helens, where we talked about how tortured our friend had been – how the way he'd been treated broke his heart. Quite definitely, the prison service finished him.

On the back of everything else, Pete's death had me in bits. The day I heard I had another panic attack. I went to the gym for four hours and afterwards was sick in the car park again. I had no phone on me; when I got home, Amy was frantic. That night I cried for an hour and a half.

That, though, was the last panic attack I'd have. I knew I had to try something, and it felt like a wussy thing to do, but it was time for counselling.

The counsellor was a lovely Eastern European woman. My appointment was for an hour, but I was only twenty minutes into my story when she said, 'I'm sorry, I can't help you.'

I started getting to my feet, embarrassed.

'No, no, I need to refer you to a psychologist. The problems you've got are way above anything I can help with.'

In March, a psychologist took things up a level. I stayed with her over sixteen sessions in four and a half months, which took us to the end of July. During that time, I got progressively worse, to the extent that, eight weeks in, I was a man possessed. But I stuck at it.

Through it all, the psychologist was brilliant.

Every session went over its allotted hour; it sometimes lasted two. Mainly she just sat and listened, chipped in now and then, as I talked about the things that tormented me.

I told her about battering that con. I spoke about the death of Pawel Nicpon – his screaming face, and how his smell continued to haunt me. I opened those inner boxes and the full chamber of horrors emerged.

'That's terrible,' she'd say.

'I'm not making it up.'

'I know you're not. I'm telling you it's terrible in itself.'

And as if that wasn't bad enough, there was all the other more mundane stuff, like how badly officers were treated by management, their colleagues and faceless bureaucrats. I was also very self-critical, a habit she told me I had to get over. As with Pete, the psychologist's diagnosis was PTSD. 'Suffers recurrent nightmares,' said her report.

I remember chatting with an ex-squaddie not long before I finished, who insisted that PTSD only applies to the military. But PTSD is not just about war. A mate and his missus were in a car on the M1, their two kids in the back, five and six. A truck turned over, causing a pile-up. The car was mashed to fuck, his missus was decapitated, and it took over and hour to get him and the kids out. These children saw it all: you're telling me they won't be traumatized? First responders

– police, nurses, firefighters – all see things that scar them. If someone says they have PTSD don't knock them for it.

One day a prison governor phoned me up to ask when I was coming back.

'Whoa,' I said. 'Who says I am? I'm in a bad way, guv, and you might have seen the last of me.'

He asked if I'd sorted any help out, and I told him about the psychologist. 'Oh,' he said. 'I've been having some therapy myself.'

Talking stirred everything back up, but it became a crutch too. For three or four hours afterwards I'd be in a good mood – euphoric, even. But by evening, clouds descended. It was as if I'd been on some psychological bender – horrendous.

I never contemplated suicide. The psychologist asked me that, early doors. Basically, I just needed someone to agree: 'Yeah, that wasn't good.'

I'd thought I'd ask Amy to share a few thoughts on her experience of this time, which she agreed to do. Here they are:

> I remember you coming home smelling of shit that time. I had to undress you at the foot of the stairs, run you a bath. Carrying that uniform to the washer made me feel sick.
>
> Another night, I'd done tea, cleaned the house and had everything prepared for a

relaxing evening. You were in a horrible mood, though, and I got no welcome. You just got changed and laid on the sofa refusing to speak. That hurt and made me feel alone, which is how I felt most of the time. Upsets at work always came back to the family.

Prison changed and brought out the worst in you. I never knew which version of you would arrive home, even when you rang to prepare me with how your day had gone.

I was mad at the people you worked with. They took you for granted and asked favours. Then when you were ill no one would cover for you.

I felt like a single parent. There was no balance between your job and personal life. We missed you a lot and would often cry and get upset when you set off.

I remember the sense of relief at your first sick note from the doctor, knowing you wouldn't have to go back to Strangeways for a while. And even bigger relief when you got another. I knew that would be that, not only due to the injury, but also blood pressure and stress. I could relax, knowing I'd take care of you; return you to your old self.

Your time in counselling was difficult. We had bad days after every session as it brought feelings of anger to the surface. Billie and me drew the short straw again.

At times I questioned our relationship. Were we strong enough to get through this?

All in all, I feel the experience made us stronger. And you certainly know who your real friends are. It was hard work, but we made it out the other side and can laugh, joke and smile about our life and the people in it again.

As a family, we are rock solid. The Sam I fell in love with is back, a loving fiancé and wonderful father.

I'd been away from Strangeways for eleven months when the decision was taken to call it a draw. Amy didn't want me to go back and my doctor was very supportive, agreeing that for the sake of my health and mental well-being I needed to get out of there. People go on about mortgages, but when something makes you miserable, stop doing it. Live in a caravan in Filey if you must. There are people in HMP Manchester now who were in the job before I began, and I'm sure that conditions are even worse. Yet they will stay in that place until they die or are killed by it, whichever comes first. I finally decided that was not going to be me.

On 2 August 2016, I left Amy and Billie waiting in the car park and arrived for my interview with the new governor ten minutes early – old habits die hard. My case manager was also present, and there were reports from the psychologist and my doctors. The governor was sympathetic, confirmed it would be best if I left rather than take another job in the prison service and we shook hands. Even more than me, Amy and Billie couldn't wait to get out of the place. It had been their first and last visit.

CHAPTER 23

DON'T LOOK BACK IN ANGER

Am I proud to have been a prison officer? I'd say it's no longer so simple. You hear that word, pride, bandied about a lot nowadays, often on social media: 'Really proud of everyone today, teamwork, support #Strangeways-Family . . .' or some such bollocks. There was pride in doing a good job. Whether you're in Strangeways for twenty years or twenty minutes, its atmosphere seeps into your soul, and it becomes a real battle to stay yourself. I'd like to think I did that. I am proud of how I conducted myself and behaved.

The Bertie Bassett era was fantastic: leadership and teamwork were outstanding; you felt part of something worthwhile. You'd turn up every day ready to go and knowing you had his backing. I am proud to have met some wonderful people. KK, Bradders and others will be lifelong friends.

But going on about pride isn't helpful. I know how it is at HMP Manchester today and that's bad, really bad: when front-line officers have nowhere to go the word has no meaning. People are turning up for work on wings that are on the verge of a riot, terrified, fizzing with adrenaline and making themselves poorly. They don't want to be there but feel they've no option. It saddens me.

I'm no angel, me. No Yorkshire martyr, and quite definitely no Confucius. I've spent a lot of time at the bottom of the ladder and can see the problems. Our prison service has plenty.

Rehabilitation is what I had after my shoulder injury: seeing a physio, doing exercise, resting, getting better. When it comes to criminal behaviour, though, most often it's time and money wasted. David Caplan at the funeral had done four or five sentences for bank robberies and he's probably heading towards thirty-five years of age now. He'd not learnt his lesson. In America, he'd have been given ten years first up, then twenty and then thirty. Three bites at the cherry and he's an old man. That's how it should be. Our system isn't working; the sentence should fit the crime. Innocent lives are being ruined.

Prisoners worked out long ago that shooting someone means twenty years. Knife them and look at fifteen. The victim is still dead, so what was the difference? We had one lad in for killing a drug rival. Ran into him in his car, reversed over the kid, dragged him down the road and made mincemeat out of him. The killer went home, got drunk and when the police came he told them he'd been pissed. He got a five-year sentence, out in three. Increasingly nowadays, it's acid attacks. If someone pays somebody else to scar a person physically and mentally for life, they need to be hit with massive jail time. It's absolutely shocking. Face it: criminal is what they are.

My grandad, though, always used to say, 'Don't bring me problems, Sam – bring me solutions.' So let's have a go, eh?

Most important is education, and I'm not talking prisoners now, but our kids. When I was at school, we knew the Green Cross Code by heart. 'First find a safe place to cross . . .' I can still recite it. Catch them young. When kids embark on a life of crime they are as good as lost. Some become hardened offenders and the cycle repeats.

Education in jail, once guys end up there, should be practical or else it's useless. A lot of courses in prisons come from colleges who have idealist liberal agendas. They're aimed too high for most inmates, who don't give a shit about identity politics. There is an enhanced thinking course inside, for example, that a healthcare orderly had to do as part of his 'sentence plan'. Before long, we got a call asking us to fetch him back from the classroom. He'd told them he'd done the course before and they said, fine, it was available on every sentence. The tutor asked what, if anything, he felt he'd got out of it. First and foremost, he said, it had made him a better criminal.

In my experience there are very few reading and writing lessons in jail, though I hear the new Thameside prison in London is different. That's the type of guidance needed. Presumably we want them to get jobs and become useful to society. Well, if they can't write there'll be no CV, and employment will be harder to get, won't it?

When people leave jail they need purposeful activity, so that needs addressing. When I left Manchester, they had a sewing shop where prison clothes were made. Some people did that, enjoyed time out of the cell and made a bit of brass. But it's not really purposeful activity, is it? No one leaving prison is going into the sewing trade. Back in the day, we had bricklaying and plastering shops with qualified brickies and plasterers showing them how. That was useful, and they were very well attended. One officer I worked with had an extension built and was away on holiday when the builders started it. When he got back, to his amazement, two of the lads laying the bricks were ex-cons from Strangeways. Plasterers earn good money, so lads left jail with a practical qualification. That's what the majority of prisoners need.

I look back on the YTS that got me into engineering when I left school. They were all the rage back then. Similar broad-based modern apprenticeships are exactly what we need now. Every lad I was with on that course got a job at the end of the two years. For someone inside to be released six months' early they should have to sign up.

The private sector seems to do this better. At Forest Bank, we had an automotive shop where lads would rebuild alternators, a double-glazing shop too. That makes sense. Businesses would approach the prison and start a manufacturing partnership. They had assembly lines, made furniture and at one point even sunbeds and blinds. The prisoners got a decent wage, learned a skill and it helped to keep the jail running. Prisoners need focus and a feeling of feeding into society while getting appreciation back for their efforts. It gives them hope. A fair few will blow the income on something antisocial – this isn't a fairy story – but at least you are giving them an opportunity to make something of themselves, rather than just throwing them back out into the jungle until they are in the slammer again.

Probation – let's say a prisoner has a two-year sentence. Actual time served will be less, and once freed they are monitored. If you are a bank robber, you turn up at an allotted time every week to tell your probation worker what you've been up to. You could be on the run from the Bank of Scotland. It's not really monitoring someone, is it?

When prisoners come out they're often sent to probation hostels for a while. But this system can sometimes work in crazy ways. There's a lad who lives on a street near us who was sent to a hostel in Bury, and reported that his room had a broken socket. He was accused of having done it, got sent back to jail and had to complete his time. But even if he had done it, is a broken plug socket worth two years? A teacher might get that for grooming a pupil. In any case, people sent to these hostels often have family willing to take them in – spouses, grandparents, aunties – which in my opinion is the best chance a lot of them have of going straight. Tag them if necessary.

Electronic tagging is used nowhere near widely enough. There were objections when the system went private; it became a standing joke, wrong sorts of headlines – they tagged one bloke's false leg: with a job to do, he left it at home. But it's time to use tagging properly: if a dog gets lost in Cornwall, chip technology can find the owner's name and address and they'll get their pooch back. If tagging places you at the scene of the crime, that's a reason not to commit the crime in the first place, isn't it? Satellite tracking can make sure curfews are kept.

Part of a drug addict's terms and conditions for release from prison are that if you use while you are out you come straight back. Addicts get disability living allowance, DLA, and it can equate to between £1,500 and £2,000 a month – as much as a prison officer earns! All you're doing is setting them up to fail. What addicts need more is life management. I Wing at Strangeways, the detox wing, had new doors put on at great expense. They had big hatches in the middle of the door, which it turned out were for nurses to push sandwiches and hot chocolate through on a night without having to open them up. It's easy to take the piss out of things like that, and I did myself when I first saw them. But when you weigh up what they are meant for – making sure people on the rattle get enough nutrition and are fattened up – it actually makes sense. By the time I left, and I believe even now, they had never been used. They'd rather give them methadone with all the problems that brings instead.

So when drug addicts come out of prison, give them enough money for rent, necessary bills and food perhaps, no more, but tied up with obligations like learning to read and write. Again, it might give them self-worth and purpose, a fresh start. They'd be monitored, given help to budget their resources. Not prepared to sign up to that? Finish your sentence.

Community service gets a bad rap – a lot of it thanks to so-called reality telly showing gangs of lads smoking spliffs while some poor supervisor works his balls off doing the work of twenty. Moss Side gang-bangers or whatever, to get out they should do community projects. I'm no gardener, but give me twenty ex-cons and a piece of fly-tipped land and I'd happily have them clearing it tomorrow. Thirty-nine hours a week? I'd be up for that. Again, it's purposeful activity. The choices you give them have to be tough choices.

These are all ways to address the growth of the prison population, which is way too large and getting bigger all the time. How else, though? Well, a good start would be to deport all foreign-national prisoners. I don't have the figures, but personal experience tells me that far too many have no right to be in the UK in the first place. I don't have the numbers for how many Brits are banged up abroad either, but take our own bad boys back as a bargaining chip if that's going to help and those figures stack up.

And at the same time, to increase prison officer numbers we should be attracting foreign nationals in. To enter Australia at the moment it seems you've to be a hairdresser under forty. They must need people who can fashion a trendy mullet. Yet there are Brits currently buggering off to be prison officers in New Zealand. The government wants 2,500 new prison officers, which sounds a lot but isn't, not least because 50 per cent will leave within the first twelve months. I reckon the bottom line figure needed is 8,000. That will make up the shortfall and replace people like me, lost through sickness and stress, and the thousands that were let go through voluntary redundancy in 2013. That cost-cutting exercise lost a lot of experienced staff, and according to reports cost the tax payer £56.5 million in payouts (compared to £5.7 million in 2012). We need fewer prisoners, more staff – what the papers call a twin-pronged approach. Common sense, really.

Here's hoping someone in authority recognizes that change must come, and that it needs to start now. Not in ten years' time, because by then it will be far too late.

As we drove away from Strangeways that day and it receded and shrank in the rear-view mirror, I was unemployed for the first time since my twenties.

There was trepidation, sure. How would we manage? Mainly, though, there was relief, although I wasn't out of the woods yet.

In September, I signed up for a level five course, equal to a foundation degree, in reflexology. Although it was something I wanted to do and I was helped loads by Alison, who ran the course, and the other girls who'd signed up, it added to my mental burden. Through October and November I was in bits: it was the March and April horror show all over again. I was still struggling to handle feelings of rage, neglect and even betrayal. I started to develop a bit of OCD, a condition I'd once taken the piss out of people for having. The course was getting on top of me too until, after another fling with medication, I realized I had to move on.

The moment came at half six one morning, while I was out walking Steve. I threw the mother of all wobblers. I stamped my feet – nobody was there but us two, luckily – and if there'd been anything inanimate to punch I'd have done it. The dog wasn't howling, I was.

We've all had times in our lives when we are

down. When that happened in mine I'd go on a three-day binge and destroy myself with food and alcohol. Then at the end of it I'd think, *Well, I can't feel any worse,* and begin to work my way back up. But this time that wasn't an option: Billie and Amy were struggling to deal with my shittiness as it was. So I decided right there and then: *I am not going to be ill any more.*

This is not in any way knocking people who can't do that. I am a strong character and I decided, at last, to remember it. I was so fed up with all the suffering. Having made up my mind, I went home, took all my tablets out of their foil and threw them down the bog. I got rid of every-thing – blood pressure statins, the works. I felt like I needed a grand gesture to start putting this shit behind me, so I made it.

For a month, I didn't tell the doctor or Amy. Drug-free, I toned down the weights at the gym and turned up the exercise. I started eating right – went on a health kick and binned the junk food. I hadn't been drinking for months, so staying off booze wasn't as hard as it once would have been. Generally, I got myself in better shape. People saying the wrong thing was always a threat – 'Too ill to come into work, but well enough to go to the gym . . .' – that sort of crap. I switched off that noise as it only led to tears of frustration.

By the time we got to Christmas the clouds began to lift. The reflexology, a bastard at first, now gave me focus. I was also starting to enjoy that feeling of control, of being a person with self-will. I don't say this is the best route to normality for everyone; it just worked for me.

The year turned, and where the last few years seemed to have been one long and painful crawl, 2017 flew by, weeks and months passing more quickly all the time. My mood improved. People began to say I was more like my old self. However, I wasn't completely in the clear, and I'm still not. It wouldn't take much to swing it around again – churning up all my memories for this book was always going to be a risk. Obstacles wait to trip you up. There will likely be setbacks, but the future does look bright. A lot brighter than it did in September 2015, quite definitely.

At Christmas 2016, sorting through my things, I came across my prison diaries, which every officer lives by. You carry them with you: they contain details of your shifts. It was those that gave me the idea of collecting all these thoughts and incidents together. Cathartic, I think they call it. And on the whole that's how it turned out.

With *Strangeways* written, I want to get back to the reflexology course and start my own business in that line soon. Amy is about to begin a course herself: she wants to go into the caring profession.

Writing this book has helped me to realize how easy it is to overlook the value of family, friends and colleagues, and made me aware of just how lucky most of us are. None of us is going to be around forever. Your family shapes you in good ways and bad; I'm grateful for the honest values of my grandparents and Mam. They didn't have much, but they always had hope.

Unlikely as it may sound, I'm grateful to the prison service too. It has an important role to play, and it also shaped my character down the years. By being so honest and open about what went on, I hope to help it do better, that's all. But ask me, 'Do I miss it?' and the answer must be no. Those days behind bars are over; the sentence is done.

I'm free at last.